DAN WAL
D0120226
MAGIC,
AND
MARADONA
CUP FOOTBALL'S FINEST TALES
WITH GERSHON PORTNOI
LIBRARIES NI
WITHDRAWN FROM STOCK
SIMON &
SCHUSTER
London · New York · Sydney · Toronto · New Delhi
A CBS COMPANY

First published in Great Britain by Simon & Schuster UK Ltd, 2016
A CBS company

1 3 5 7 9 10 8 6 4 2

Simon & Schuster UK Ltd
1st Floor
222 Gray's Inn Road
London WC1X 8HB

www.simonandschuster.co.uk
www.simonandschuster.com.au
www.simonandschuster.co.in

Simon & Schuster Australia,
Sydney

Simon & Schuster India,
New Delhi

A CIP catalogue record for this book is
available from the British Library

Hardback ISBN: 978-1-4711-3631-3
eBook ISBN: 978-1-4711-3633-7

Designed by Jacqui Caulton
Printed and bound in Slovenia by GPS

CONTENTS

FOREWORD BY ALAN SHEARER

I have two things in common with young Daniel: our love of football and a mild obsession with golf. I know he has to be a bit more serious these days when he sits on the sofa for *BBC Breakfast*, but he'll never lose that passion for sport.

He is annoyingly good at golf and has even – scandalously – won his own charity golf day. We are currently an unbeaten partnership, with a 100 per cent record. He's a great presenter, really understands his football, but is nowhere near as good at playing the game as he thinks.

We were on opposite sides in a charity game at Wembley a few years ago. He was attempting to mark me and just before kick-off remarked that I would spend the entire game in his pocket.

Wor Al and I at Golf de Saint-Cloud. No, I am not wearing long white socks.

I know it was tongue-in-cheek, but I did enjoy leaving him for dead on a couple of occasions and I may have elbowed him in the neck by accident in the first minute – just to let him know I was there and nowhere near his pocket.

Dan sent me a copy of his first book – *The Thronkersaurus* – and I don't mind telling you that it has a home in the Shearer toilet. I look forward to reading this one all about the highs and lows of cup football.

The FA Cup was always a frustrating tournament for me. I got to the final twice and lost twice. We felt we had a good chance in 1998 against Arsenal, but it wasn't to be. I hit the post in the second half, but the Gunners got another and that was that. The following year we got there again, but this time were beaten by the Manchester United Treble winners. I'd like to say we were robbed on both occasions, but it's probably not true.

I have much fonder memories of Wembley in Euro 96. I know we lost in the semi-final, but I can genuinely say we couldn't have given any more and that was the highlight of my England career.

It wasn't my first taste of a major tournament. In 1992, I was one of the turnips who lost to the Swedes. There were rumours of discontent between Gary Lineker and the boss, Graham Taylor. Graham actually told me I was going on for Gary in that game against Sweden, but he must have told Alan Smith the same thing. Alan got the nod and the rest is history. That was followed by the miserable qualifying campaign for the 1994 World Cup. I was out for eight months of that through injury, and looking back I like to think I could have made a difference. Whenever I play golf with Ronald Koeman, I still bring up that free kick!

We made the next World Cup under Glenn Hoddle and again it was penalties. That game against Argentina was amazing. I remember shouting at Michael Owen to 'pass it' a few times, but then just watching him carve their defence to pieces. David Beckham's sending off was a big moment, but we still had the chance from the spot. I have a photograph of me on the pitch at St Etienne before that shoot-out, looking up at my family in the ground. I love it because it looks like I'm excited and enjoying myself, though the reality was I was absolutely bricking it. I couldn't even speak.

I was so happy to score, and remember talking to David Batty on the half-way line and telling him: 'Whatever you do, don't

The photo that hangs in the Shearer house. All is not quite as it seems.

change your mind.' He said he was going to smash it. I wish he had. A few hours after we lost, I asked him why he put it to the keeper's right instead of smashing it. He said he changed his mind in the last second of his run-up. That uncertainty killed him.

The image that I can't get out of my head is the Argentinian team celebrating on the bus afterwards. We were waiting for our transport while watching them banging on the windows and taunting us. I'm sure we would have done the same, but I can still see Gabriel Batistuta smiling at me. I feel it should have been us. And I still think I should have wiped the smile off his face!

My final major tournament came two years later. Losing 3-2 to Portugal was a disastrous result from being 2-0 up, and then we had the elation of beating the Germans in a major tournament for the first time since 1966. The less said about the final game, against Romania, the better. Dan loves a stat, and when he reminded me that that is still the only game Romania have ever won at the European Championships it didn't go down well. Let's just say it was up there with Batistuta.

That time it didn't come down to penalties, but spot kicks have always been crucial in my career. Plenty of my goals have come from 12 yards, and it was something I always worked on. I never missed one in a major tournament.

I remember doing a piece with Dan in Brazil about how to best prepare for them. It was about 30 degrees and we were both sweating like pigs, but I talked to him about how I always used to put the ball down the same way. The valve had to be pointing up and the writing had to be facing the goalkeeper. Don't ask me why.

To go back to that game against Romania, I'd been told that they had a spy watching us when we were training in the stadium in Charleroi the night before the game. So I took ten penalties and made sure I put every one of them in the same place – to the keeper's left. The next day it worked a treat. Bogdan Stelea was already going the wrong way in anticipation and I went to the keeper's right instead. That was to be my last goal for England.

I should also point out that I don't just remember the ones that ended up in the back of the net. It still annoys me that I never scored at Birmingham City. St Andrew's remains the only league ground I played at where I drew a career blank. I missed a penalty there once.

I scored one at Highbury – the only one I ever scored there. We turned up for the game in December 2001 just 25 minutes before kick-off because of horrendous traffic. We had only five minutes to warm up and then it was straight out onto the pitch. Somehow we won 3-1. I had a great record against Arsenal when we played them at our place, but Tony Adams was one of the few defenders who was able to match me physically. Ninety-six per cent of them – just like Dan at Wembley – I could budge with a nudge. Adams was unbudgeable and we had some great duels over the years. He was also a great leader for England, and I wish that together we'd been able to win something with our country.

As for 2016... well, I loved working on the Euros as a pundit and it was great to see all the home nations make the last 16, but ultimately it was another disappointing summer for England. I know people are always quick to blame the academy system that pampers young professionals, but until we learn to settle on a system and pick the people to fit it we are never going to succeed.

Look at what Wales did in that tournament. They may have lacked the individual talent of some of the more established nations, but they were truly a 'team' who followed a clear plan where everyone knew what was expected of them at both ends of the pitch.

Anyway, enough about the misery, it has been a real pleasure for me to write this foreword and take a brief look back at my life in football. I really hope you enjoy reading the book. Dan has brought together some brilliant stories from his impressive career and, let's be honest, who doesn't love a stat or a bit of trivia (as long as it's not about Romania)?

Well. Here we go again. A huge and significant 'thank you' to all those who read *The Thronkersaurus*, talked about it, enjoyed it and took it to the toilet.

It was lovely to meet many of you at various book signings, and a particular thank you to John, who came to the festival in Cheshire and told me that he was going to go and read it on the bog that very night. The thought of John on the John has haunted me ever since.

This second tome has been bubbling away for a while. I love cup football and this is a collection of stories, tales, facts and trivia from many of the wonderful domestic and international competitions around the world.

At last count, I have been to 13 FA Cup finals and a host of World Cups and European Championships and various other bits and bobs around the globe. I am currently writing this introduction sat in Nice airport, waiting for a flight back to Paris hopefully in time to watch Northern Ireland take on Germany. The flight has already been delayed for three hours and I am sitting next to a rather distressed German fella clad in lederhosen and a Lothar Matthäus shirt.

I need to talk to you about the title of this tome. Quite a few of my suggestions were sadly rejected. *Thronkersaurus Next* and *ThronkerMOREus* didn't get past the initial phone call, and when I dipped into social media for suggestions there were some rare beauties. *Game Of Thronks* came from Ron Chakraborty, Gordon Wallace was the first of many pointing me towards *Thronky McThronkface* and Sacred Coo's offering of *Englebert Thronkerdink* was sadly met with a firm 'no' from the head honchos at Simon & Schuster.

Other rejects included: *Thronkersaurus Reloaded*, *Beyond The Thronkerdrome* and *Thronkersaurus 2: Tokyo Drift*.

And so to *Magic, Mud and Maradona*. As you delve into this, please remember I am not attempting to put right all of the sport's wrongs. It is not my intention to preach to you about my take on football, but merely share some stories about the game we love. I may have to wear a tie on *BBC Breakfast* these days, but the sporting heart still beats with the same passion as ever.

I know some people will read it cover to cover, but you are more than welcome to adopt the dip-dip technique and synchronise your sessions with toilet visits. If it's good enough for Shearer, it'll do for the rest of us. I also need to thank Wor Al for penning the foreword.

Don't tell him, but I still remember working with him for the first time just after he'd signed for the BBC many moons ago. When he called me 'Dan' while we were discussing a World Cup draw, the little kid inside me who'd wept over England heartache whispered 'Alan Shearer actually knows my name'. It's my absolute privilege to now know him as a friend, karaoke compadre and golfing comrade.

I've even forgiven him for elbowing me in the throat during that charity match at Wembley. That wasn't my immediate

Welcoming Shearer into the National Football Museum Hall of Fame alongside Iain Dowie.

thought as I lay twisted on the floor gasping for air but, after years of physiotherapy, I've come to realise what an honour it was to get 'Shearered'.

As well as Al's words, you'll see that many of your Friday Team News pun suggestions have made it on to these pages. Thanks again for all the effort that goes into those each week. It still makes me laugh when people collar me at a train station wondering why their suggestion of 'Jesper Donkeyar' only made the bench of the #SeasideXI.

It's also been lovely to meet so many parents who gave the first book to their kids, children who bought it for their mums and dads, and other humans who selfishly purchased it for themselves. I really hope you enjoy this one too and I look forward to chatting to you about it. Just don't give me too much toilet detail. I'm talking to you, John.

When people talk about the 'magic of the cup', what they normally mean is a little tiddler of a team taking down a giant. There is something beautiful about the Sutton United, Warrington Town and Blyth Spartans of this world.

Every one of you reading this could probably name a player who will be forever etched in your FA Cup memory. It might go back 50 years, five years or five months, but they still mean something however much the competition has changed since then. As a religious watcher of Ceefax and Teletext, Roy Essandoh always held a special place for me. The fact that Wycombe signed him following an advert on Teletext still makes me giggle to this day. The fact that he scored the winner against Leicester City in the FA Cup quarter-final makes it even more special. I know Roy was released soon after, but that was his moment in the sun, that was his 15 minutes and we are all able to share in that.

Roy the Boy. He may have been a one-game wonder – but what a game.

I mentioned the mighty Spartans and it's the north-east warriors that I want to shine a little light on here. They have a rich history in the competition that goes back many years. They've made the first round on 31 occasions and the heady heights of the third round four times. One of those happened in 2014 when Tom Wade's side managed to see off Hartlepool on a freezing cold second-round Friday night in the north-east. I hosted the game on the BBC and it sticks in my memory for a number of reasons:

1. We got in trouble with Jeff Stelling for allowing Alan Shearer to go into the Blyth dressing room before the game. Shearer told the players 'one of you can be a hero out there' and subsequently Jarrett Rivers delivered the goods. We did offer the same Shearer service to Hartlepool, but they understandably turned us down.
2. The fact that Mr Shearer and fellow pundit Trevor Sinclair turned up dressed like Brian Harvey from East 17 and Inspector Gadget.
3. The fact that some fella with a tinfoil helmet jumped over the hoardings at half time and accidentally broke our big screen, which had taken hours to wheel into position.

Blyth marched on into round three and were drawn at home against Birmingham City. *Football Focus* decided to use their Croft Park ground as its base that weekend and we received the

It was chilly that night in the north-east. Alan now has a new coat. Trev still rocks the hat.

warmest of welcomes from the Northern Premier League team. They opened every door and gave us access all areas. On one wander through the home team dressing room we stumbled upon a laminated piece of paper which was quickly put on social media and subsequently shared and retweeted millions of times over the next few hours. It's easy to see why:

You'll struggle to find a better list anywhere in the land.

There is so much to enjoy about this list. I love the fact that someone has urinated in the shower enough times for it to make the list in the first place, although £2 seems nowhere near enough to deter potential pee-ers. Failure to wear flip-flops is also frowned upon, and most of the fines relate to issues around kit, uniform and behaviour in the shower. Perhaps it gives us all an insight into the importance of team spirit that non-attendance at a team night out carries double the fine for missing a match.

I know Blyth Spartans are a non-League football team, but I think there are life lessons in here for all of us. We could all do with a bit more Blyth in our lives. We'd be much happier and our showers would be a lot cleaner.

DRESSING ROOM DUST-UPS

What goes on in a dressing room should stay in a dressing room, so the unwritten code of the entire sporting industry tells us. But that's not much fun. Strolling around the Blyth Spartans changing room was great, and reminded me of the shroud of secrecy that usually protects these holiest of holy football Meccas – and how brilliant it is on those rare occasions where we are privy to the showdowns that have taken place in the heart of the footballers' workplace. Here are my favourites:

DID ANYONE ORDER A PIZZA?

FIGHTERS: Pizza v Alex Ferguson

DO THEY HAVE PREVIOUS? No, Fergie is more of a red wine, meat and potatoes man.
THE INCIDENT: Arsenal's 49-match unbeaten run was ended at Old Trafford so Cesc Fàbregas (allegedly), and others, hurled their dressing-room pizza slices at Sir Alex when he came in to say 'well played' (or something similar).
FINAL SCORE: Pizza stain 1 Fergie's suit jacket 0
WHAT HAPPENED NEXT? Arsenal have never bothered winning the league since, Fergie won it plenty more times, pizza got eaten more than it was thrown.

DINNER TIME

FIGHTERS: John Sitton v Leyton Orient

DO THEY HAVE PREVIOUS? Yes, in the dressing room every week throughout Sitton's tumultuous reign of terror at Brisbane Road.

THE INCIDENT: Trailing at home to Blackpool at half time, Sitton could take no more and promptly challenged two of his players to a fight and advised them to 'bring your dinner because you'll need it by the time I'm finished with you'.
FINAL SCORE: Sitton 1 Orient players Terrified
WHAT HAPPENED NEXT? Sitton was sacked, Orient were relegated and everyone lived happily ever after.

PUTTING THE BOOT IN

FIGHTERS: Fergie v David Beckham

DO THEY HAVE PREVIOUS? Let's just say Sir Alex wasn't exactly a big fan of Beckham's showbiz lifestyle.
THE INCIDENT: Manchester United lost to Arsenal in the FA Cup, Fergie got a touch miffed and kicked a boot, which cut Beckham above the eye.
FINAL SCORE: Fergie 1 Beckham 0
WHAT HAPPENED NEXT? Beckham appeared in the papers the next day with wound clearly in shot and eventually moved to Real Madrid to pursue his career away from the hairdryer.

HANDBAGS

FIGHTERS: Wayne Rooney v David Beckham

DO THEY HAVE PREVIOUS? None that we know about.
THE INCIDENT: Rooney took exception to being told to calm down by Becks after some on-pitch petulance earned him a yellow card during England's infamous 1-0 defeat away to Northern Ireland. He told the skipper to, ahem, go forth and multiply, then allegedly called him a 'flash so-and-so' in the tunnel before the pair squared up in the dressing room. All this, and it was only half time.
FINAL SCORE: Team-mates stepped in to separate the warriors, leaving us with a stalemate of Rooney 0 Beckham 0
WHAT HAPPENED NEXT? England lost but qualified for the World Cup. Rooney eventually calmed down, then everyone opined he wasn't the same player without that fire. Beckham, not the sort

of bloke to get into a fight, regained his composure, straightened out his hair and found his Zen.

WHO YOU CALLING CHICKEN?

FIGHTERS: Brian Laws v Ivano Bonetti

DO THEY HAVE PREVIOUS? Not one jot.

THE INCIDENT: After Grimsby lost 3-2 to Luton, player-manager Laws launched a dressing-room tirade and Bonetti hit back. Literally. By throwing sandwiches and a punch, according to Laws. What followed depends on who you believe. Either way, Bonetti ended up with a broken cheekbone. Whether it was inflicted by a plate of chicken wings or a right hook, both thrown by Laws, remains a mystery.

FINAL SCORE: Laws 1 Bonetti 0

WHAT HAPPENED NEXT? The press had a field day, as the incident filled the back pages. Bonetti was moved on to Tranmere on a free, Laws left the club later that year. No one knows what happened to the chicken wings.

RED RAG TO A BULL

FIGHTERS: Joey Barton v Alan Shearer

DO THEY HAVE PREVIOUS? Barton definitely has previous, although not necessarily with Wor Alan.

THE INCIDENT: As Newcastle fought to avoid relegation, Barton was sent off at Liverpool. Temporary manager Shearer bravely laid into him after the game, but Barton countered by telling his boss that he was a 's**t manager with s**t tactics'.

FINAL SCORE: Shearer 2 Barton 2 (Shearer gets an extra goal for writing the foreword to this tome)

WHAT HAPPENED NEXT? Shearer suspended Barton, Newcastle were sadly relegated and both men wound up in pundit land.

EARLY BATH

FIGHTERS: Lawrie McMenemy v Mark Wright

DO THEY HAVE PREVIOUS? Quite possibly, but nothing documented.
THE INCIDENT: At half time during a Milk Cup tie against QPR, centre-half Wright exchanged strong words with team-mate Steve Williams and his Saints gaffer McMenemy. As the team returned to the pitch, McMenemy pushed Wright into the shower room and punched him, so the defender retaliated by shoving his manager across the room and into the bath, before McMenemy came back for more. Proper Laurel and Hardy stuff.

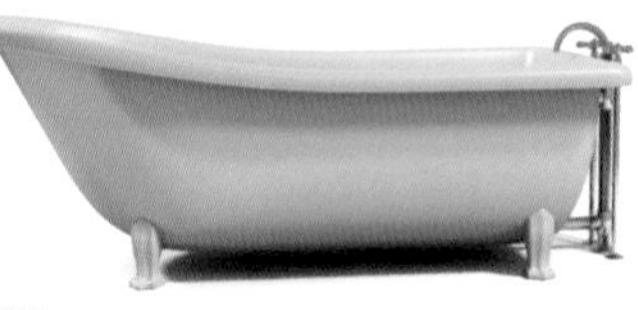

FINAL SCORE: McMenemy 1 Wright 1
WHAT HAPPENED NEXT? Wright wanted out, saying: 'That punch-up was the last straw for me.' But he stuck around to help Southampton finish fifth and went on to score a famous World Cup goal for England against Egypt in Italy. McMenemy also ended up with England as assistant manager to Graham Taylor – but the less said about that, the better.

A CLOUGHIE JEM

FIGHTERS: Brian Clough v Nigel Jemson

DO THEY HAVE PREVIOUS? Cloughie had previous with everyone. Jemson, not so much.
THE INCIDENT: Jemson showboated during the first half of a reserve-team game, so Clough rebuked him with a half-time punch in the stomach and the killer line: 'Don't you ever try those fancy tricks again while your mum and dad are in the stand.'
FINAL SCORE: Clough 6 Jemson 0
WHAT HAPPENED NEXT? Cloughie's legend lived on long after him, while Jemson went on to score more than 100 goals, without any party tricks, before becoming Ilkeston Town player-manager.

FOOTBALL'S MOST UNIQUE NAME ENDINGS

Any team can be a United, City, Town or Rovers, but it takes something special to be a Spartan. Here's a quick look at some of the great team-name endings in British football, with one South American classic thrown in for good measure.

BLYTH SPARTANS

Club founder Fred Stoker thought naming the north-east club after the formidable Greek army would inspire them every time they went into battle on the pitch.

LEYTON ORIENT

The team was formed by members of the Glyn Cricket Club, and the story goes that one of them was employed by the Orient Shipping Line and asked for that to be reflected in the name. And so it was.

HAMILTON ACADEMICAL

The South Lanarkshire club was formed by the rector and pupils of the local school Hamilton Academy – the only professional British club to start off life as a school team.

TOTTENHAM HOTSPUR

The club, originally called Hotspur FC, were named after 14th century knight Sir Henry Percy, whose bravery and attacking instincts earned him the nickname Hotspur – you do the math(s).

SHEFFIELD WEDNESDAY

The Wednesday Cricket Club (named after the day they played) needed something for their players to do during the winter so formed a football club. Turns out they were better footballers than cricketers.

CREWE ALEXANDRA

The Alex were named after Princess Alexandra. Who? She was the Princess of Wales in the 19th century who went on to become Queen Consort to Edward VII. You did ask.

ACCRINGTON STANLEY

When Accrington resigned from the Football League in 1893, local team Stanley Villa took the town's name and added part of their own, which was named after the Stanley Working Men's Club on Stanley Street.

KIDDERMINSTER HARRIERS

The Midlands club were formed out of an athletics and rugby club, hence the whole Harrier thing.

PLYMOUTH ARGYLE

Nobody knows for certain the origins of Argyle other than the club were part of general sports outfit Argyle Athletic Club. Theories include the name coming from army regiment Argyll and Sutherland Highlanders, nearby pub The Argyle Tavern, or the famous Argyle diamond pattern on the kit. You decide.

DEPORTIVO WANKA

Stop giggling at the back. The Peruvian Andes outfit were named in honour of the indigenous Wankas people who used to dwell nearby.

NON-LEAGUE'S GREATEST CUP TEAMS

Spartans have a tremendous history – as I detailed earlier, in case any of you weren't paying attention – so I thought this would be an apt moment to celebrate some of the cup achievements of our greatest teams from outside of the professional game.

SPURS

Stop laughing Arsenal fans, they were once a non-League team and one so good that they won the FA Cup back in 1901, the equivalent of Enfield winning at Wembley in today's era. Probably. Spurs were a Southern League club at the beginning of the last century, but still beat Sheffield United after a replay (they only scrapped those in 1993) to lift the trophy.

HAVANT & WATERLOOVILLE

The 2007-08 cup run which culminated in the minnows twice leading Rafa Benítez's Liverpool in the fourth round was utterly ridiculous. After coming through around 20 qualifying rounds, the Hawks beat York City and Notts County in rounds one and two (proper) before defeating Swansea, who were on their way to the League One title, 4-2 in a third-round replay. Then came Anfield where 1-0 and 2-1 leads couldn't be sustained and they eventually bowed out 5-2.

WOKING

Tim Buzaglo and Woking shot to fame in 1991 when the non-Leaguers stunned Second Division West Bromwich Albion with a 4-2 third-round away win, before losing 1-0 to Everton in round four. Trailing 1-0 to the Baggies at half time, Woking's second-half performance tore Albion to shreds as Buzaglo notched a 15-minute hat-trick to steal all the cup headlines for himself. Not that he enjoyed the limelight that followed. Asked a decade later for his reflections on the aftermath of that tie in which he appeared on *Match of the Day*, he said: 'I hated it.'

BLYTH SPARTANS

They are getting a lot of love in this chapter, but with good reason. We've touched on their recent exploits, but let's go back to 1978, when the Northern League club managed to reach the fifth round of the FA Cup. They overcame eight hurdles to get there, including a fourth-round win over Stoke City, who had been playing in the top flight the season before. In the last 16, Blyth should have beaten Wrexham 1-0, but a controversial thrice-taken late corner saw the Welsh side equalise. That led to a replay which was held at St James' Park in front of 42,000 fans, including Sunderland and Newcastle die-hards who had all come together to get behind Spartans. Despite the extra support, the north-east side lost 2-1 to end an extraordinary adventure. And for Spartans' Steve Carney and pit worker Alan Shoulder the dream continued as the cup run earned them contracts with Newcastle United. Fairytale indeed.

CHASETOWN

The Staffordshire club became the lowest-ranked side to reach the third round of the FA Cup in 2008. The British Gas Business Southern League Midland Division side played ten ties in all that season, defeating Port Vale in round two to earn a game against second-tier Cardiff, who were six leagues above them. Incredibly, the minnows – whose team included a postman, customs officer and decorator – took the lead but eventually succumbed 3-1, having won a whole load of new fans.

AYLESBURY UNITED

They may not have achieved as much as other non-Leaguers on this list, and plenty of others not on this list, but their 1995 duck walk at QPR secured the club's place in cup history. Making their eighth first-round appearance in 11 seasons, the Ducks defeated Newport IoW and launched a goal celebration that got the nation talking, mainly because elaborate goal celebrations were still in their infancy back then. The players got down on their knees and waddled in a line together in a move that was repeated in the second-round win over Kingstonian and, even though they lost 4-0 to Rangers in round three, they still treated their fans to another rendition of the duck walk.

SUTTON UNITED

In 1987, Coventry City won their only FA Cup. Eighteen months later, they were humbled by Sutton United as the non-Leaguers triumphed 2-1 in one of the most famous cup shocks in history. Goals from Tony Rains and Matt Hanlan won the game for Sutton, but let's not dwell on their subsequent 8-0 hammering by Norwich in round four.

ALTRINCHAM

There was a time when the Greater Manchester club were the finest non-League side in the country. Between 1979 and 1982, they reached the third round of the FA Cup every season, and also hold the record for knocking out the most league clubs in the competition's history, with a total of 16 including famous names such as Blackpool, Birmingham City and Sheffield United.

EYEMOUTH UNITED

Back in 1960, East of Scotland side Eyemouth shocked Scottish football, or fitba as I believe it's spelled up there, by reaching the quarter-finals of the Scottish FA Cup, the first non-League side to do so. After receiving a bye in round one, Eyemouth overcame league clubs Albion Rovers and Cowdenbeath before losing 2-1 to eventual finalists Kilmarnock in the last eight.

WHAT HAPPENS AFTER THOSE 15 MINUTES OF FAME?

Roy Essandoh enjoyed his amazing moment in the sun thanks to his text-based televisual information service-inspired heroics for Wycombe Wanderers. But what happened next for Roy – and the other temporary stars who experienced a taste of FA Cup glory? Let's find out.

ROY ESSANDOH

After heading Wycombe into the FA Cup semi-finals, Essandoh became a non-League journeyman moving between the likes of Bishop's Stortford (twice), Billericay, Kettering, Grays and Cambridge City. Towards the end of his career, the Ceefax striker became a personal trainer and is available for hire right now.

TIM BUZAGLO

Woking's hat-trick hero was also a decent cricketer and represented Gibraltar in World Cup qualifiers several times until 2001. He went on to work as a porter at a school for Americans in Cobham, close to Woking where he still lives, and is constantly reminded about the West Brom game.

MICKEY THOMAS

The Welsh wonder scored a tremendous free kick to help Wrexham knock out Arsenal in 1992, capping off a career in which he'd enjoyed more than his 15 minutes as he'd also been a Manchester United player at one point. But he was soon enduring an 18-month sentence in prison after a counterfeit currency scam in which he laundered money through Wrexham trainees. As Thomas later quipped: 'Roy Keane's on fifty grand a week. So was I 'til the police found my printing machine.'

RONNIE RADFORD

The scorer of arguably the most famous FA Cup goal ever, for Hereford against Newcastle in 1972 (it was an equaliser as you will soon find out), went on to become the Worcester City player-manager and Bath player before retiring in 1975. He worked as a joiner and carpenter before retiring to spend time with his grandchildren in Wakefield. Sweet.

RICKY GEORGE

Radford scored the equaliser, but it was George who struck in extra time of the third-round replay to create one of the cup's greatest ever shocks and send Newcastle tumbling to defeat at the non-Leaguers' Edgar Street ground. George went on to own a share in the horse Earth Summit which won the 1998 Grand National, before releasing a 2001 autobiography summing it all up, called *One Goal, One Horse*. Not as good as *The Thronkersaurus*, but a decent effort nevertheless.

MATT HANLAN

The scorer of Sutton's winner against Coventry in 1989 was a self-employed bricklayer who was back at work on the Monday straight after the game. He also played for Wycombe, Dorking, Molesey and Carshalton before romantically finishing back at Sutton. Hanlan is currently a director of a property company who regularly makes his long-suffering children sit through the DVD of Sutton v Coventry.

RAY CRAWFORD

Crawford scored hundreds of goals in a career that saw him play for the likes of Ipswich and Wolves and even England twice, but he will always be remembered as the man who notched a brace in Colchester's 3-2 win against Leeds in 1971. He eventually became the Portsmouth youth team coach and brought through the likes of Steve Foster, Graham Roberts and Chris Kamara, whoever he is. Crawford is retired and lives in Portchester.

DUDLEY ROBERTS

In the 1969 fifth round, the centre-forward scored the first goal of Third Division Mansfield's amazing 3-0 humbling of a West Ham team containing England World Cup winners Geoff Hurst, Martin Peters and Bobby Moore, as well as Billy Bonds, Trevor Brooking and Harry Redknapp. The Stags could not repeat the trick in the quarter-finals as they were knocked out by Leicester, who went on to reach the final. Roberts subsequently had spells for Scunthorpe and Doncaster before working for the electricity board, and then as a local photographer.

A BRIEF HISTORY OF PUNDIT STYLE

I thought Alan Shearer and Trevor Sinclair were dressed like Brian Harvey and Inspector Gadget respectively at the Blyth Spartans match, which made me look into some of the more dubious outfits worn by football pundits on the telly over the years. These are my favourites:

JIMMY BULLARD'S POST-NIGHTCLUB CHIC

The loveable former Fulham midfielder was a studio guest for the 2015 Arsenal v Hull live FA Cup tie and turned up in what can only be described as the kind of get-up you might expect to see someone wearing after a heavy night on the tiles, while stumbling around for a cab at 3am. Only Jimmy could get away with that.

BARRY VENISON'S SHIRTS

The 90s ITV regular was famous for his shirts – but not in a particularly positive way. He wanted to get noticed and his increasingly garish jacket/shirt combos ensured he always was, if not for the right reasons – it was a look which was also replicated by Peter Schmeichel several years later.

Just one of Motty's sheepskin numbers. We shall talk more about the importance of a good coat later.

JOHN MOTSON'S SHEEPSKIN

Motty was far too serious to mess about with flamboyant shoes or cuff links – the man who made the sheepskin coat famous stayed faithful to his trademark throughout his career and was rumoured to have kept it on even when appearing on the radio. OK, I made that bit up.

JOHN BARNES' JACKETS

When the former England and Liverpool star hit our screens in the 90s, he took the Venison approach and decided to dazzle with a selection of seriously savage jackets. Which brings us nicely on to...

ROBBIE SAVAGE

The Welshman has never been shy when it comes to his dress sense and has often taken flak for his colour combinations. A recent suit jacket-over-gilet look provoked the most ferocious response on social media, where judgement is always swift and merciless.

ADRIAN CHILES

When working for ITV during the 2014 World Cup, Adrian opted for the shorts and smart shirt look on Copacabana beach. It's always a tough look to pull off, especially when you are sitting next to chiselled pundits like Gus Poyet and Patrick Vieira.

ANY 70s PUNDIT

I know it was a glorious era of flares, kipper ties and all that, but ITV's World Cup panel of 1974 embodied everything that was wrong with that era. Malcolm Allison, Paddy Crerand, Derek Dougan, Brian Clough and Bob McNab were all groundbreaking pundits, but seemed to be on a mission to outdo each other in the sartorial stakes.

WHEN THE TEAM NIGHT OUT ISN'T COVERED BY THE FINE LIST

The Blyth Spartans fine list may have carried a harsh penalty for missing a team night out, but there have been many players who would've wished they'd stayed away from an evening on the town with their team-mates, as they tend not to go to plan.

THE SPURS FOOD FIGHT

Let's kick off with some good, clean fun from the 60s as Tottenham gathered for their Christmas party. The manager Bill Nicholson sent the trainer Cecil Poynton to the pub to remove the players, but his arrival prompted a huge food fight with nuts and sausage rolls flying in his direction, according to Jimmy Greaves. Poynton was forced to retreat and the youth-team players were next in the target line as the gathering descended into chaos.

KEANE FOR A NIGHT OUT

Possibly due to events in the 60s, but more than likely nothing to do with that, four decades later Spurs manager Harry Redknapp banned his players from having a Christmas bash. Robbie Keane decided to fool his manager by telling him he was taking the team on a quiet golf trip, but instead took the Tottenham squad on a heavy night out in Dublin, much to Redknapp's ire. Keane was loaned to Celtic the following month.

ENGLAND EXPECTS... PLAYERS TO GET DRUNK

Everyone knows about Gazza's famous 'dentist's chair' goal celebration at Euro 96 after his memorable strike against Scotland – it referenced a particularly heavy night out in a Hong Kong bar, pictures of which appeared in the national press before the tournament began. England had been in the Far East as a warm-up to the main event, and their night out was captured in the papers with a shot of Gazza, Teddy Sheringham and Steve McManaman with their clothes ripped and looking worse for wear. Images of Gazza and Sheringham strapped to the dentist's chair as drink was poured down their necks didn't go down too well either. But it all turned out fine in the end – apart from losing on penalties in the semi-final.

CRAIG BELLAMY'S GOLFING GAFFE

Liverpool were at a training camp in Portugal before a Champions League tie against Barcelona in 2007, when Rafa 'The Gaffer' Benítez gave the players permission to go out for dinner and have one beer. As John Arne Riise said afterwards: 'Some had more than one.'

The players had a private room in a karaoke bar and Craig Bellamy kept insisting that Riise should perform ('Ginge is going to sing'), but the Norwegian was having none of it as karaoke was not his thing. The pair squared up with Riise insisting he wouldn't sing. Later that night, Riise was in bed in his hotel room when the door opened, but it wasn't his room-mate Daniel Agger. It was actually Bellamy armed with a golf club, who proceeded to smash his teammate on his backside. The story leaked out and made the back pages in Britain, and Bellamy marked the notorious event by scoring in the Nou Camp and performing a golf swing goal celebration.

BARTON'S STINK

The infamous Manchester City 2004 Christmas party featured a fancy dress theme in which Joey Barton dressed as one of the Beatles. But the players had returned to their civvies when a ruckus took place between youth-team player Jamie Tandy and Barton. The midfielder claims the youngster had set his shirt on fire, so he grabbed the first thing he could find – which was a lit cigar – and launched it at the back of Tandy's head, but the youth player moved and received some burning ash straight in his eye. Both players were subsequently fined by the club, Barton to the tune of £60,000.

CELTIC MAKE IT SNAPPY

When players from the Glasgow club went for an evening out in Newcastle in 2002, three of them spent the night in a local police station when a *Daily Record* photographer reported camera equipment worth £12,000 stolen or damaged. Neil Lennon, Joos Valgaeren, Johan Mjallby and Bobby Petta were all taken into police custody, with Lennon subsequently released and the other three sleeping in the cells.

CRAZY LIKE A FOXE

We've all been there. You've had a few drinks, and before you know it you've mistaken the bar for a toilet. No? Well, it happened to West Ham's Hayden Foxe on a 2001 night out with his team-mates at the Sugar Reef club in Essex. Foxe urinated on the bar which resulted in the whole Hammers party being turfed out of the club and the Australian being fined two weeks' wages.

CATTLE BATTLE

The Manchester United 2007 Christmas party was a Rio Ferdinand production which didn't quite go according to plan. The team embarked on a marathon drinking session in Manchester's Great John Street Hotel from which their partners were banned, but around 80 specially selected women were invited to party with the players. Complaints followed, and Sir Alex Ferguson was not best pleased, with Christmas cancelled forever.

STIG GETS SHIRTY

Danish hardman midfielder Stig Tofting was enjoying the AGF Aarhus Christmas party until his shirt was torn. In the mêlée that followed, Tofting punched four of his team-mates – perhaps because he couldn't be sure who was the real culprit. The obligatory fine from the club soon followed.

So many of these issues have been caused by a little too much alcohol. Sometimes you feel it would be wise to sit at home with a takeaway. Which brings us beautifully to a #TakeAwayXI. Take it away...

#TakeAwayXI

Team Name: Barbecue Spare Hibs
Reserves: Dim Sunderland
Stadium: KFC Stadium
Management Team: Sillet Of Fish, Sir Alex Burgerson

First Team:
Brad Friedelivery

Didier Pakora
Chicken Tikka Mangala
Lahm Bhuna
Celestine Kebabayaro

Mushy Pienaars
Hamann Pineapple
Landon Donner Van
Naani

Benteke Fried Chicken
Garlic Fred (c)

Subs:
Sushi Jaaskelainen
Prawn Kakas
Smicer Delivery Boy
Andrew Wimpy
ChowMein Defoe
Big Chamakh

I would like to talk to you about what it feels like to be super famous. It happened to me for one day only at the World Cup in 2014. It was a window into the life of a famous footballer. It all took place in the heart of the Amazon rainforest just before England's opening game of the tournament.

Manaus was hot... boil-in-the-bag hot... fry-an-egg-on-your-car-bonnet hot... lobster-shoulders-in-ten-minutes hot. When you stepped outside the hotel at 7.30 in the morning, it was already 33 degrees. I remember having a conversation with Gary Lineker a few days before we flew to the jungle and he was reminiscing about playing in 40-degree heat in Mexico in 1986. I threw in a story about playing a game against my mates in Benidorm in 36-degree heat in the 1990s. I was about a third of the way through the story when it dawned on me that this was a ludicrous example to give. It was about two-thirds of the way through when Gary looked at me as if to say: 'Are you really equating a kick-about with your mates to a crucial game against Poland at a World Cup?' I stopped talking.

Anyway... back to Manaus, where it was Italy and not Poland who were England's opponents. The game was actually being played in the evening, so the heat was going to be much less of an issue than people were making out. It was still hot, but not 'chest-sweat' hot. The BBC team arrived about a day and a half before the game and we were staying in the same hotel as the Italian team. As you can imagine, security was incredibly tight. They had their own floor (15th), their own restaurant, their own chef and their own lift.

I wasn't aware of the lift thing, so as soon as we arrived I wandered into the same capsule as Andrea Pirlo, Mario Balotelli and Gianluigi Buffon. They gave me a similar look to the one

Sweating for England in Manaus with Messrs Neville and Murphy.

Lineker gave me during the Benidorm story, but I stayed strong and pressed the number 9.

Mario was looking at me with a slightly confused expression on his face. Like he'd seen me before. I took it as an invitation. 'Noel Gallagher, Mario. I interviewed you with Noel Gallagher.' I took his 5 per cent smile and miniature snort as recognition that he felt it was the best interview he'd ever been involved in. Buffon still wasn't happy I was in his lift. I am 6ft 6in, but somehow he seemed to be looking down on me like he was some sort of Italian behemoth.

As the bell went 'ding' on the ninth floor I confidently strolled out. Pirlo looked at me as if to say: 'You're not cool enough to share a lift with me, punk.' He was right. He looked effortlessly stylish, even in full Italian team tracksuit with matching trainers. His beard was just as magnificent close up as it is from a distance. Powerful, bushy and incredibly masculine.

The day before the game, the Italians – along with England – were training at the stadium and the fans had calculated what time they would be heading back to the hotel, so there were about a thousand of them waiting outside. Our wildly dangerous taxi driver dropped us off at exactly the same time as the players. I let them all go through first, including the bearded hero Pirlo who gave me the 'lift look' again, before dazzling the crowd with his manliness. The masses were going wild taking hundreds of selfies and autographs were being fired off left, right and centre.

I left it about 60 seconds and then decided to run the gauntlet. The fans must have still been in a post-Pirlo state of

The day the Terriers took over the Amazon.

frenzy, because as soon as I came round the back of the bus they went wild. There were hundreds of people convinced they were in the presence of greatness. I did my best to resist the rush, but I got dragged in for photographs with kids, selfies and autographs before eventually being led away by some rather burly security.

That was my one day of superstardom – well, four minutes anyway. I like to think there were quite a few Italians who arrived home from Brazil and had this conversation with their family…

Italian number 1: Would you like to see my photos?
Italian number 2: Yes.
Italian number 1: This is when we met the team at their hotel.
Italian number 2: You met Pirlo?
Italian number 1: Yeah. Great beard, isn't it?
Italian number 2: The best.
Italian number 1: The whole team was there.
Italian number 2: Oh yeah… Darmian, Chiellini, Marchisio… er… who is this sweaty guy with the red face?

When I returned from Brazil, normal life resumed very quickly. A fella approached me in the street and said 'excuse me'. I was thinking – here we go – it's Manaus all over again. Someone call security. 'How can I help?' I offered expectantly.

'I know you from somewhere,' he said excitedly. 'Did you used to work in Burger King in Birmingham?'

FOOTBALL'S GREATEST BEARDS

Once, a great football book took a look at the greatest upper-lip hair in the beautiful game. It was a wonderful thing for anyone lucky enough to have seen it. Now, a football book aspiring to greatness attempts to list the greatest beards that the beautiful game has to offer, inspired by a very close encounter with Andrea Pirlo, owner of the modern game's most wondrous lower half of facial hair.

PART I: BEARDS OF THE 70s & 80s

These days, beards are two a penny. Some women even have them. There are hipsters wherever you look. There is even a name for people who ally a beard with a checked shirt – a lumbersexual! A few decades back, the growth (no pun intended) of facial hair took off, and these first-wave beards are celebrated here.

The beard and headband combo is tough to beat.

Sócrates – The coolest ever beard in football.

George Best – Football's first showbiz star was a bearded natural.

Ricky Villa – A technical masterpiece to match a technically gifted player.

Paul Breitner – The epitome of German hairiness in the 70s. I believe his countrymen refer to this as a 'vollbart'.

Trevor Hockey – To this day, it's still unclear where the late Welsh international and Birmingham legend's head hair ended and facial hair began.
Danny McGrain – A no-nonsense beard befitting of a Celtic captain.
Leonardo Cuéllar – Mexico cult hero of the 1978 World Cup. More hair than the Dulux dog.

PART II: 90s & NOUGHTIES BEARDS

The beard backlash began as we entered the late 80s and early 90s so it took a brave man to sport facial hair. But this lot all bucked the trend with virtuoso solo efforts, and are to be applauded for their individuality.

Alexi Lalas – One of the beautiful game's ugliest but most iconic efforts. Without it nobody would ever have known who USA international Lalas was.
Alan Cork – A beard that was worth waiting for, as it came towards the end of the former Wimbledon man's career. It got Sheffield United all the way to Wembley.
Gennaro Gattuso – As we've already discovered, there's nothing you can tell Italian footballers about style and looks.
Abel Xavier – The men in Middlesbrough and Liverpool have never been the same since Xavier dyed his immaculately coiffured facial hair.
Djbril Cissé – Beard art was taken to a whole new level of topiary by the eccentric Frenchman.
Olof Mellberg – Stuck to his guns and kept those impressively hairy chops going through thick and thin.

PART III: ON-TREND BEARDS

I never received this particular email, but at some point during the 2010-11 season, beards became cool again. And here I present to you the finest footballing specimens who went with the flow and binned the razor...

Andrea Pirlo – The Sócrates of his generation, and therefore the coolest contemporary beard in football.

Roy Keane – Just because he'd retired didn't mean that he wasn't still going to wade in.

Tim Howard – The representative of the Goalkeepers Union™ is superb.

A wonderful example of an upside down head.

Stuart Sinclair – The Bristol Rovers player's effort led to this chant, to the tune of 'Sloop John B': 'He's Stuart Sinclair, he's Stuart Sinclairrrrrr, Angry little pirate, who's covered in hair.' I know you're singing this in your head right now.

Adam Clayton – Football League favourite Clayton managed to dye his beard in the blue and white colours of Huddersfield which, fortunately, was the team he played for at the time.

Davide Moscardelli – The Lecce striker became famous in Serie B for his facial hair as much as his goals.

Raul Meireles – Raul is a tad alternative in the looks department but has always stayed faithful to the chin hair. A proper Portu-geezer.

Joe Ledley – An impressive monster effort. I've seen it up close and it is thick, rich and remarkably soft.

PART IV: THE ROBERT PIRÈS AWARD FOR THE WORST BEARD IN FOOTBALL

There can only be one entrant and therefore one winner of this category – Robert Pirès's 'Brazilian wax' facial hair is a stain on our sport.

Not sure anyone on the planet could get away with this.

FOOTBALL'S GREATEST HOAXES

For a minute or two in Brazil, more than one person mistook me for a member of the Italian World Cup squad and, to be honest, it felt good. It didn't take long for me to be rumbled as a largely insignificant TV presenter. But what about those who got away with their football hoaxes? Let's find out more...

KARL POWER

Arguably sport's most famous prankster, Power's *coup de grâce* came in 2001 when he managed to be part of the Manchester United team's photo seconds before kick off in their Champions League tie away to Bayern Munich. The hoaxer got on to the pitch by posing as a member of the TV crew. In subsequent stunts, Power also posed as an England cricketer during the Ashes, beat Michael Schumacher to the podium at the British Grand Prix, played on Wimbledon's centre court and was finally banned from Old Trafford for life after re-enacting a Diego Forlan goal against Liverpool before a United home match against their rivals.

RÉMI GAILLARD

Power's French counterpart managed to get on to the pitch at the end of the 2002 French Cup final in which Lorient defeated Bastia at St Denis. Clad in the winners' kit, Gaillard joined in all the post-match on-pitch revelry, and even shook hands with President Jacques Chirac. Mange tout, mange tout.

THE FAKE SHEIKH

In one of the great tabloid stings, former England manager Sven-Göran Eriksson was caught out in Dubai by a sheikh claiming he was ready to buy Aston Villa

and appoint the Swede as manager. The sheikh was, of course, *News of the World* reporter Mazher Mahmood, who then spilled the beans on many of Sven's indiscretions during their meeting, including stories about David Beckham, Michael Owen and Wayne Rooney.

ALI DIA

No proper football book published in the UK is allowed to be printed without a reference to the great Southampton hoax perpetrated by Ali Dia, supposed cousin of George Weah. The story goes that Saints gaffer Graeme Souness received a phone call from Weah about his cousin and that the Scot agreed to have a look at him. Exactly what happened next is unclear, but Dia found himself on the bench for Southampton days later in their match against Leeds, where he was brought on and subsequently replaced when Souness discovered that his grandmother could probably have done a better job. Turned out that phone call wasn't actually from Weah at all.

YARDIS ALPOLFO

Glasgow Rangers put one over on their fans when they announced the signing of 17-year-old Turkish striker Yardis Alpolfo from Galatasaray for £5 million in 2003. The deal was widely reported across the media until it was discovered that an anagram of the teen's name was April Fools Day.

REX SECCO

Staying on the elaborate wordplay theme, the silence of a quiet international weekend in September 2015 was broken by rumours which surfaced on Twitter that Arsenal were set to sign unheard-of 16-year-old Rex Secco for £34 million. The usual social media meltdown followed, with Rex Secco trending, and opposition fans queuing up to ridicule Arsenal for wasting money. But all was not as it seemed. The following day at the Soccerex conference, social media company The Social Chain revealed they had been behind the story to prove how influential they were and had made up the player, whose name was an anagram of the conference.

RICKIE LAMBERT

When Southampton striker Rickie Lambert appeared in an official Saints website video, dressed in a New Zealand kit, claiming that he was looking into playing international football for New Zealand, most people forgot to check the date.

On 1 April 2013, Lambert, who was the leading English Premier League scorer at the time but had yet to receive an England call-up, spoke about his grandfather being a Kiwi and his connection to the country: 'I've made no secret of the fact that I would love to play international football, but I haven't yet managed to break into the England squad. New Zealand has always had a special place in my heart, given that my grandfather was born there. Everything I've heard from their footballing authorities and their foreign office has been encouraging, so I'm really hopeful that this can get sorted out sooner rather than later.'

It wasn't long before a subsequent video was released, with Rickie turning his New Zealand shirt around to reveal an 'April 1st' message on the back. A few months later, Lambert scored on his England debut and made it to the following summer's World Cup finals – no joke.

WORLD CUP 58

In 2002, a documentary was broadcast on Swedish television claiming that the 1958 World Cup never really took place but was instead a project planned by American and Swedish TV companies, the CIA and FIFA. The programme suggested that the hoax World Cup was a Cold War exercise in which the Americans were researching the effect of TV propaganda. With several former Swedish players and football officials involved in the film and lending it credibility, many viewers were duped and it wasn't until the very end that it was revealed to be a hoax. The programme-makers wanted to highlight how historical facts could be manipulated and show how dangerous Holocaust denial was.

BALOTELLI AND THE MAVERICKS

Don't worry, the Italian has not formed a new hipster band – but I was mighty impressed by his sheer indifference. It takes a certain kind of footballer to have that 'not give a damn' attitude and Mario is one of a select few who can truly claim to have maverick status. Here are seven rare talents that nobody could quite pin down:

ROBIN FRIDAY

WHO: The former Reading and Cardiff striker was an alcoholic, womanising drug addict and heavy smoker, who also happened to be one of the most talented footballers of the 70s.

HIGHLIGHTS: Dancing naked in nightclubs, umpteen red cards, two player of the year awards for The Royals and, when he moved from Reading to Cardiff, he didn't buy a train ticket to Wales and had to be bailed out by Bluebirds manager Jimmy Andrews.

MAVERICK RATING: 10/10

RENÉ HIGUITA

WHO: Without doubt, the craziest goalkeeper ever to play the game, Higuita created a style all of his own.

HIGHLIGHTS: His world-famous scorpion kick at Wembley when he saved Jamie Redknapp's speculative long-range shot with an acrobatic two-footed punt clearance was just the tip of the iceberg. Higuita regularly came out of his area and embarked on mazy dribbles into the opposition half. Oh, and he was also an associate of Colombian drug lord Pablo Escobar.

MAVERICK RATING: 11/10

Tried this in a pool in Spain once. Pulled 14 muscles.

ZLATAN IBRAHIMOVIĆ

WHO: Swedish striker who says it like it is on and off the pitch, no matter who's listening.

HIGHLIGHTS: Claiming that the 2014 World Cup would be a poorer tournament without him after Sweden lost a play-off to Portugal pretty much sums up Zlatan's attitude. His quote upon leaving Paris St Germain is another example of the career he could have had if he wasn't plagued by self-doubt: 'I came like a king, left a legend.'

MAVERICK RATING: *7/10*

BRIAN CLOUGH

WHO: The former Derby and Nottingham Forest manager who said what he liked and liked what he said. Won a fair few trophies, too.

HIGHLIGHTS: 'I wouldn't say I was the best manager in the business. But I was in the top one.' The Cloughie classics are too numerous to do him justice here, but he was unique in every sense of the word.

MAVERICK RATING: *10/10*

LEN SHACKLETON

WHO: The 'Clown Prince of Soccer', and arguably the game's first-ever maverick, played football to entertain in a 297-goal career for Bradford Park Avenue, Newcastle and Sunderland.
HIGHLIGHTS: His party pieces included combing his hair while on the ball, sitting on the ball during a match, and playing one-twos with the corner flag. Look, it was the 50s, OK?

MAVERICK RATING: *8/10*

EDMUNDO

WHO: Eccentric Brazilian striker who was infamous for his volatile behaviour on and off the pitch.
HIGHLIGHTS: He once left Fiorentina mid-season to return to Rio to attend the carnival. For his son's first birthday party, legend has it that Edmundo hired circus animals to perform, and fed beer to a monkey.

MAVERICK RATING: *8/10*

JOSÉ LUIS CHILAVERT

WHO: Fiery Paraguay goalkeeper who also managed to score 66 career goals from free kicks and penalties.
HIGHLIGHTS: Threw punches at Diego Maradona and Faustino Asprilla, and also received a suspended prison sentence for attacking a physiotherapist. 'I've had a lot of fights on the pitch, but what did people expect?' he said. 'With the face I've got I have to play the bad guy. It's a lot easier that way. Being the good guy just isn't me.'

MAVERICK RATING: *9/10*

This whole chapter has been inspired by that magical time in Manaus in 2014. I went back to Brazil for the Olympics in 2016. Maybe that will provide inspiration for another book, but for now an #OlympicXI will have to suffice.

Team Name: Adlington Stanley
Stadium: Track AnField
Management Team: Niall QuinnChronised Swimming, Keith Curling

First Team:

Headwind Van Der Sar

Breen & Jerk
Pinsent Kompany
Bould Medal
10000 Pieters

Torvill & Dean Whitehead
Delap of Honour
Mersonal Best (c)
Juan Hundred Mata Final

Dzeko-Roman Wrestling
Doping ScanDahl Tomasson

Subs:

Figueroa Skating
Mark Van Pommelhorse
Jessica Ennis Bergkamp
Olympic Frings
Steven N'Bronzi
DeJong Jump

POLISH PROBLEMS

'What's the nearest you've been to death?' That was a rather fruity question that came my way when I was talking to some kids at a school in London a few years ago. The previous week they'd had someone in who had circumnavigated the globe, so expectations were high.

It did get me thinking about perilous experiences and my mind went back to some dark days in Poland at the European Championships in 2012. In the build-up to the tournament I'd just taken part in the *Men's Health* six-pack challenge, eaten a wheelbarrow-load of broccoli and cottage cheese and lost about a stone and a half in weight.

I'd also had a serious bout of man-flu just before flying to Poland and I remember sweating profusely on the plane. After about a week in Warsaw, I woke up one morning with blood-red eyes. I looked a little bit like a character from *The Walking Dead* about two minutes before they start chomping on someone's arms.

I made what would be the first of many visits to a Polish clinic and received some medication for kerato-conjunctivitis. I thought that would be the end of it, but two days later I noticed my ankles were much more swollen than normal. My mate in the office made a joke about my 'cankles', I ate half-a-dozen Polish biscuits and thought nothing more of it. At the start of the second week, I started to feel a weird pain in my stomach – like I'd swallowed a larger than average walnut.

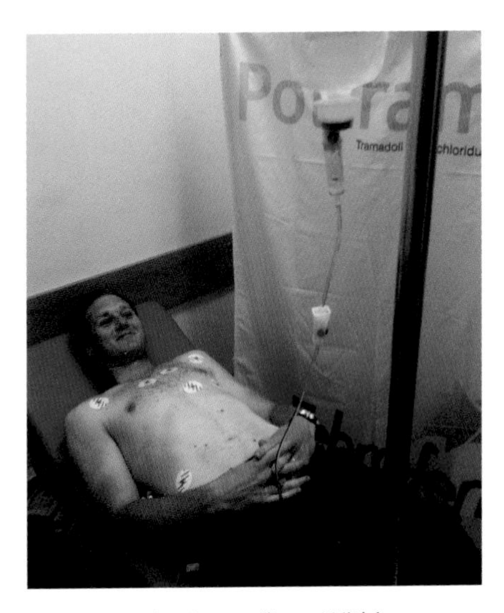

Not sure why I'm smiling. Within a minute of this being taken I was in the back of an ambulance.

Rather than going away, the pain was becoming more pronounced and the ankles now looked like a pair of tennis balls. It was starting to hurt when I bent forward, so as I left the International Broadcasting Centre in Warsaw at the end of a shift, I popped into the first-aid office. Within three minutes I was in the back of an ambulance. My resting heart-rate was down to 30 bpm and my blood pressure was through the roof. The pain in my stomach was something to do with my kidneys – all related to the ankles and the red eyes.

I lay in the back of the ambulance thinking that this wasn't quite what I planned when I left the UK. My head was spinning with possible outcomes as the driver rattled over speed bumps and hurtled around corners. Richard Hughes – my friend from the BBC – had jumped in the ambulance just before we left and our wonderful Polish fixer – Urszula – was with us, too. She was lovely and we all called her Ula.

I was raced into the hospital, into a wheelchair and into the room of a gargantuan nurse called Igor. He started attaching wires to my chest and asking me questions in Polish. Ula was filling out forms, so I had no idea what was up for discussion. Igor pulled out a massive needle the size of a Pepperami and started jabbing away at my arm. I shouted at him to stop and called Richard, whose grasp of Polish was just as disappointingly average as mine.

We managed to stop Igor and his big needle, but within an hour I was undergoing an emergency scan. Then came the wait. I was left sitting in a room with two elderly fellas for what seemed like an eternity, waiting for a visit from the consultant. Around 2am a middle-aged lady in a white coat strolled in carrying a clipboard with scan pictures on it. She said 'hello' in English and then something in Polish. Everyone left the room apart from me and Ula. I felt the back of my throat go dry but tried to smile. 'Please tell me everything she says,' I asked Ula, who reached out to hold my hand as the consultant started taking her through the scan results.

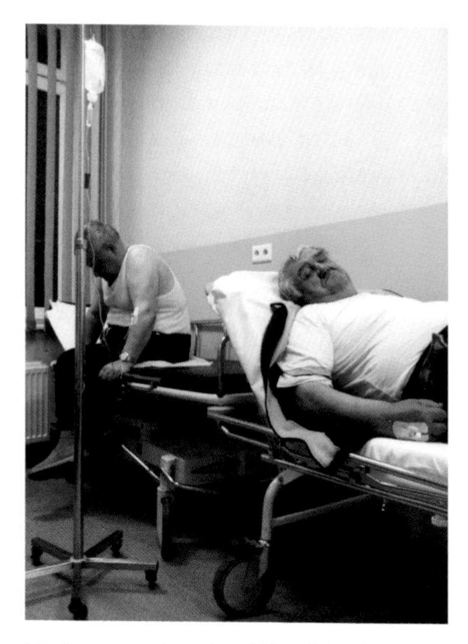

My two ward mates. We all had a great time.

I was hanging on her every word, desperately trying to understand medical Polish. Ula turned and explained that I'd suffered acute kidney failure. They were inflamed – that was the pain in my stomach – and they were down to about 30 per cent functionality. She was pointing at the scans and then said the word 'tumour'. I squeezed Ula's hand tightly and hurriedly said: 'Can you ask her again? Does tumour mean the same in Polish as it does in English? Is she saying I've got cancer?' As Ula checked, and double-checked, I held my breath... 'Yes,' she said. For some reason, I laughed.

'You need to have another scan,' said Ula. Richard is the perfect person to have around at a time like this. He came back into the room and we talked about guff for some 15 minutes. I prayed in silence a few times and thought about whether I should ring my wife in the middle of the night to tell her what had just been relayed to me. I decided against it and was whisked off for another scan to confirm the diagnosis.

I was very thankful for the care, Richard's presence and Ula's kindness but the hospital was some way short of state-of-the-art. As I was wheeled down another dimly lit corridor to another wing, it was tough to focus on the positives. There was another scan and another seemingly endless wait.

At 3am the hospital's top man came in. He spoke perfect English, didn't have a clipboard and was wearing jeans and a t-shirt. He was smiling. I started smiling and he said he had good news. 'You haven't got cancer, Mr Walker.' I was very glad I hadn't called my wife.

The Medical Corridor of Uncertainty Warsaw.

'Your kidneys are a mess, but we can fix it. We'll start right now.' I was flat on my back within minutes and they started pumping eight litres of saline fluid into my body. 'This will make you big, Mr Walker, but I hope it will work. You're lucky you came in when you did.'

Richard, Ula and I left the hospital about 7am that morning. Over the next few days I did get massive. Before the drugs kicked in, my kidneys couldn't process the extra fluid in my body. I had an A4 face and couldn't even get my trousers above the thigh area. I briefly ventured out in Poland for a cup of tea with some colleagues, but people tend to look at you rather strangely if you can't do your trousers up.

Thankfully, within a few days the gut retreated, the eyes whitened and the pain in the stomach became a distant memory. I still have my kidneys checked every six months, but they are now back to somewhere where they need to be, and Richard and I are able to laugh about our one night in Warsaw.

I didn't tell the schoolkids about this when they asked me 'what's the nearest you've been to death?' Instead, I told them about the time I nearly fell off the roof of St Paul's Cathedral. Thankfully, that didn't involve Igor or a huge face.

THE FITTEST FOOTBALLERS

Don't worry, this isn't the kind of feature you'd read in *Heat* magazine about the beautiful game's most beautiful people. Memories of my six-pack challenge made me want to find out which footballers worked as hard in the gym as they did on the pitch. And in some cases, possibly even harder.

GEORGE ELOKOBI

Not necessarily the most glittering career, with a six-year spell at Wolves the highlight, but he can certainly lay claim to one hell of a torso. Memories of myself at my peak. When filming *Football Focus* at Molineux, the boot box arrived as we were live in the dressing room. I made a joke about it being Elokobi's lunch. Unfortunately, he was standing right behind it. I hid in the showers for a good hour.

What a specimen. Muscular magnificence from Big George.

CRISTIANO RONALDO

Never one to miss an opportunity to go topless, Cristiano's body has been a lifetime's work, so we all have to know about it. As Rio Ferdinand said: 'If you've got a bod like that, you might as well fling it out there.'

MARIO BALOTELLI

A mercurial talent with a mercurial body whatever that actually means. Essentially, he's ripped. And hench, as the kids like to say.

The only man who could beat Elokobi in an arm wrestle.

ADEBAYO AKINFENWA

The man who invented Beast Mode On has been terrorising lower division defences for years with his sheer bulk and surprising pace for a big lad. And that's not the only time you'll read about him in this book.

TIM HOWARD

You'd never guess it, but underneath the goalie top lies an impressively toned physique that rivals anyone on this list. Apart from Drogba, Richards, Akinfenwa and Elokobi. Obviously.

DIDIER DROGBA

The best way to describe Didier is like the Premier League or Champions League version of Akinfenwa. OK, that's not the best way but you take my point.

MICAH RICHARDS

The one-time England player's career may have taken a turn for the worse, but there's no denying that he has abs which are worthy of an international call-up – if that is indeed possible. I once saw him in a muscle vest at Manchester City's training ground. It was definitely a well-titled item of clothing for him.

NOBBY STILES

You might not think it to look at him, but Mark Lawrenson swears that our Nobby was 'as buff as anyone around these days'. Mr Stiles was apparently also the proud owner of significantly bony elbows and – allied with the guns – was able to use them to great effect.

THE FOOTBALLERS WHOSE BITE WAS WORSE THAN THEIR BARK

Any excuse would have done for this one, but my poor kidney-induced zombie-style red eyes meant that it would be rude not to have a little taste (sorry) of the footballers whose hunger (and again) for success saw them get carried away on the pitch. Luis Suárez, this one's for you.

LUIS SUÁREZ

There's only one player to start with here and that's Dracula himself – the man who has been done for biting three different opponents. His role of dishonour started with *hors d'oeuvres* in Holland when he bit PSV Eindhoven's Otman Bakkal, continued at Liverpool with a main course of Chelsea's Branislav Ivanović, while afters came in the shape of Italy's Georgio Chiellini in the 2014 World Cup. It's not yet known whether he's going for petits fours. His antics did provide me with one of my favourite ever lines of voiceover, though. During my summary of the tournament played out just before the final, there was a line that said: 'Chewy Luis made the news. He can dribble, he can nibble but this party isn't all you can eat.'

JOSS LABADIE

Suárez isn't alone, not according to the FA at any rate. A disciplinary commission ruled that Labadie had twice been guilty of biting an opponent. First, while playing for Torquay, he bit Chesterfield's Ollie Banks and was banned for ten matches. Then, at Dagenham & Redbridge, he was hit with a whopping six-month suspension for biting the finger of Stevenage's Ronnie Henry – Labadie insists he was innocent in both cases.

JUAN ARANGO

Venezuela captain Arango was suspended for two matches for having a nibble at Jesus Zavala's shoulder during a 2015 Mexican league match between Tijuana and Monterrey. The referee missed the bite and the pair even exchanged shirts after the match (although Arango might have been disappointed that Zavala's had a hole in).

OLIVER KAHN

The far-from-shy Bayern Munich goalkeeper once nibbled the neck of Borussia Dortmund's Heiko Herrlich during a Bundesliga game – but not in an affectionate way. Kahn escaped punishment, presumably because everyone had already had such a good laugh at his expense for his naughty nuzzling.

He can't dribble, but he can nibble.

GLENN RULE

The ironically named Stockport County player was handed a ten-match ban by the FA after allegedly biting Stalybridge Celtic's Aaron Chalmers in a National League North game at Edgeley Park. Although no video evidence was available, Rule was found guilty of biting Chalmers on the thigh. Yes, that's right... the thigh.

JERMAIN DEFOE

The Tottenham striker was hacked down by West Ham's Javier Mascherano in a 2006 Premier League game at White Hart Lane and, in his frustration, crawled over to the Argentine and bit him on the arm. Not only was he not punished, but everyone thought it was quite funny. How times change.

FRANCISCO GALLARDO

Gallardo's bite is unique for two reasons. Firstly, he bit his own team-mate and secondly, he bit him on his, er, manhood. The Sevilla midfielder was over-excited after José Antonio Reyes had scored against Real Valladolid and, for reasons only he will know, decided to join in the celebration bundle in a way neither man would ever forget. He was fined and suspended for 'violating sporting dignity and decorum'. Quite right.

THE SWISS PINE MARTEN

The only animal on this list (although you could make a case that they all are), the furry forest creature invaded the pitch during a Swiss match between Zurich and FC Thun. Countless attempts to catch him failed until a magnificent diving tackle from Zurich's Loris Benito snared the bushy beast. Perhaps inspired by Suárez and others, the pine marten refused to go quietly and took a chunk out of Benito's finger for his trouble.

FOOTBALLERS' FOREIGN ADVENTURES

My Polish hospital shocker may have been dramatic, but it paled into insignificance when compared to some of the sagas which have been played out by football teams travelling abroad. Let's start with a tale that featured a totally blameless England player, in stark contrast to the rest of these.

BOBBY BEHIND BARS IN BOGOTÁ

Imagine David Beckham being imprisoned shortly before the Germany World Cup in 2006. That's pretty much what happened to Bobby Moore in 1970 as England travelled to Mexico to defend their trophy. Moore was accused of stealing a bracelet from a jewellery shop in the lobby of the team's Bogotá hotel where they were staying to play a pre-tournament friendly against Colombia. Moore was eventually released without charge – because the story was utter nonsense – but not before the England team had left for Mexico without their captain.

Not that everyone was innocent on that particular trip. Striker Jeff Astle had to be carried through a Mexico airport draped in a photographer's cape after having one, or possibly 15, too many, while the players used to play a game called Dogfight whenever they attended a local dance (nightclub to you and me), which was the drawing of lots for ugly dance partners. The louts.

WHEN (GAZZA'S) IN ROME

There are so many stories about Paul Gascoigne's antics while playing (or being injured) for Lazio, but perhaps the best happened on his first night. Gazza was given a minder when he arrived, but wasn't overly keen on the close attention so managed to lose him momentarily. He then put his shoes on the ledge of an open window in his hotel room and hid in a cupboard, so that when his minder came to see if he was OK, it appeared that he'd leaped to his death.

THE GREAT BRAWL OF CHINA

The Chinese Olympic team visited the UK in 2007 and played a friendly against QPR, although it has to be said that if ever the word friendly was used inappropriately here was Exhibit A. After various niggles between players, a full-scale war broke out as kung-fu kicks and punches were exchanged and corner flags were even raised as potential weapons. At the end of the 30-man mêlée (yes, substitutes and coaching staff were also involved), China's Zheng Tao was left unconscious with his jaw broken in three places, police were called to the training ground, and Rangers assistant manager Richard Hill was arrested and later released without charge. Seven Chinese players were sent home in disgrace, while the FA banned Hill from all football for three months (even watching it on the telly at home) and fined QPR £20,000 for failing to control their players.

LEICESTER GO LA-LA IN LA MANGA

As a reward for earning a place in the 2000 League Cup final, the Leicester squad were sent to luxurious Spanish resort La Manga for a three-day break. The players flew out the day before manager Martin O'Neill, and attempted to drink the place, and a nearby Irish pub, dry. One of the team clearly couldn't find the toilet (we'll give him an excuse), so went in one of the plant pots in the hotel reception, and Stan Collymore then let off a fire extinguisher in the hotel bar, covering more than 40 people in foam. Before O'Neill had even managed to fly out the next morning, the team had been thrown out of the resort and were heading back to Blighty in disgrace.

Incredibly, four years later, the Foxes were allowed to return to the resort and, this time, three players were charged with sexual assault and had to remain in Spain until the charges were dropped.

FINNISHING TOUCH

In between those two Spanish sojourns, Leicester embarked on a 2002 pre-season tour of Finland – a much tamer affair than the drunken do in La Manga. One night, some of the players enjoyed a game of cards – it was all very genteel. Well, it was until Dennis Wise and Callum Davidson had a minor disagreement. Davidson returned to his room and went to sleep. Wise, who had once let off fireworks in a hotel corridor during a Wimbledon pre-season tour of Sweden, was about to unleash something far more damaging as he broke into the defender's room and punched him, fracturing his jaw. After a protracted legal dispute, Wise was eventually sacked by Leicester.

THE THAILAND THREE

Completing the four-part Leicester hall of shame is the tale of three young players disgracing themselves on a holiday to Thailand in 2015 – a story which might have contributed in some way to Leicester winning the unlikeliest Premier League title of all time.

Tom Hopper, Adam Smith and James Pearson filmed a sex tape with three Thai ladies while verbally and racially abusing them. Unsurprisingly, the video was leaked and the players were all sacked by the club, who, as the whole world now knows, have Thai owners.

Pearson was the son of then manager Nigel, whose volatile relationship with the club's owners deteriorated with their decision to dismiss his son. Two weeks later, Pearson Sr followed Pearson Jr out of the door and was replaced by Claudio Ranieri. We all know what happened next.

THE MIGHTY QUINN

Manchester City's pre-season tour of Italy in 1992 was pretty unexceptional, unless you regard a street fight between Niall Quinn and Steve McMahon as exceptional. Oh, you do? Read on then.

The Barcelona Olympics were ongoing and when the well-lubricated players discovered a boxing ring in the middle of a town square, they could not resist a drunken version of the Games, focusing mainly on boxing, naturally. At one point, Quinn

and McMahon were in the ring and the Irishman thumped McMahon and split his nose. There was blood everywhere, so Quinn removed his shirt and entered a club wearing only his cut-off jeans, which led to the creation of the Maine Road terrace chant 'Niall Quinn's disco pants are the best', but that's a different story and a different book.

McMahon found Quinn in the club and got his own back by flooring him, which led to a chase through the streets of Penola, at the end of which Quinn caught McMahon and gave him a shove straight through a shop window. When manager Peter Reid demanded to know what had happened the following day, McMahon had no recollection of most of the evening but paid for the damaged window anyway.

BARTON BARRED

Another Manchester City pre-season in Thailand (there are common themes to all these foreign adventures) in 2005 ended early for Joey Barton when he became involved in a heated exchange with Everton fans in a Bangkok bar. Barton and Richard Dunne had been given the night off by manager Stuart Pearce, so were having a few drinks and talking to the Everton fans who were in town as the Toffees were in the same pre-season tournament.

One of the Everton party said something incendiary about Robbie Fowler to Barton, so the City player advised that the fan disappear. A scuffle ensued in which Barton was kicked, which he returned with a slap (not a punch), but it turned out that the recipient was only 15. In his attempts to get Barton to apologise to take the sting out of the situation, Dunne became angry and also had a scuffle with Barton. The Irishman was so incensed that he kicked a wall in frustration, broke his foot, and was soon following Barton home in a cast. All in all a pretty shambolic night out all round.

POOR POMPEY

They might have gone into administration, been relegated from the Premier League and had a transfer embargo imposed, but Portsmouth's 2010 pre-season tour of North America would give the club the boost it needed. What could possibly go wrong? Well, nothing apart from:

- A 42-hour journey from London to San Diego due to the cancellation of a connecting flight
- Two players, including a goalkeeper, sent home with injuries after playing Edmonton
- Stranded in Chicago due to bad weather grounding a flight from Edmonton to Washington to play DC United
- Sleeping for just four hours before that match due to the bad weather, which meant the travel time totalled 27 hours
- Losing 14 bags during that flight, including one containing all the kit and therefore having to play in DC United's kit
- The match against DC United turned out to be the hottest day of the year and was played in 38-degree heat, meaning all the sleep-deprived players lost at least 4kg
- Another goalkeeper was lost to injury during the match and Hayden Mullins was sent off, along with two DC players

Apart from that, nothing at all.

MARINE MAYHEM

George Graham took his Arsenal players to Portugal during the 1986-87 season for a short break – and we all know that these things tend to pass off without incident. Six players were in a local nightclub strutting their stuff to some local ladies when they became embroiled in an argument over the Portuguese princesses with some US Marines.

The dispute continued outside the club with a car chase in which Charlie Nicholas hurled a bottle of vodka into the Americans' windscreen causing them to swerve off the road. Police became involved the following morning and gaffer Graham's golf game was interrupted by a telephone call informing him that half of his squad had been arrested for attempted murder. Down at the police station, a 'compensation package' of £2,000 for the Marines was agreed and everyone was allowed to go home.

Nobody knows what became of the nightclub ladies.

KEAN AS MUSTARD

Fulham were on a pre-season tour of Germany and Austria under the guidance of Chris Coleman and his assistant manager Steve Kean. One night, the players were drinking in the hotel's canal-side bar when Coleman warned them that they had to be in their rooms by midnight, but not for any pumpkin reasons. The players continued revelling and by 2am, they were actually joined by Coleman and Kean who took a 'if you can't beat them, join them' approach. Well, it was pre-season.

A couple of hours later and everyone present was pretty drunk, so Jimmy Bullard thought it would be a good idea to hurl one of Kean's flip-flops into the canal. An argument ensued, but Bullard refused to retrieve the footwear, so Kean went to search for it. As Bullard and his team-mate Mark Crossley watched Kean standing perilously close to the canal looking for his flip-flop, a thought occurred to them both – in an instant, Bullard jumped over the table where they'd been sitting and launched himself at Kean with a full-length rugby tackle, throwing them both into the water. There was a bit of a fracas in the canal, and Kean then continued to chase Bullard around the hotel gardens as the rest of the Fulham squad looked on in hysterics.

The morning after the night before, Bullard came down in the lift and, as the doors opened, there was Kean waiting to get in. He smiled at the footballer, gave him a wink and said: 'Blinding night, last night.' Which, when you think about it, is how all these stories should really end.

Bearing in mind that the many of these stories involved some sort of hospital visit, I think it's only fitting that we settle in for a #MedicalXI*. Ready? Excellent.

* Any similarities you spot between this and the #InjuryXI in *The Thronkersaurus* are entirely unintentional and not because I forgot that we had already done that one. Honest.

#MedicalXI

Team Name: Bed Panathinaikos
Reserves: Plaster of Paris St Germain
Stadium: GalPharmacy
Training Ground: Operating Theatre Of Dreams
Management Team: Powell Movement, Lawrie McEnema

First Team:
Headwound Van Der Scar

Alan Scrubs
HepaTitus Bramble
Papa BUPA Preop

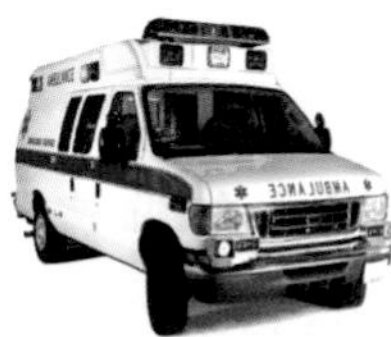

NHEssien (c)
Diego MarrowDonor
Steven Pien-aar Pien-aar Pien-aar
Marouane FellA&E

Robin Van Nursie
Zlatan IntravenousDrip
Djibril CisseSection

Subs:
Radek Gurney
X-Ray Parlour
Stress FractureGas

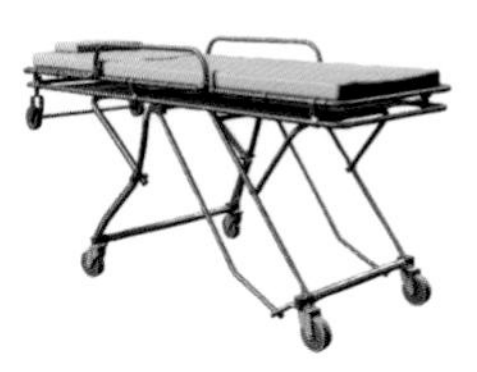

THE CLARET MUG

Over the years I have given Alan Hansen a number of reasons to dislike me. The lofty Scot left a big hole when he departed the *Match of the Day* studio and ever since he's had a bit more time to polish up the golf swing. It has never required too much additional shine. Apart from a dodgy few wafts at the Ryder Cup celebrity match at Gleneagles, it is normally in rather good nick.

I have witnessed the well-oiled machinery on numerous occasions. The first time I met Hansen on a golf course, he and Kenny Dalglish were climbing over the fence onto the driving range at the Open at Royal Birkdale back in 2008. I am sure they could have just strolled in through the front door, but they were avoiding the crowds.

The first time we played together was at Royal Lytham a few years later. My game was in what I like to call an 'agricultural phase'. I was in transition from a big loopy, wristy take-away to a shorter, more cultured, economic swing. I had been invited by MasterCard to play in a corporate event hosted by the golfing god Tom Watson. Now I knew Hansen was a big fan of Watson, so I called him and invited him along. Alan has an encyclopedic knowledge of golf. I once foolishly questioned his knowledge of Nick Faldo's major wins and he spent ten minutes trotting out his career stats to prove his point. It was as ugly as a Jim Furyk backswing.

I was right about the lure of Watson, though. Hansen was there in a heartbeat and we were waiting on the first tee for the five-time Open champion to grace us with his presence. Mr Watson was his usual mixture of gentleman, sportsman and raconteur. Hansen lapped it up, played like a demon and more than made up for my distinctly average display.

We played with Tom for six holes, and by the end of the round we had a score that had a chance to challenge the leaders. Hansen had to go to a dinner date with Mr Dalglish, so left me with strict instructions to hand in the scorecard and collect any gongs. The prize for first place was a gorgeous replica Claret Jug presented by Watson himself. Hansen called me a few hours later to see how things panned out...

Hansen: How did we get on, Dan?
Me: We finished second on countback, Al.
Hansen: Second? Second? Are you sure? What did the winners get?
Me: They got 78 points, too, but had a better back nine.
Hansen: We had 79, Dan! 79!
Me: No. It was definitely 78.
Hansen: Dan, listen...
Mr Hansen proceeded to take me through our scores on every one of the 18 holes and – annoyingly – he was correct. I had miscounted. The conversation continued.
Hansen: How did you get it so wrong?
Me: Sorry, Al.
Hansen: Countback? Countback? Dear me, Dan. I hope the prize was crap.
Me: [silence]
Hansen: Dan?
Me: Yes?
Hansen: What was it? Don't tell me it was any good.
Me: It was a mini Claret Jug.
Hansen: Was Tom there?
Me: He handed it out.
Hansen: You're kidding me, Dan?
Me: No. Sadly not.
Hansen: What did we win for second?
Me: A jumper.
There was a long silence.

There was also quite a long time before we played again. Our next encounter saw a grudge match with ITV at the World Cup in Brazil. It was Hansen's last tournament and he and I were taking on the collective pundit power of Glenn Hoddle and Lee Dixon.

Hansen told the Tom Watson story before we'd even reached the first tee, and again on the back nine, but we were playing well. My game was in shape and Al was popping in the occasional putt. We were in the seemingly unassailable position of being four holes up with just five to play.

Hoddle started hitting every fairway and deadly Dixon started holing every putt. Four up with five to play soon became three up, two up, one up and then, somehow, level going up the last. Hansen's game had fallen to bits. It was 35 degrees and he was struggling. I missed a putt from 10 feet for birdie, Dixon holed his from 8 feet and two grown men started dancing about on the green. Hansen, heartbroken, looked across at me and said: 'They are never going to let us forget that.'

He was right again. Despite picking up a mere three points on the last five holes, Hansen has blamed me 100 per cent for the loss. Sometimes Dixon texts me simply '4 up with 5 to play never wins' in the middle of the night. Sometimes I see him across a room and he holds up four fingers on one hand and five on the other, with a big smile on his face. The last time I saw Hoddle, he started giggling as I walked into the room and simply said: 'Remember Brazil.' I do Glenn. I will never forget it.

I'm still haunted by this image. Look at his face, just look at his face.

SNATCHING DEFEAT FROM THE JAWS OF VICTORY

It seems that Al and I were in good company with our throwing away of what looked like a completely unassailable lead. And let's not forget that one man's capitulation is another man's incredible comeback, as Lee Dixon never fails to remind me. Here are some of my favourite football chokes (or comebacks) to make me feel better about myself. The standard of this lot is so high that there wasn't even room for the Premier League classic, Spurs 3 Manchester United 5.

TOON TOSS IT AWAY

The flagship. The standard-bearer. The mother of all seemingly unassailable leads. With 14 games to go in 1996, Kevin Keegan's Newcastle were 12 points clear of Liverpool and Manchester United. They had led the league since August. They were champions elect.

But then United went on one of those runs they used to go on in the 90s, winning 12 of their last 14 games. So what happened to Newcastle? First of all, Keegan signed Faustino Asprilla in January, which meant Peter Beardsley was pushed out wide to accommodate the Colombian. Les Ferdinand, who alongside Beardsley had scored 21 times until that point, scored only four more goals that season.

Then there was the epic 4-3 defeat at Liverpool which certainly didn't help, and that was followed shortly after by Keegan's infamous 'I would love it...' moment live on TV after he had been irked by Alex Ferguson's comments that Leeds should play their best against Newcastle to make sure the title race was even. Job done. I hosted an evening with Mr Keegan recently and he said it's much better now – people only mention it once or twice a day.

The Big Swede did the business against the Germans.

GERMAN INEFFICIENCY

If Germany are winning 4-0 with 28 minutes left of a game at home in Berlin, there is only one winner. This is Germany we're talking about. In two years' time, they will be world champions. By rights, this game will end with maybe one or two more German goals and none conceded. But the Zlatan Ibrahimović-inspired Sweden side they were playing against in 2012 hadn't read the script. By all accounts, they'd probably been reading *Roy of the Rovers* or *Billy's Boots*, as four goals without reply, including a Rasmus Elm equaliser in stoppage time, left Germany and the rest of Europe completely stunned.

BAYERN BOTTLE IT

Included as much for Manchester United's cheek as well as Munich's choking, this was the moment that provided us with Ferguson's 'Football, bloody hell' classic quote. Because that just about sums up United trailing 1-0 in injury time in the 1999 Champions League final, having been behind for almost the entire game after Peter Schmeichel's error allowed Mario Basler to score early on, yet still winning without even bothering to go into extra time. For three crazy minutes in Barcelona, the Germans forgot how to defend corners and the Reds scored twice through Teddy Sheringham and Ole Gunnar Solskjaer to become European champions. Sometimes when I close my eyes I still see Sammy Kuffour of Bayern Munich beating the earth in frustration.

NOT HUNGARY ENOUGH

Hungary had not lost a game for five years. They were the best team in the world, playing in the 1954 World Cup final against a West Germany team who they had beaten 8-3 in the group stages of the same tournament. Not only that, they were 2-0 up against the Germans in the final after just eight minutes. But heavy rain hampered the Magyars' game and the Germans hit back to level the match, and then struck an 84th-minute winner to stun Hungary and the world. There remain accusations of doping whenever the game is discussed, but this remains a solid-gold Hungarian choke.

SAINTS SURRENDER

When you're 3-0 up against a team from a division below with half an hour left of an FA Cup fifth-round tie, you may as well start making plans for the quarter-final because you are as good as there. And it seems that's exactly what Saints players must have done against Tranmere at Prenton Park in 2001, because there's no other explanation for what happened next.

I was sat in the press box that day and remember Paul Rideout starting the comeback, but it was still 3-1 with 71 minutes on the clock. Then, Rideout struck again and completed his hat-trick on 80 minutes to level the tie. With my golfing nemesis Glenn Hoddle's Southampton struggling to come to terms with what had happened, Stuart Barlow popped up with a late winner causing the former England boss to label his team a 'disgrace'.

DISGRACE

TOTTENHAM'S TERROR

Another 4-3 capitulation, but this was arguably worse as Tottenham's opponents at White Hart Lane in this 2004 FA Cup tie were a Manchester City side who had been reduced to ten men at half time. The visitors were going into the break 3-0 down, which would've been bad enough, but then Joey Barton was dismissed for dissent as the teams left the pitch to compound City's misery.

I was at this one, too, and remember watching quite a few fans deciding they'd had enough and start the long trek home before the teams resurfaced for the second 45. However, an early goal after half time from Sylvain Distin changed the atmosphere. There were 20 minutes left when Paul Bosvelt made it 3-2 and then Shaun

Wright-Phillips equalised on 80 minutes to send City fans wild with delight. And those supporters went positively berserk when Jon Macken's 90th-minute header won the tie. True comeback madness.

UNITED WE FALL

In the days before United always won the league, and shortly before the Premier League even existed, Alex Ferguson's team once capitulated in a very un-United like way, weighed down by the historical burden of not having won the title for 25 years.

This was 1991-92 when United had the title, if not the points, in their own grasp as they trailed Leeds by just a point with two games in hand, and only six games of the season remaining. Having won the League Cup and the UEFA Super Cup (played mid-season back then), there was some fixture congestion which led to a ridiculous four matches in six days for Fergie's side.

It started well with a win against Southampton, but a draw with Luton was followed by a home defeat to Nottingham Forest. Fergie was on the edge and he lost it Keegan-style when United were beaten at West Ham, a team already relegated. The Scot ranted that it was 'obscene and almost criminal' for a relegated team to suddenly raise their game like that. The cheek of it!

Even worse was to come, as United's third defeat in a row followed at bitter rivals Liverpool, and Leeds became champions. At one stage United had been six points clear, but they took just 13 points from their final 11 games. Although they kind of made up for it for the following 20 years.

MILAN'S MISERY

We all know the story, but that doesn't mean it shouldn't be on this list. AC Milan were 3-0 up at half time of the 2005 Champions League final against Liverpool. They had at least nine fingers on the trophy. Even at 2-0, BBC Radio's Alan Green had said on air: 'This final is over.' I remembered talking to John Aldridge at half time in Istanbul and he was weeping into his moussaka in the press room. 'It's an absolute mess, Dan. There's no way back. I might as well stay in here. Not sure I can face another half like that.'

Liverpool and Rafa Benítez had other ideas, though. Steven Gerrard, Vladimír Šmicer and

Xabi Alonso levelled the tie up, and Jerzy Dudek's save from European Footballer of the Year Andriy Shevchenko's penalty handed Liverpool the shoot-out win and a fifth European Cup. I saw Aldridge at the airport on the way home and he said he always thought there was a way back. Must have been something in the moussaka.

I stayed up for two days straight on that trip. We were either busy or travelling for 48 hours and by the time I came down from the crane above Anfield at 7pm the night after Istanbul, I was ready for a bit of Rip Van Winkle action.

ROYAL RUMBLE

The craziest cup tie you will ever come across, I'm not entirely convinced that this 2012 League Cup fourth-round match isn't just a figment of my imagination. Reading were 4-0 up before half time – or four up with 45 to play if you like – and on their way to found five. A Theo Walcott goal on the stroke of the break reduced the arrears, and Olivier Giroud pulled another back but that was it. Kind of.

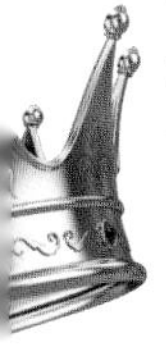

The Royals led 4-2 with two minutes to go. Then Laurent Koscielny struck to make it 4-3, and in the 95th minute of normal time Walcott equalised. Into extra time it went, and Arsenal led for the first time through Marouane Chamakh, but a Pavel Pogrebnyak leveller made it 5-5. The tie seemed set for penalties until Walcott completed his hat-trick and Chamakh added another, both in the final minute, to finally see off Reading. Ludicrously it finished 7-5.

ANGOLA'S ANGST

The opening match of the 2010 African Cup of Nations was supposed to be a party for hosts Angola and when they were 4-0 up against Mali with 11 minutes to go, the festive atmosphere was in full swing. Incredibly, 15 minutes later they'd only drawn the game. Even with two minutes to go, Angola were 4-1 up. Not winning was inconceivable. Mali made it 4-2 at that point and as the game entered stoppage time, surely there was only one result possible? Correct, if that result was a draw. A 93rd-minute goal from Seydou Keita, followed by another a minute later from Mustapha Yatabaré, ensured the hosts' party had been well and truly pooped.

ENGLAND BOO BOYS

There was a cruel chant which used to be sung about my golfing tormentor Lee Dixon – occasionally, I sing it quietly to myself to feel better about *that* day in Brazil. The words were quite simple: 'If Dixon plays for England so could I.' For one reason or another, despite being a top fella and footballer, Lee was targeted by England fans, but he wasn't the only one.

JOHN BARNES

He may have scored England's most famous ever solo goal, against Brazil in the Maracana in 1984, but his failure to regularly convert his superb club form for Liverpool onto the international stage meant the patience of some fans wore thin and he was routinely booed in the latter stages of his England career.

CHRIS WADDLE

Amazingly, one of England's Italia 90 stars also fell victim to the fans' jeers when he failed to reproduce his outstanding performances for Spurs and Marseille whenever he wore an England shirt. This still annoys me to this day because The Waddler is in my top three footballers of all time.

DAVID BECKHAM

After being sent off for England against Argentina in the 1998 World Cup last-16 match, Becks became public enemy number one in England. Wherever he played the following season, the boos rang out, so Becks did the decent thing and promptly won the Treble with Manchester United to shut everyone up.

EMILE HESKEY

On the face of it, seven goals from 62 appearances is not a great return for a striker, and that's pretty much why Emile Heskey received regular rollickings while playing for England – in his defence, the fans didn't really understand what role manager Sven-Göran Eriksson was asking him to play, but Heskey probably didn't either.

CARLTON PALMER

The man who once bashfully told me he would become England manager one day would most likely have received the same welcome as gaffer as he did when regularly used as a midfielder by Graham Taylor – not a friendly one. The fans didn't rate Palmer and made their feelings very clear.

DAVID BENTLEY

The outspoken flair player snubbed a call-up to play in the Under-21 European Championship for England in the summer of 2007. A few months later, he played for the senior team at Wembley and the fans let him know what they thought of that decision.

FRANK LAMPARD

Whether it was the whole Lampard/Gerrard playing together debate or something else, it's fair to say that Lamps never shone for England in the same way as he did for Chelsea. That frustration boiled over when Lampard came on as a substitute at Wembley against Estonia in 2007 and was greeted by a load of booing. Weirdly, he'd been cheered at HQ just a few months before when he was announced as England Player of the Year. The fickle finger of football strikes again.

WAYNE ROONEY

As England's players trudged off the pitch following their worst performance in the worst football match ever played (the 0-0 draw against Algeria in the 2010 World Cup, in case you need reminding) they were roundly booed, and Rooney took exception by informing an on-pitch camera: 'Nice to see your own fans booing you. If that's what loyal support is... for f***'s sake.' As a result of that, and England's subsequent surrender to Germany in the last 16, he and several other England players who featured in the 2010 Community Shield at Wembley a couple of months later were booed by fans throughout the match.

ASHLEY COLE

Poor Ashley was given pelters at most grounds, but his most infamous moment for England came when a poor pass allowed Kazakhstan to score at Wembley. The fans weren't happy and subsequently booed every time Cole touched the ball. It is a tough school on occasions, this international football lark.

OWEN HARGREAVES

Prior to the 2006 World Cup finals, England fans didn't really get who Hargreaves was. Born in Canada, then playing for Bayern Munich in the Bundesliga meant some supporters thought he was some kind of German infiltrator and, as such, they booed him. Following that World Cup in which he shone for England, with a particularly heroic effort against Portugal in the quarter-final, funnily enough, the booing stopped.

PETER CROUCH

How could anyone boo Peter? In the 2006 World Cup warm-up matches, England played at Old Trafford as Wembley was still being rebuilt – given that Crouch was a Liverpool player at the time, he was probably an easy target. That, and the robot dance.

If in doubt, bust The Robot out.

THE MASTERS – FOOTBALL'S GREATEST GOLFERS

Hansen may not rate my game – or my counting – very highly, but that's his prerogative. All footballers fancy themselves on the fairways, but which players are actually half-decent at spoiling a good walk? Here's my guide to the beautiful game's best golfers.

JIMMY BULLARD – PRO

One of those people who's good at everything, Bullard could hit a 180 in darts and make a century break in snooker while he was

Bullard is no dullard. King of the swingers.

still a kid. He was a scratch golfer who turned pro after he retired from football, and currently plays on the Euro Pro Tour, the third tier of European professional golf. Every now and again, I remind him of a game we had at Worsley Park in Manchester when he put three balls in the drink on the 12th and walked off in a huff. He has no recollection of the incident.

NEIL COX – HANDICAP 1

He may not have had the glittering career of others on this list, but the former Watford defender is a phenomenal golfer who once came through regional heats to play in the final qualifying round for the Open Championship.

ANDRIY SHEVCHENKO – HANDICAP 2

Sheva owns a property in the Wentworth Estate and is a member of the famous golf club where he's managed to hone his game to the extent that he's appeared in the odd Challenge Tour event. He plays every day. That's *every* day.

ALAN HANSEN – HANDICAP 3

Al may well have taken up a career in golf were it not for the Hibernian manager Eddie Turnbull. My former playing partner takes up the story: 'Golf has always been my first love. I stopped playing football between the ages of 15 and 17 to concentrate on playing golf. My father wanted me to be a footballer, so just to placate him I went on trial at Hibs when I was 17. It was a week before I was playing in the Scottish Boys' Strokeplay at Montrose.

'Eddie Turnbull brought me into his office after five days and said he wanted to sign me on professional terms. I said: "What, I'll just pack in playing golf? I'm going to Montrose to play in the Scottish Boys' Strokeplay, I'm never playing football again." He said: "Are you an idiot?"'

DWIGHT YORKE – HANDICAP 4

The former Manchester United forward may want to save some of his fancy pundit clothes for the golf course as he's a decent player. The story goes that he was introduced to golf by former Villa team-mate Dean Saunders and never looked back.

JAMIE REDKNAPP – HANDICAP 4

The former Liverpool and England midfielder used golf as a crutch to lean on when his career ended at the age of just 31, and has performed brilliantly playing alongside Luke Donald at the Dunhill Links Championship in the past. And he appreciates that golf is there for good: 'I can't play football anymore because of my knee, but I can hopefully play golf for the rest of my life.'

GIANFRANCO ZOLA – HANDICAP 5

'I wouldn't call it a passion,' says Zola, when asked about his love of golf. 'I think it is more than that. It is madness.' The little genius was first introduced to the madness by Gianluca Vialli when the pair were at Chelsea in 1996. 'It was Vialli who took me to play golf and I've been crazy about it ever since.'

MATT LE TISSIER – HANDICAP 5

Le Tiss is mad about golf and rates himself as the best ex-footballer on the course. Although he says he's not as passionate about it as his former team-mate Paul Telfer. 'He [Telfer] actually wasn't that interested in football; he was far more into golf. Paul would even play a round on Saturday morning before a game! I never got to that extreme.'

TEDDY SHERINGHAM – HANDICAP 6

Sheringham started playing while at Millwall, and has never looked back. He fondly recalls his England days playing alongside Shearer, [Gary] Neville and Owen – on the golf course, not the pitch – but has strong words about another national team-mate: '[Paul] Scholes is a bandit. He reckons he has a handicap of 14, but he can drill the ball miles.' I played with Teddy, alongside Peter Schmeichel and Paul Lawrie at the BMW Pro Am a few years ago. Teddy was steady.

CARLOS TEVEZ – CADDY

He's not a bad player himself, playing off 13 which is very respectable, but Tevez once caddied for his compatriot Andres Romero at the 2012 Open Championship at Royal Lytham.

FOOTBALL'S GREATEST PAIRS

As Al went off to have dinner with his former team-mate Kenny Dalglish to leave me to mess up the scoring, I realised that some football folk were just born to be together. And it got me pondering about the game's greatest pairs, the players who go together like a horse and carriage, whether they were defensive rocks, midfield maestros or striking sensations. Then I realised that there are absolutely loads of them so, before you all start arguing about the ones I've missed, here are my favourites.

REAL DEAL

WHO ARE YA? Alfredo di Stéfano and Ferenc Puskás, the Messi and Ronaldo of their time, except these two played for the same Real Madrid team

WINNING COMBO: Real Madrid won everything with the pair, including the 1960 European Cup in which Puskás scored four goals and Di Stéfano a hat-trick in the famous 7-3 final win over Eintracht Frankfurt at Hampden Park

VITAL STATS: Di Stéfano scored 216 goals for Real, and Puskás netted 225

RESEMBLE: Spock and Captain Kirk – they were on another planet

DOUBLE DUTCH

WHO ARE YA? Ruud Gullit and Marco van Basten, AC Milan and Dutch legends

WINNING COMBO: Just the 1988 European Championships, and the 1989 and 1990 European Cups

VITAL STATS: Between them the pair scored 125 goals for Milan (Van Basten 90, Gullit 35) while van Basten was on target five times as they led their country to its only major trophy in Germany

RESEMBLE: Posh and Becks – they pioneered sexy football

RHYMING COUPLET

WHO ARE YA? Mark Bright and Ian Wright, the Crystal Palace dream team up top

WINNING COMBO: Their goals helped win The Eagles promotion to the top flight, a record third-place finish, and came within a whisker of winning the FA Cup in 1990 – although they did lift the Zenith Data Systems Trophy...

VITAL STATS: Wright scored 117 goals for the club, Bright notched 92 for a joint total of 209

RESEMBLE: The Chuckle Brothers – always played with smiles on their faces

UNITED THEY STAND

WHO ARE YA? Steve Bruce and Gary Pallister, the Manchester United defensive pair who started a dynasty of success at Old Trafford

WINNING COMBO: Four Premier League titles and three FA Cups

VITAL STATS: 133 clean sheets, 0.89 goals conceded per game, 57 per cent of games won and only 17 per cent lost

RESEMBLE: Reeves and Mortimer – pair of north-east diamonds

THE SAS

WHO ARE YA? Alan Shearer and Chris Sutton, Blackburn's very own Special Air Service up front

WINNING COMBO: Their goals shot Rovers to the 1994-95 Premier League title

VITAL STATS: 46 goals between them, 31 for Shearer and 15 for Sutton, landed Rovers an unlikely championship

RESEMBLE: Blues Brothers John Belushi and Dan Aykroyd – only one success on the big stage, but what a great one it was

THE BOYS FROM BRAZIL

WHO ARE YA? Ronaldo and Rivaldo, Brazilian magicians in front of goal

WINNING COMBO: The samba skills™ of both were instrumental in winning Brazil's historic fifth World Cup in 2002

VITAL STATS: Ronaldo's eight goals earned him the Golden Boot while Rivaldo scored in each of his country's first five games

RESEMBLE: Batman and Robin – everyone remembers Ronaldo in 2002, whereas Rivaldo was a bit like his sidekick

GUNNER SALUTE

WHO ARE YA? Tony Adams and Steve Bould, Arsenal defensive lynchpins in the 80s and 90s

WINNING COMBO: Three Premier League titles and two FA Cups in nine seasons together

VITAL STATS: In Arsenal's 1991 league title triumph, Adams and Bould (alongside Winterburn, Dixon and Seaman, of course) conceded only 18 goals in 38 games.

RESEMBLE: Statler and Waldorf – nothing got past that mean pair

THE OTHER BOYS FROM BRAZIL

WHO ARE YA? Romário and Bebeto, Brazil's early 90s version of Merson and Shearer

WINNING COMBO: Fired the South Americans to the 1994 World Cup and introduced the world to the 'baby rocking' goal celebration

VITAL STATS: 94 goals combined for their country, in the finals Romário scored five (and a penalty in the winning shoot-out) while Bebeto notched three times

RESEMBLE: Havaianas – so efficient, you barely noticed they were there

Not sure if it was the first baby celeb, but it's certainly the most memorable.

CATALAN CREW

WHO ARE YA? Xavi and Iniesta, the greatest midfield pair in the modern era – eclipsing Keane and Scholes, Petit and Vieira and any others you want to bring to the table

WINNING COMBO: One World Cup, two European Championships, two Champions Leagues, six La Liga titles, the list goes on...

VITAL STATS: Both players have career successful pass rates of more than 90 per cent which, when you think about it, is bonkers

RESEMBLE: A Spanish Ant and Dec – great at what they do but hard to tell apart from a distance

TRICKY TRIO

WHO ARE YA? Dwight Yorke and Andy Cole, Manchester United's Treble-winning wonders. 'When we started playing together, it was like meeting a special woman and falling in love,' says Cole.

WINNING COMBO: The 1999 Premier League, FA Cup and Champions League

VITAL STATS: 53 goals combined that season was the firepower behind their team's extraordinary success

RESEMBLE: Ricky Gervais and Stephen Merchant – one always giggling, the other playing it straight, but it worked

GOLDEN GAFFERS

WHO ARE YA? Brian Clough and Peter Taylor, the incredibly successful manager and assistant manager duo

WINNING COMBO: Two European Cups, a league title and four League Cups with Nottingham Forest, one league win with Derby County

VITAL STATS: Worked together for pretty much 18 years – no other manager/assistant relationship like it in football

RESEMBLE: *Minder's* Arthur Daley and Terry McCann – Arthur needed Terry more than he liked to imagine

6 THINGS THAT FOOTBALLERS LIKE DOING OFF THE PITCH APART FROM GOLF

Surprisingly, it's not just golf that keeps footballers busy after training or post-retirement – some of them are also interested in doing other things, too. Here's my guide to the six essential non-golfing activities footballers like.

FISHING

We're always told this is the nation's biggest participation sport, so it stands to reason that footballers would be getting involved, too. The likes of Matt Taylor, Tony Hibbert, Jimmy Bullard, Gazza, Mark Noble and Jack Charlton have all indulged in regular angling, confirming its popularity.

OWNING PUBS

It's a bit of a blast from the past, but players from a certain era – those not lucky enough to be paid an absolute fortune – moved into the pub trade after hanging up their boots. Everton's Dixie Dean (he of record goalscoring feats) ran the Dublin Packet in Chester, former England striker Tommy Lawton owned Nottinghamshire's Magna Carta Inn, while several Leeds players pitched in to run Leeds bar Brahms and Liszt. Even today's players get involved, as Frank Lampard and his dad own The Pig's Ear in Chelsea.

GAMBLING

Unfortunately, this is an extremely popular pastime for footballers past and present, with the extra money doing some of them no favours. The likes of Michael Chopra, Keith Gillespie and Paul Merson have all lost small fortunes to the bookies – they should have stuck to golf.

PROPERTY PORTFOLIOS

Once the domain of the super-rich, now it's Premier League footballers who are building up handsome property collections in some kind of real-life Monopoly game, but without dice, Community Chest or Chance cards. Robbie Fowler is the most famous example of a player who invested wisely in property, to the point that when he played for Manchester City, fans used to sing 'We all live in a Robbie Fowler house' to the tune of 'Yellow Submarine'.

TRAINING RACEHORSES

It's related to gambling, but it's far more legitimate as many players have gone into the world of racing as trainers or racehorse owners. Fergie owns his fair share of horses, Michael Owen trains and owns them, while Mick Channon is now equally famous for training horses as he was for playing the beautiful game.

CHEEKY NANDOS

More often the pursuit of the B- or C-List footballer. You can't just go to Nandos, it has to be a 'Cheeky Nandos' – although how cheeky it can be when it happens every day is debatable. Nile Ranger, Michael Duberry and Josh McEachran all shout about it, but the ultimate aim of the footballer is to secure the restaurant chain's exclusive VIP Black Card, which guarantees them free food for life.

Let's finish off by returning to golf. Alan Hansen has played the golden grass of Augusta on numerous occasions. Most of us can only dream. The closest we'll get is this... a #MastersXI.

#MastersXI

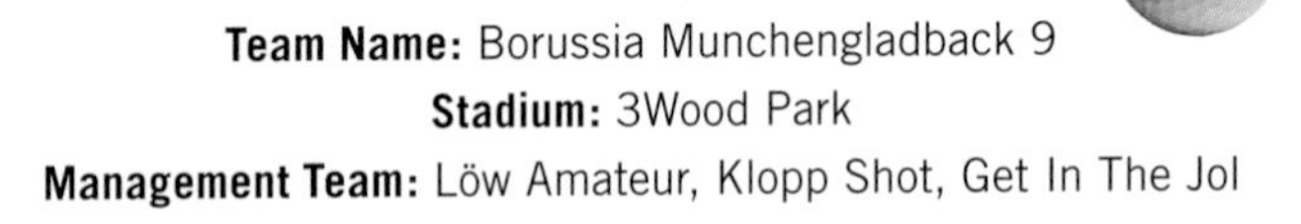

Team Name: Borussia Munchengladback 9
Stadium: 3Wood Park
Management Team: Löw Amateur, Klopp Shot, Get In The Jol

First Team:

Caddyshaka Hislop

Titleist Scramble
Dogleg Luzhny (c)
Joan HandiCapdevilla
Büttner's Cabin

Schlupp And Down
Brolin Wanchope
Nicky Putt

Gimme Floyd Hasselbaink
Benni McParthree
Spieth Houchen

Subs:

Par Mertesacker
Damien Duffner
Davis Ndlovu III
Peter Odemswingie

THE WEMBLEY ARCH

'How are you with heights?' was how the conversation started. 'I'm OK. I had some issues at the top of St Paul's Cathedral once [that story again], but I think I'm OK these days.'

The reason for the question was a plan to send some poor idiot up to the top of the new Wembley arch for the FA Cup final between Arsenal and Aston Villa in 2015. No prizes for guessing who the 'idiot' was. They gave me a week to think about it. When I was told about the long list of TV types who'd been offered the chance to do it and either chickened out or puked at the last minute, that was all the motivation I needed. I was in.

The arch is one of the most recognisable structures in the world and it's not just there for show. Like many of you, I am aware of the statistics. It supports the entire north side of the stadium and 60 per cent of the south stand and it's the reason there are no pillars inside the stadium. It's wide enough to fit a channel tunnel train through it, weighs the same as 275 double-decker buses and – at 315 metres – is the longest single span of roof structure anywhere in the world.

The one fact that didn't leave my brain was the height above the floor: 133 metres. That is roughly the same height as the London Eye. I could tell you how many otters on top of each other that corresponds to, or we could just agree that it's high. 'All I will say, Dan, is don't be sick from the top of it. From that far up it'll take quite a lot of time to clean things up.'

Those were the wise words from the chief safety officer at Wembley the day before the cup final. He'd been unsure about the weather conditions, but was finally happy that the rain had gone away and the wind had died down enough to get into a tiny little lift and travel from one side of the arch to the other. I put on about four layers of clothing and stepped into one of those safety harnesses that gently crushes your man goods while stopping you from falling to certain death somewhere near the centre circle.

'This is where Ray Stubbs pulled out,' said the Scandinavian engineer as he skipped across the walkway that led to what he called 'the cage'. He didn't want to be named, so we'll call him Swedish Dave. I stared at the back of his head as he opened up the worryingly flimsy door and attached all sorts of hooks to my harness. I must confess that my pants shook a little when I noticed that the lift was operated by wedging one bare piece of metal against another to complete the circuit. The cage jolted into gear and we began the slow 15-minute progress to the top of the arch.

As we moved up, I was trying my hardest not to think about death. The view was helping. The pitch looked immaculate, and as we moved up above the roof the rest of London came into sight. I was just pointing out Canary Wharf to my cage compadre when our little vehicle came to a jolting stop and starting rocking around uncontrollably. The contents of my stomach jumped upwards and it was only the reassuring smile of Swedish Dave that stopped my two Weetabix and a banana covering the seats of the Royal Box.

Swedish Dave whacked the metal rod with a big spanner, pressed a green button and we were off again. I talked incessantly for the next ten minutes, trying to take my mind off our increasing

This smile is right out of the 'grin and they won't know you're wetting yourself' textbook.

distance from terra firma. As we approached the summit, Swedish Dave stopped our little cradle. I should probably point out at this stage that I wasn't on a jolly. The whole reason for the trip was to film a line for the opening sequence of *Football Focus* the following day. We dangled in the cage for what seemed like ages as the drone camera got into position. 'Welcome to Wembley, welcome to *Football Focus*' was repeated five or six times as the drone hovered about and fought annoyingly high winds.

Just as we completed the final take, my phone went off. I thought it would be the editor of the show checking that everything was OK. 'Hello Daniel, it's your mother. Are you OK?' Mumma Walker has mastered the awkwardly timed phone call. The first week I took over from Bill Turnbull on *BBC Breakfast*, I was also covering the FA Cup. I got up at 3.30am on Monday, Tuesday and Wednesday, worked all day Thursday, travelled to Reading v Crystal Palace on Friday, arrived in Liverpool at 2.30am on Saturday morning to present *Focus* from Goodison Park and then went on to Salford to host *Match of the Day* that evening. She was worried that I wasn't getting enough sleep, so she rang at 6.55am on Saturday morning to let me know her concerns. When I lovingly informed her that she was adding to my raging insomnia, she claimed 'this is what mothers do' and laughed.

She also laughed that day at Wembley when I told her that I was quite a few otters above the Wembley pitch and swaying gently in the breeze with a fella from Scandinavia. Swedish Dave and I took a few snaps and began the journey back down to the other side of the stadium.

'Has anyone ever fallen out of this?' I asked.

'Shouldn't you have asked that before you got in?' responded a giggling engineer. Despite the worryingly vague answer to my safety concern, the descent went perfectly. My attempt to act all manly failed miserably when I hugged Swedish Dave for about two seconds too long as we stepped out of the cradle. We wandered back to the security room, and it really was a 'wander' because it's quite hard to walk correctly when there's harness working its way up your crevice.

If you add in the safety briefings, waiting for the right weather and all the form-filling, the whole thing took the best part of five hours. Five hours for five seconds of TV.

THE FOOTBALL FAMILY

Sometimes, someone from your family – usually your mum – just has to get involved in your life when you least expect it. My mater called me up when I was on top of the Wembley arch. Fortunately, I wasn't broadcasting live at that point, but there have been many occasions when a member of a footballer's family has become part of the story, for better or worse...

MRS TERRY

It's hard enough when you're working on rebuilding a damaged reputation, so the last thing John Terry needed was his mother on the front pages after being arrested for shoplifting. And if one family member wasn't good news, Mrs T was caught red-handed alongside her boy's mother-in-law.

MRS ROONEY

When Coleen Rooney innocently posted a tweet saying 'Happy Father's Day' to her husband and father of her two children,

If Coleen really wants to be heard, she needs to add the other hand to make a funnel.

Mummy's little hero.

Wayne, the day after England's 2014 World Cup defeat to Italy, several fans took that as an opportunity to criticise Wazza's performance in the game. But Coleen stood by her man, telling one punter: 'You take his place then! Let's see how you get on!'

MRS RONALDO

Word has it that Cristiano Ronaldo's mum calls all the shots when it comes to her boy's career. And Maria Dolores Dos Santos Aveiro really gave her little Ronni cause for embarrassment by admitting on camera in the documentary *Ronaldo* that she didn't want him in the first place: 'He is a child that I wanted to abort,' she said. 'God didn't want that to happen and I was blessed because of that.'

MRS SUNG-YUENG

In a far more mild-mannered affair, the wife of then Celtic player Ki Sung-yueng jumped to her man's defence after he criticised his South Korean national team manager on social media. 'Thanks for selecting me to the national team even though I play for a mere second-tier league in Europe,' he sarcastically wrote after the South Korean boss had slammed the standard of the Scottish Premier League. Unfortunately, those comments didn't go down well and Ki was forced to apologise, but his actress wife, Han Hye-jin, stood by her man with stoic realism. 'Some say it is a time when Ki Sung-yueng will need his wife's support. I believe we'll have to receive beatings when we have to since my husband and I both have jobs which expose us to the public. We are trying to weather hard times right now, but I believe we'll get a chance to rise again with time.'

All of which is a world away from Coleen Rooney.

MR ADEBAYOR

Never one to hold back his feelings, Togo striker Emmanuel Adebayor has gone public on the shortcomings of his family more than once. He lambasted his younger brother Rotimi on Facebook, accusing him of stealing a Marc-Vivien Foe shirt, a signed Zinedine Zidane jersey and a Cartier necklace he'd bought for his mother. And this is the same brother who Emmanuel also claimed had stolen up to 21 mobile phones from team-mates at a French football academy.

In another Facebook rant, Adebayor also took other family members to task for taking money from him and ended his revelations by writing that 'the main purpose is not to expose my family members. I just want other African families to learn from this. Thank you.'

MR ZAHA

Shortly after Wilfried Zaha was transferred from Crystal Palace to Manchester United, the press revealed that his older brother Herve was a 'general' in the feared South London gang DSN or the Don't Say Nothing crew. The footballer's brother's Bebo page profile declared: 'General Zeltor on dis ting say no mre,' which was enough to convince many tabloids to run the story – well that, and Herve's 2012 conditional discharge for criminal damage.

MRS IRELANDS

Former Manchester City star Stephen Ireland's grandparents shot to fame overnight back in 2007 when the midfielder tried to get out of international duty for the Republic of Ireland by first claiming that his grandmother had died. When some careful journalistic digging found that she was alive and kicking, he said it was his grandma on the other side. When she too was revealed

to be breathing oxygen freely, he claimed it was his divorced grandfather's partner who had died. Which was also a lie.

'I decided at that stage that I must tell the truth and admit I had told lies,' Ireland finally conceded at the time. 'I realise now that it was a massive mistake to say my grandmothers had died and I deeply regret it. I would like to apologise to my grandmothers and all my family. I have learnt a valuable lesson from this mess and hope those I have hurt will forgive me.'

I think there is a lesson for us all there. I had a mate at university who always handed in work late. Like Mr Ireland, his regular excuse to lecturers was that his grandmother had sadly passed away and 'it's been a tough few weeks for the whole family'. At the end of our second year he was dragged in by the head of the history department who said: 'Ed. We have every sympathy for you, but according to our records you've had at least nine grand-parents.' He had to come clean. I was best man at his wedding a few years later and amazed to find out that he actually had a full set! It constituted a significant chunk of my speech.

MRS DEFOE

Despite fierce opposition from neighbours in Chigwell, Jermain and his mum – Sandra St Helen – went ahead with a planning application to build a nightclub in the basement of an Essex mansion. The application to Epping Forest District Council was in the name of Defoe's mum and plans included a cards room, swimming pool, hot tub, hair salon and a five-a-side football pitch in the gardens. Permission was granted by the council, but it's not known whether Defoe and his mum went ahead with their palace of fun.

MS NILES

When you're one of your Premier League club's most promising young stars, the last thing you need is your mum showing up at games and causing a stink. Unfortunately, that's exactly what happened to Arsenal's Ainsley Maitland-Niles, whose mother Jules was banned from the club's training ground after an incident in which police had to be called during an Under-21s match. Ms Niles was allegedly involved in a confrontation with a club official and her son's agent, and was arrested on suspicion of assault – although she was subsequently released without charge.

MRS MESSI

It was just a normal trip to the shops with her mum for 20-year-old model Macarena Lemos (real name) until she saw an angry older woman coming towards her armed with a phone and a frying pan. It was none other than Leo Messi's mum, who believed Lemos, a former girlfriend of her boy, had spoken to a magazine about him.

'She was following me and taking photos until I turned around and asked her what was going on,' explained Lemos. 'That's when she started insulting me. What was she doing there in the electronics section, with a frying pan in her hand? She was following me with a telephone and a frying pan. She seems to think I said something to a magazine, but I never did. They are confused.'

MRS KONCHESKY

It's unlikely that Paul Konchesky's mum has been back to Liverpool since going to watch her son play for the Anfield club. The left back struggled for form and the fans weren't overly complimentary towards him. But Carol Konchesky wasn't having any of it and used Facebook to let rip: 'The Liverpool scum don't know class when it hits them in the face.' It wasn't long before Mrs K's Facebook page was history.

MADE-UP FOOTBALL STATS

Let's be honest... most of us like a stat. I am mildly obsessed with them and – just like those beauties about the Wembley arch – I think a good one always adds a little something special. The best stat I have ever heard is that Barcelona have played three games in their history during a Papal conclave and won all of them 4-0. That is just simply unbeatable.

But does anyone actually know if any of these stats are true? Has anyone tried to fit hundreds of double-decker buses on a set of scales? Here's a load of stats that I haven't bothered checking whatsoever, but they just feel like they should somehow be right.

1,765,382 – minutes that Zlatan Ibrahimović has spent talking about himself since records began

3,109 – the number of Arsenal players who have been sent off during Arsène Wenger's reign

3,109 – the number of times Arsène Wenger missed seeing the incident that led to an Arsenal red card during his reign

209,804,307 – mirrors used by Cristiano Ronaldo since he turned professional

Number 21, 657.

22,631 – the number of career yellow cards received by Lee Cattermole

3 – according to FIFA bylaw 23, sub-section 2, clause 8, José Mourinho is not allowed to stay in any one job for a period of more than three years

5,674 – number of times managers of Premier League clubs have refused to speak to the press after they've lost a game

0 – number of times a Premier League manager has refused to speak to the press after they've won

54,019 – defenders left sitting on their backsides by Lionel Messi

5,902,881 – amount in Swiss francs spent on lunches by Sepp Blatter during his reign as FIFA president. Per year

48,759,889 – number of times footballers use 'you know' during interviews each week

SUPER STADIA

Being up on the Wembley arch was an amazing experience which got me thinking about some of the world's great football stadiums, or stadia if you really insist – which I know you do. Like our now world-famous arch, I've selected some of my favourite designs from around the world, most of which I have been fortunate enough to sit in.

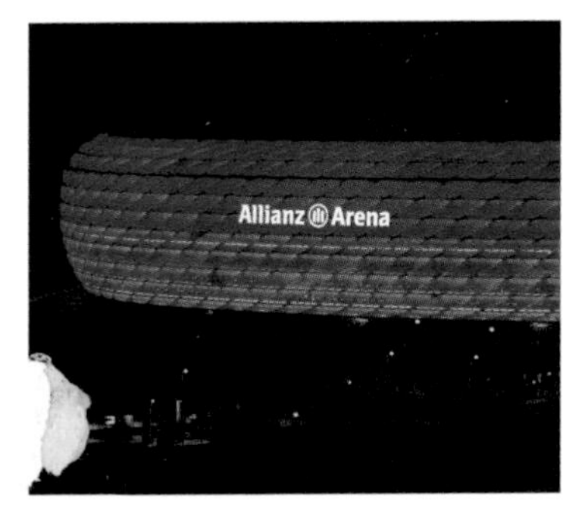

Allianz Arena, Munich

Azteca Stadium, Mexico City

Cape Town Stadium, Cape Town

Rungrado May Day Stadium, Pyongyang

Estadio Axa, Braga

Arena Das Dunas, Natal, Brazil

Bate Borisov, Belarus

Estadio Chivas, Guadalajara

Sapporo Dome, Sapporo

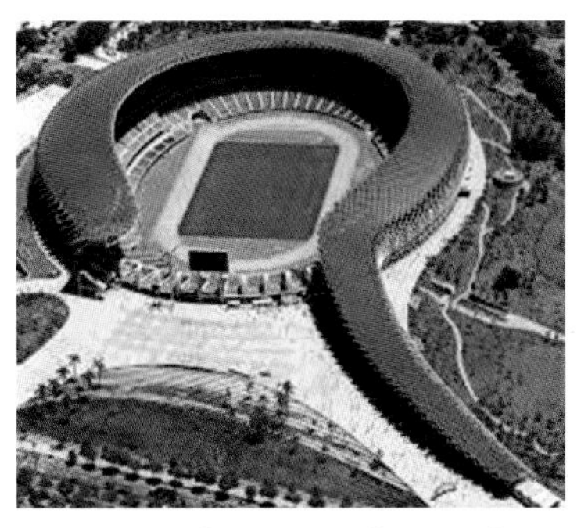

Dragon Stadium, Kaohsiung, Taiwan

We've talked a lot about stadia in this chapter. One thing that unites all these famous footballing venues is a good pitch so, in order to honour all those groundsmen and women out there... here is your #GardeningXI.

#GardeningXI

Team name: Weeds United
Stadium: Elland Rhododendron
Management Team: Tony Tulips, Russell Spade & Roberto Di Patio

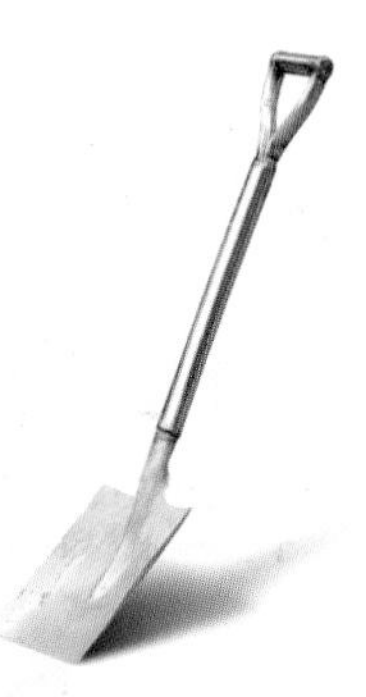

First Team:
Gravel Srnicek

Hanging Gardens of Gabbidon (c)
Gazebo West
Skrtyliser

Helder ComPostiga
TramPaulinho
FlyMo Sissoko
Paddling Polacios

Watering Kanu
Weed Malbranque
Romelu LeCatPoo

Subs:
Ballack & Decker
Trowel Meireles
Gregory Van Der Wielbarrow
Plant Holt

Getting the FA Cup coverage back on the BBC has been brilliant. I know the competition has changed a lot over the years, but I still have a real fondness for it. Quite apart from the great games it throws up and the glamour of the final at Wembley, it has been magnificent to take the show on the road and host *Football Focus* from some of the clubs that rarely get the publicity they deserve.

It was great to do the show from Wealdstone back in the first round of 2015-16. The mighty Raiders gave us an incredible welcome, packed the clubhouse and when I foolishly asked super-fan Russell Grant if he was wearing his lucky pants, I gave him the perfect opportunity to reveal a little too much: 'Don't be daft, darling – I'm going commando.'

Rod Stewart's double life behind the Stourbridge bar.

Round two took us to Stourbridge, where most of the show was devoted to the fact that Rod Stewart works behind the bar. Look at the picture and tell me it's not true. The Stourbridge faithful have also starting singing 'Barmy Llamas' in a subtle twist on the oft-sung 'Barmy Army' number. Apparently it happened naturally during one particular game. Someone heard a subtle variation, started singing along and all of a sudden a new song was born.

We met the inflatable llama during the show, but sadly there had been a 'puncture scenario' at a recent game. There was a young man responsible for the llama – I seem to remember his name was Andrew. When I asked him if this injury meant the tradition was over he said, in the most wonderful Brummy twang: 'It's OK. We've got a puncture repair kit.' You need to say that to yourself in a Birmingham accent to appreciate the full magic of it.

However, the most embarrassing incident on the FA Cup trail came at Wrexham in 2014. They were preparing for their second-round tie against Maidstone United and welcomed the *Football Focus* cameras. We took Mickey Thomas along with us to recreate 'that' free kick against Arsenal back in 1992.

The Gunners were the league champions and had the England goalkeeper between the sticks, but there was nothing that Big David Seaman could do to stop the rocket from Mr Thomas. It was a beautiful free kick, but I always feel a little sorry for Steve Watkin. Everyone talks about Thomas's free kick, but his goal only levelled things after Alan Smith had given Arsenal the lead. It was Watkin's 86th-minute winner that sent the Welsh side through. Watkin remains the forgotten man of that memorable cup win.

I wish my actions at Wrexham would also be long forgotten after I thoroughly embarrassed myself. As well as the free-kick recreation, we also had a wander around the boardroom and had a chat with the chief executive, Don Bircham. The room was adorned with some great moments from Wrexham's history and also had various honours boards, including a rather elaborate one that listed all the club's players of the year.

During the chat with the lovely Don, I noticed that there was a little stain on it. From a distance it looked

Puncture repair kits not suitable for use on live llamas

like a bit of ketchup or tea. My mother always told me to tidy up, so I thought I would do the decent thing and wipe it clean. I picked up a little tissue and – live on TV with millions watching – decided to give it a scrub. It became clear early on that I had very much underestimated the stain. It wasn't tea or ketchup, but a rather robust varnish that was used to hold the letters in place underneath. On my second stroke, not only did the varnish come off but also a couple of the names underneath it.

I foolishly thought I could wipe away the drip with ease.

You know that feeling you get when you kick a football and you see it heading uncontrollably towards a window? That. I had been very happy with the initial contact, but this clearly wasn't going to end well. I turned round to the camera and said: 'Well, that didn't really go according to plan, did it?' I glanced across at Don, whose friendly face had changed a little as it became clear that Dixie McNeil's wonderful season of 1979-80 had been wiped from their history.

Within seconds my phone was going mad and I was apologising profusely to everyone I could see. I assured Don we would get it repaired and, thankfully, when the papers did come knocking at his door, rather than binning me off as a complete idiot, he simply said that the BBC would be getting a bill for the damage. Thanks, Don.

If there was a positive to come out of it, I did a little research into Dixie McNeil and found out that two years before he was Wrexham's top dog, he was the man who scored the winner against Blyth Spartans in the fifth round of the FA Cup in 1978. That was the season that the Spartans had beaten Stoke City, and Wrexham had denied them what would have been a remarkable cup tie against their north-east neighbours by beating Newcastle United.

So there you go, a few life lessons for us all: add Dixie McNeil and Steve Watkin to your list of 'Lesser Known FA Cup Heroes', try not to confuse Ketchup with varnish, and NEVER clean an honours board on live TV.

LIVE AND KICKING OFF

Admittedly, I would have preferred not to have tried to erase Wrexham's football history live on television, but I was certainly not alone in messing up on live TV. In an attempt to deflect attention away from my horror show, here are some other poor unfortunate souls.

MUCKY MICAH

Put a 17-year-old on live TV moments after he has just scored his first goal for his club to keep them in the FA Cup, and you never really know what might happen. For Micah Richards, who had just rescued Manchester City in an FA Cup tie against Aston Villa at Villa Park, it was all too much. The wonderful Garth Crooks asked Richards how he was feeling and the teenage defender replied: 'It was just great to be out there... f***ing hell, I just can't believe it!' Profuse apologies followed.

Biblical name, rather unbiblical choice of lingo. Yellow card.

NOW YOU SEE HIM...

Sky Sports reporter Nick Collins was talking to the nation live outside Wembley ahead of an England v Scotland international when he suddenly lost his balance. What the viewing public couldn't see was that Collins was perched on some kind of platform to make sure that the stadium was in view behind him – the platform gave way, Collins fell and disappeared out of shot. Viewers then saw a smirking Jim White in the studio ad-libbing the best he could without bursting out laughing. 'That's the kind of thing that you hope never happens to you on live television, but it obviously happened to Nick there,' he said.

HEADS UP

German football presenter Jessica Kastrop was broadcasting pitchside in the build-up to a 2010 Bundesliga game between Mainz and Stuttgart as the players warmed up. As she was in mid-flow, a stray pass from Khalid Boulahrouz thumped her on the back of the head, knocking her forwards. Later on, the player apologised to Kastrop on air, giving her a bunch of flowers and a goalkeeper's helmet, by way of a joke. A once-in-a-lifetime horribly embarrassing and painful incident, right? Wrong! Four years later, Kastrop was pitchside before Bayer Leverkusen took on Hoffenheim when exactly the same thing happened. If only she'd been wearing that helmet.

PIRATE RADIO

Towards the end of Bournemouth's home game against Spurs in 2015, in which the visitors were winning 5-1, the Cherries' PA system suddenly boomed into life – it seemed that the man responsible for communicating with the fans didn't realise it was on, as he was caught saying: 'It's like men against boys, it's f****** unbelievable', which was highly embarrassing for him and the club. Except all was not as it seemed. In fact, the culprit who had broadcast to the entire ground was none other than Barnaby from the Spurred On TV YouTube channel (Yes, him!). He was wearing a radio mic for his post-match broadcast, which was using the same channel as the PA system, thus enabling him to air his views to the entire stadium. Oops.

FINAL SNORE

Poor Dong Lu. He had a dream job, as he was Chinese broadcaster LeTV's football commentator who called all the big games, including Champions League matches. But it all went wrong late one night, when Dong started to get tired during a Real Madrid v Paris Saint-Germain game – we've all been there. Due to the time difference, the match started at 3.45am in China and by the second half the 45-year-old commentator had seen enough. During the 78th minute of the match as Paris's Adrien Rabiot and Angel di Maria exchanged passes inside the Madrid half, all that Dong could muster was 'zzzzzzzzz' as loud snores echoed around China. Unfortunately, it was his last commentary gig as he was fired after the match.

KLOPP STROP

After Liverpool's amazing come-from-behind victory against Dortmund in the 2016 Europa League quarter-finals, BT Sport's reporter asked the Reds manager Jürgen Klopp if his team were now close to the Champions League, as the tournament winners were given a place in the competition. 'Please, please don't ask me this s**t,' said Klopp. 'It's so hard, I don't know, I know nothing about the other results.'

MONKEY MONCUR

In a case of the Micah Richardses, Colchester hero George Moncur (son of West Ham legend John, fact fans) was hauled in front of the live TV cameras after his winner against Preston saved the club from League 1 relegation. Behind him, fans had jubilantly invaded the pitch and were celebrating as he was asked to describe their noise at the final whistle. Moncur pointed to all the U's fans behind him and said: 'Mate, f****** says it all!'

MIND YOUR LANGUAGE

When the USA lost to Mexico in the 2011 Concacaf Gold Cup final in California's Rose Bowl, the post-match ceremony was conducted in Spanish, much to the irritation of America's goalkeeper Tim Howard. 'I think it was a f****** disgrace that the entire post-match ceremony was held in Spanish,' he fumed in a live interview. 'You can bet your ass if we were in Mexico City, it wouldn't be all in English.'

THE MAGNIFICENT SEVEN UNSUNG HEROES OF FOOTBALL

After almost losing the memory of Dixie McNeil's heroics, and giving you a reminder about why Steve Watkin is a real FA Cup legend, I thought I would investigate further and dig out a few other names who deserve a little extra limelight.

DAVID CORBETT

Everyone knows about the late, great Ronnie Corbett, but we should also add David Corbett to our official list of national treasures, whether that actually exists or not. David is the man who, more than any other, helped England win the World Cup. Yes, Geoff Hurst scored a hat-trick in the final. Yes, Bobby Moore was an inspirational skipper. Yes, Sir Alf Ramsey was the mastermind behind the team's success. We know all that stuff. But England could never have won the World Cup without the Jules Rimet trophy being found.

Pickles starred in *The Spy With The Cold Nose* alongside Eric Sykes.

We all know it was found by Pickles, the mixed breed collie, but why does the dog get all the kudos? The owner was Mr David Corbett! Would Pickles have been taking a walk in Upper Norwood on that fateful day in March 1966 if it wasn't for Corbett? Of course he wouldn't, because he was a dog! David Corbett, World Cup winner, we salute you.

TOFIQ BAHRAMOV

Alongside Corbett stands the other man who should share responsibility for England's greatest footballing triumph. Tofiq Bahramov. Who? You may well ask. At 2-2 in the first period of extra time in that 1966 final, Geoff Hurst's shot cannoned back off the bar and bounced down very close to the goal-line. Did it go in, and were England 3-2 ahead?

The decision was all down to one man, who the world knows as 'the Russian Linesman' – that man is Tofiq Bahramov. And he wasn't even Russian. Bahramov was from Baku in Azerbaijan and was a former Soviet Union player and then match official. His moment of inspiration in awarding the goal gave England the extra-time advantage that they would never relinquish. When he died in 1993, Azerbaijan's national stadium was named after him. The Tofiq Bahramov stadium? When Wembley was rebuilt and reopened in 2007, I think we missed a trick...

JORGE BURRUCHAGA

The 1986 World Cup is all about Diego Maradona. But let's be honest, he cheated. Yes, he scored the greatest solo goal of all time, but he cheated and that is a stain that can never be removed. Instead, one man we should forever be talking about is Jorge Burruchaga, the scorer of Argentina's World Cup final winning goal, in the most exciting final of all time.

Argentina led 2-0, but Germany came storming back with two goals in seven minutes to level the match with less than ten to go. Cometh the hour, cometh the man. Yes, he may have received a pass from Maradona, but he still had an enormous amount to do, in holding off a German defender before keeping his cool with a perfect low finish into the bottom corner. That is what heroes do.

RICKY GEORGE

As mentioned earlier in the book, Ricky George is a genuine FA Cup hero who needs to have his name in lights – so here's another plug for him. Everyone will remember Ronnie Radford's goal for Hereford against Newcastle, which prompted the pitch invasion and one of the cup's greatest-ever moments. But let's not forget that was only an equaliser. Moments later, George scored another superb goal which won the match for his lowly side and the fans were back on the pitch surrounding George. Like the hero he was.

STEVE WALSH

Who was the real hero of Leicester City's unforgettable march to the Premier League title in 2016? Was it loveable manager Claudio Ranieri? Or maybe goal machine Jamie Vardy? Perhaps it was silky-skilled Algerian Riyad Mahrez? Or maybe defensive rock Wes Morgan? They've all got a good shout, but perhaps not quite as good as Steve Walsh, the former Foxes defender who became their assistant manager and head of recruitment. It was Walsh who was the man responsible for bringing Mahrez and Vardy to the club, as well as other important players like Christian Fuchs and N'Golo Kante. And for that, he deserves a plethora of plaudits and probably a statue somewhere – although he did then join Everton. Arise Sir Steve of Walsh.

FONS LEWECK

The Fonz has always been cool and well known, but this is nothing to do with the dude out of *Happy Days* (one for the older readers, there). This is all about Alphonse 'Fons' Leweck, Luxembourg footballer and national hero. His nation were on a poor run of form – in fact, poor doesn't begin to describe a sequence of 59 defeats in their previous 60 competitive matches. That's just plain shocking. Then came a World Cup 2010 qualifier away to Switzerland. The score was 1-1 with less than five minutes left when Luxembourg worked a brilliant free-kick routine and Fons finished with a sensational strike from a tight angle to cue some of the wildest and most memorable celebrations on and off the pitch. Incredibly, the only other non-defeat in that awful run was a 1-0 win against Belarus. And the scorer of the goal in the game? The Fons. What a guy.

PC GEORGE SCOREY

We finish with another tale of a man and an animal in which the animal's fame was far greater than the man. Mention the 1923 FA Cup final between Bolton and West Ham to anyone and the first thing they would say – presuming they're football fans, of course – is the White Horse. The image of that equine beast on the Wembley pitch trying to keep the crowds off the playing area in order to get the match started is as much a part of FA Cup folklore as Alan Sunderland's winning goal or Liverpool's white suits. Yet, what about the brave copper who steered the horse through the crowds? Take a bow, PC George Scorey.

The full story is that the final was the first to be played at Wembley, but an estimated 300,000 people turned up to see it in a stadium with a capacity of 125,000. Crowds spilled onto the pitch and mounted police were required to restore order, and make sure the game took place. PC Scorey was on board Billie, the 'white horse' who was in fact a grey, but appeared white in the black and white footage of the event (another bombshell right there – the Grey Horse final just doesn't sound the same). Other horses were involved, but Wembley officials later said the match would never have started without Scorey. And if the FA Cup final hadn't been played at Wembley on that day, they may never have tried to do so again. They may never have staged football there again – PC George Scorey may well have saved the beautiful game as we know it in this country.

13 (UNLUCKY FOR SOME) WEIRD FOOTBALL SUPERSTITIONS

In *The Thronkersaurus* (another book I've written, not sure if I've mentioned it before) I brought you some extraordinary pre-match football rituals including voodoo and urinating on the pitch. Here, not keeping the lack of Russell Grant's lucky pants in mind at all, are some slightly more down-to-earth habits. Sort of.

LAST OUT

(To the tune of 'No Limit') Kolo, Kolo Kolo, Kolo Kolo, Kolo, Kolo Touré – sorry, couldn't help myself – had a weird superstition where he would always have to be the last man out onto the pitch. But he came unstuck in a Champions League game between Arsenal and Roma when William Gallas received some treatment for an injury at half time and was late rejoining the action. Incredibly, Kolo, Kolo Kolo (OK, enough) decided to wait for Gallas to come out, so the second half started without him – Touré then realised he'd better get on the pitch pronto, but was booked by the referee for entering the field without his permission.

INSIDE OUT

Former Romania and Chelsea striker Adrian Mutu had some strange habits – unfortunately, at least one of them was illegal and he got in trouble for it, but that's a different story. Another weird one was his predilection for wearing his pants inside out for every game. But he's not alone, as Spanish goalkeeper Iker Casillas used to wear his socks inside out during matches too, but has since seen sense.

SEEING STARS

France coach Raymond Domenech was a bit of a strange one, as he believed astrology was a key factor in selecting his team. Yes, you can read that again if you want. Astrology. He wasn't a fan of Scorpio, as he believed it was a negative influence and this was thought to have cost Scorpio Robert Pirès a place in the side. It didn't stop there. Domenech wasn't overly keen on Leo either. 'When I have got a Leo in defence, I've always got my gun ready, as I know he's going to want to show off at one moment or another and cost us,' he once said, going on to explain that with team selection, 'All parameters have to be considered and I have added one by saying there is astrology involved.' OK, then.

LUCKY EIGHT

Cardiff owner Vincent Tan is a colourful character, literally. He insisted that The Bluebirds should play in red, despite the fact they'd played in blue forever. Teams in red have fared better throughout football history, so he might have had a leg to stand on with that one. What he definitely wouldn't have been able to justify, though, was his preference for signing players who had the number eight in their dates of birth – apparently, the number has huge significance in Tan's native Malaysia.

Vincent Tan proving why no one in the world wears a football shirt over a normal one.

SALT OF THE EARTH

Italian club Pisa enjoyed their most successful period during the 80s when the minnows spent a long time in Serie A rubbing shoulders with the likes of Milan and Juve. At the time, the club president was Romeo Anconetani, who believed that if he threw salt on to the pitch before a game, it would bring his team luck. The superstition grew to such an extent that before a fixture against arch-rivals Cesena, 26kg of salt was thrown on to the pitch. It wasn't just salt, there was also chicken. Before a match against Padova, Anconetani set a chicken free and then ate it after the match. Of course, that may have had nothing to do with superstition. He was probably just hungry.

NUMBER CRUNCHER

Leeds fans will be familiar with the eccentricities of their owner, Massimo Cellino. When he was in charge of Cagliari, he spied a problem with the fixture list in 2011, as the club's first home game of the season against Novara was to be played on 17 September – but 17 was his unlucky number. The club never used the shirt number and Cellino tried to avoid it at all costs. So Cellino made the club press office put out a statement asking supporters to wear purple to the match, as this was *obviously* an unlucky colour and the two negatives (purple and 17) would *obviously* cancel each other out. Whether any of the fans paid any attention to this nonsense is unclear, but what is clear is that Cagliari won 2-1.

Cellino had previous with colours. When Cagliari lost their first five games of the 2009-10 season, the owner asked manager Max Allegri to change the colour of his suit. Allegri liked to wear black, but Cellino wasn't so keen as he thought it was negative. The coach switched to a blue suit, Cagliari finished ninth in Serie A and Allegri was named Italy's coach of the year.

CRUYFF'S TURNS

The late, great Johann Cruyff wasn't immune to the odd bit of lunacy. He liked to spit the pre-match gum he was chewing into the opposition half before each game began. He also used to slap his team-mate Gert Bals in the stomach before every match – it's possible he just didn't like the goalkeeper, but apparently it was a superstition.

GETTING SHIRTY

Even Maradona's mate Pelé had his strange quirks as a player. He once gave away a match shirt to a player, but a brief goal-scoring drought followed so Pelé asked someone to retrieve the piece of kit, believing that was the problem. Unfortunately, the shirt could not be found, so a different top was given back to Pelé, who suddenly started scoring again – completely unaware that he was wearing another shirt.

TUNNEL VISION

Like Kolo Touré, former Manchester United and Liverpool mid-fielder Paul Ince always liked to enter the pitch last, but he also had one other habit. Ince never put his shirt on until he was in the tunnel heading out to the pitch and would often be seen finishing putting it on as he walked across the white line.

OLD BANGER

Former West Ham skipper Billy Bonds played almost 800 first-team games for the Hammers. And before every single one, he would bang his head against a changing room door before jogging out to the pitch. Ouch.

SHOT SHY

Gary Lineker never indulged in any nonsense like inside-out socks or pants. But he did have one weird pre-match superstition which was never to shoot during his warm-up. Lineker, a perfectly sane man as far as I'm aware, was always worried he might 'waste a goal' in the warm-up, so refrained from taking a single shot until the match started.

KISS AND TELL

Some players like to indulge in a spot of pre-match kissing. Luis Suárez gets his mouth warmed up for action by kissing his wrist where the names of his children are inked, while Cesc Fàbregas likes to plant four kisses on the ring on his finger, which was given to him by his girlfriend. The ring, not the finger.

TIED UP

Everton left back Leighton Baines always walks on to the pitch with his laces tied. But he must wonder why he bothers, because the first thing he does when he gets on to the pitch is untie his laces only to immediately retie them again. 'My pre-game ritual does my head in,' he says. 'I don't know why I do it.' Which sums this section up quite nicely.

I had a mate who I used to play football with who would always hit a few keys on the piano by the door in their house before he left for a game. He was clearly mad, but that is the only link I require here to show you the #MusicalInstrumentXI.

#MusicalInstrumentXI

Team Name: Fiddlesbrough
Reserves: Panpipeinaikos
Stadium: Ewoodwind Park
Training Ground: White Harp Lane

Management Team: José Tamborinio, Steve McClarenet, Horn O'Driscoll

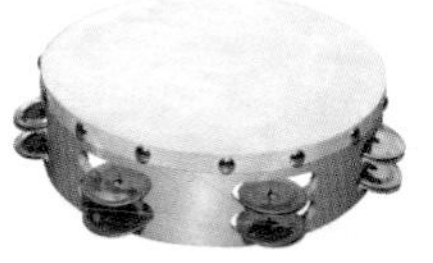

First Team:
Diggery Dudek (c)

Pascal Chimbongo
Piccolo Toure
Sun Ji Hihat

Claude Ukelele

Torsten Strings
Papa Tuba Diop
GlockenTeale

Organ Gamst Pedersen
VuvuZola
VionLingard

Subs:
Banjo Shelvey
Jon Oboe Mikel
Sax Gradel
AccorDion Dublin
DrumKitson

MISSING MARADONA

You know that time when you get one chance to do something and you mess it up? This chapter is about that. The fateful tale involves Diego Maradona and a camera – but we'll get there shortly.

We've all had those times in our lives when you want something to go well and it doesn't. At university I lived with a fella called Ed. Ed is a lovely lad, but on the first day I met him he turned up to our shared room in Earnshaw Hall in Sheffield with a mannequin wearing a Sheffield Wednesday kit! I know. He turned out to be a lot less of a weirdo than I initially thought, we are still good pals and he's the same Ed who got rumbled for losing too many grandparents.

I know he still has the kit, but I am not sure if he still has the mannequin. Anyway, what it tells you is that Ed was an obsessive Wednesday fan. We used to go to Hillsborough regularly to watch the magic of Reggie Blinker and Orlando Trustfull, and Ed read, listened to and watched everything he could about the club. This is why when Ed clapped eyes on legendary Sheffield Wednesday keeper Chris Woods in our local Tesco it all proved a little too much for him.

Woods was one of his favourites and Ed couldn't allow this opportunity to pass. This was back in the pre-selfie 1990s, so Ed bravely decided to step forth and actually talk to Chris. Ed could have happily taken Chris through virtually any game of his career, so encyclopedic was his knowledge. It's that detail which makes the conversation that took place even more excruciating.

'Hi Chris,' Ed offered tentatively before launching into his killer line. 'What are you doing here?'

'Shopping,' said Chris dismissively.

There was an awkward silence. Ed looked at Chris. Chris looked at Ed who – despite his deep knowledge of all things Owl – had nothing else to give other than, 'OK.' Chris realised that the 'chat' was going nowhere and his stare returned to the bin bags and sink-unblocker in front of him. An embarrassed and heartbroken Ed shuffled off to the frozen food section to gently weep.

The mere mention of Woods these days is enough to crush Ed. His mind instantly goes back to the time he met his hero and failed at life.

I had a similar experience with my childhood hero Glenn Hoddle. I was once at Gatwick Airport waiting to pick my dad up from America and the Spurs team were just about to fly out for a foreign trip. I used to spend months at a time pretending to be Hoddle, so when I clapped eyes on the great man I felt I needed to mark the occasion by getting his autograph. I was only about 11 or 12 at the time, so I scrabbled around for a pen and paper and plucked up the courage to join the queue for a scribble.

As I was nearing the mercurial midfielder, I was thinking through how to start the conversation. I'd seen him score twice against Stoke a few months before and I thought that might be a good way in. I had it all planned out and then – with about five people in front of me in the queue – the rest of the team started picking up their bags. Their flight had just been given the final call. Glenn stayed as long as he could, but just as I got to the front of the queue came the crushing blow delivered by assistant boss Peter Shreeves: 'Sorry mate. He's got to go.'

'Really sorry,' said Hoddle as he threw his leather man bag over his shoulder and drifted off through the departure gate. I kept that blank piece of paper in my bedroom drawer for a while. It was a dark time.

These days it's all about the selfie. Footballers can't go anywhere without leaning in for a 'quick selfie' with their adoring public. The grateful amateur snappers have a permanent reminder to share on social media, show their family and annoy their friends with every Friday night. But what about those moments when you get those pictures that don't go according to plan? Those moments when you have one opportunity to get the shot and it goes wrong? I want to tell you about one of those pictures.

The venue is the Argentinian broadcasting studio in Rio de Janeiro. The date is the second week of the World Cup. Gary Lineker was interviewing his old mucker Diego Maradona. Maradona had a nightly chat show and the BBC team were grabbing him at the end of that to talk about the World Cup, England and anything else we could in the short time provided. The place was packed. There was a small BBC team there and one of the producers was called Matt and the other was Mark. At the end of the interview, Gary had his picture taken with Maradona for the BBC website and then Mark thought he would take that perhaps once-in-a-lifetime opportunity for a lad from the West Country to wedge his mug next to one of the greatest footballers in history.

Diego's people agreed that it was OK and Mark quickly handed his phone to Matt and asked him to do the honours. Now, as I am sure you all know, normal protocol in these situations is to take five or six pictures in the hope that at least one of them is a winner. If you're a real technology-embracing millennial, you might even throw in a variation of landscape and portrait and possibly go down on one knee. Which is why everyone was surprised that Matt took only one picture. Just one. The conversation went like this:

Mark: Matt, can you take a photo of me and Diego please?

Matt: Sure [takes phone]. OK... ready... [presses button]. There you go [hands phone back].

Mark: Did you get it OK? [Diego is removed by one of his people and everyone is quickly ushered out of the room].

Matt: Yeah... it's fine. I checked it.

The thing is. Matt hadn't checked it. Matt had actually done a very bad thing. Matt had taken one of the most pointless pictures of all time. In later years I have seen Mark trying to convince people that the out-of-focus and blurred flash of black hair belongs to the great Diego Maradona. No one believes him. Matt still clings to the defence that he was carrying a camera bag and it was hard to steady the shot.

Mark claims this is him with Diego Maradona.

MARADONA'S MADDEST MOMENTS NOT INCLUDING *THAT* GOAL

No chapter in any book featuring the most talented footballer of the 20th century would be complete without a look back at some of his most temperamental moments. And with that timely note to myself to make sure this chapter is complete, here is that very section on Maradona's most mischievous mayhem.

DIEGO v PHOTOGRAPHER

Irked by the ever-present paparazzi in his life, Diego lost his rag in 2000 when he punched and broke a photographer's car window. And, like a movie superhero, he even had a killer line ready to explain himself: 'If, in 1986, I said the goal against the English came from the Hand of God, today I announce this broken glass comes from the Hand of Reason.'

DIEGO v THE PRESS

Now I'm not saying that Maradona has an uneasy relationship with the media, but many of his less sane moments do happen to feature members of the fourth estate. Like the time a few months before the 1994 World Cup when reporters had gathered outside his house in Buenos Aires for reasons only they will know, with the result being that they made Diego angry. In fact, they made him so angry that he emerged from his property holding an air rifle which he then fired towards the reporters, four of whom and a photographer were injured by pellet fragments. Somehow, Diego received only a ten-month suspended prison sentence for his actions.

DIEGO v CAMERAMAN

You're cruising into work in your Mini when you see a cameraman by the side of the road. Do you: a) Give him a wave and continue driving into the Argentine Football Association training complex or, b) Drive into his leg and then shout out of the window: 'What an a**hole you are. How can you put your foot under the wheel, man?' Maradona chose b).

DIEGO v PEACE

The Big Man can still shift when it comes to avoiding the press.

The mild-mannered one went to play in a charity match in Colombia in 2015. The Match for Peace, ironically named as it turned out, ended in a penalty shoot-out in which Diego struck the winning spot-kick. A huge scrum ensued, with press and cameramen swamping Maradona, and we all know how situations like that play out. This time, Diego just kicked out at a steward and smacked a reporter's phone out of his hand. Peace, man.

DIEGO v ATHLETIC BILBAO

The traditional post-match swapping of shirts with a member of the opposition team is not for Diego. Following Barça's 1-0 defeat at the hands of Athletic Bilbao in the 1984 Copa del Rey final, a huge brawl erupted between both sets of players and coaching staff, with little Diego leading by example using the unheralded post-match tradition of 'flying karate kicks at anyone in a Bilbao kit'.

DIEGO v PELÉ

The Argentine saves most of his contempt for two things in football – FIFA and Pelé. And when the two combine, Maradona is never shy about making his feelings clear. The rivalry with Pelé stems from a war of words between the pair, both widely considered the best players of the last century. Maradona has cast doubts on Pelé's sexuality in the past, claiming the Brazilian football god lost his virginity to a man, or 'debuted with a lad' in his own words.

When he heard that Pelé had criticised his coaching ability, he declared that 'Pelé should go back to the museum'.

But the Argentine said nothing when FIFA decided to create a player of the century, which was voted by the public on the football governing body's website. Maradona won convincingly, polling three times as many votes as Pelé, but FIFA weren't happy with the outcome so added a second award, which they gave to the Brazilian. At the ceremony, Diego maintained his silence by picking up his player of the century gong and then promptly walked out before Pelé was given his special award. Later, he explained himself by saying: 'The people voted for me. Now they want me to share the prize with Pelé. I'm not going to share the prize with anybody.'

DIEGO v THE WORLD

How do you go about celebrating your team's World Cup qualification? By ranting against all your enemies in a foul-mouthed outburst that was broadcasted and repeated all over the world, that's how.

Maradona coached Argentina to the 2010 World Cup finals, with a 1-0 win over Uruguay booking their spot in South Africa. As soon as the microphone was placed near a jubilant Diego, he let rip... I have slightly changed the quote to avoid an overly offensive attack on younger ears.

'To those who did not believe in us – and ladies forgive me – they can... [at this point Mr Maradona made reference to a sexual act on a few occasions and then returned to his main point]. I am black or white. I'll never be grey in my life. You lot take it up the a**, if the ladies will pardon the expression. This is for all Argentinians except for the journalists. I would like to thank the team for giving me the privilege to lead Argentina to the World Cup. Thank you to the Argentinian people who had faith. This is for those who did not believe in the team and treated me like dirt, but we still qualified with honour. They will now have to accept this. I want to thank the players and the fans – no one but them.'

FIFA banned him from football for two months.

DIEGO v GEORGE W. BUSH

Not content with taking on the football fraternity, Diego also gave the treatment to US President George W. Bush in the form of a political protest. When Bush visited Buenos Aires in 2005 for the Summit of the Americas, Diego used his new role as a TV personality to lead the opposition to the American leader's presence on Argentine soil. 'As far as I'm concerned, he is a murderer; he looks down on us and tramples over us,' enthused Maradona. 'I hate everything that comes from the United States. I hate it with all my strength.'

Inspired by their hero, thousands of Argentinians came to a public counter-summit rally to support the ex-footballer and demonstrate against Bush. 'I'm proud as an Argentine to repudiate the presence of this human trash, George Bush,' said Maradona at the rally before his traditional shooting and kicking of the assembled media. OK, that last bit wasn't true.

DIEGO v FRANCE

Maradona is not afraid to take out entire nations in one fell swoop.

During the 2010 World Cup, Diego was angry about the tournament's Adidas Jabulani match ball and chose to vent his anger at Michel Platini, who he suggested should try it himself. 'Platini, I'm not surprised with him because we've always had a distant relationship,' said Diego at a press conference. 'Hello, Goodbye! We all know how the French are, and Platini is French and believes he is better than the rest.'

Plus ça change.

DIEGO v ARGENTINA

And when Diego has finally exhausted all other options, he'll blast his own players. Literally. During the South Africa World Cup, astonishing footage emerged of an Argentina training session in which the losers of a match were made to stand on the goal-line as the winning team took pot-shots at them by smashing footballs towards them from close range. Diego's world is a mad, mad, mad, mad world.

MISBEHAVING MANAGERS – THE NOT-SO-MAGNIFICENT SEVEN

Like Diego, not all managers set their players the greatest of examples. For every mild-mannered Roberto Martínez, there's a loose cannon Paolo Di Canio-type going apopleptic in the technical area. But touchline histrionics are just the tip of the iceberg for some gaffers who overstepped the line just that little bit more...

STEVE EVANS

I'm not saying Steve Evans pushes the boundaries, but his middle name might just be 'controversy', although I've not checked his passport so I'm not sure.

While manager of Boston United, Evans oversaw the Lincolnshire club's promotion to the Football League, although he did that by 'conspiring to cheat the public revenue' according to a judge and jury at Southwark Crown Court in 2006. The Boston squad that won promotion to the league in 2002 was full of players who were being paid inflated wages, written into secret contracts which enabled them to recruit the best players whom they otherwise wouldn't have been able to afford.

In all, Evans and his chairman Pat Malkinson cheated the taxman out of £250,000. Evans escaped a prison stretch, instead receiving a 12-month suspended sentence and a 20-month ban from football by the FA. Boston were docked four points, which were held over until the following season, meaning Dagenham & Redbridge, who finished level on points with Boston, were denied a promotion. It's fair to say that Steve has a slightly different version of events.

As a footnote, Evans went on to successfully manage my team Crawley Town a few years later. When he left, the players rather cruelly joined in a popular rendition of Chubby Checker's hit 'Let's Twist Again', with the immortal opening line: 'We're gonna sing a song 'cos the fat man's gone...' Harsh. Very harsh.

JOHN BECK

Another divisive manager made his name with Cambridge United by guiding the minnows from the old Fourth Division to within a whisker of the inaugural Premier League. Beck's tactics were simple. He employed an unashamedly direct long-ball game, but also used some other dubious methods to give his team an edge. The corners of the Abbey Stadium pitch were left with longer grass so that the long balls would stop more easily. He would throw iced water at his players shortly before kick-off to get them up for a game. The away team's dressing room would be flooded hours before a game so that it felt damp when the visiting players arrived. And once they'd dealt with that, the visitors' tea would also arrive laced with far too much sugar.

Somehow, it all worked and Cambridge were in the play-off race in the 1992 Second Division, but all was not well in the camp. After 20 minutes of a home game against Ipswich, striker Steve Claridge had the temerity to cut inside his man and beat him, instead of keeping the ball out wide as per the Beck doctrine. Furious, Beck substituted Claridge, which led to a half-time brawl between the pair, other players and coaching staff. Claridge and striker partner John Taylor were sold the following week, Cambridge lost in the play-offs and the club eventually slid back down the leagues.

LUIS ARAGONÉS

When he was managing Spain in 2004, Aragonés thought José Reyes, of Arsenal, needed some encouragement to fire him up for the challenge of playing for his national team. So he decided to tell Reyes that he was a superior player to his club team-mate Thierry Henry to boost his confidence. Unfortunately for Luis, the words he chose – 'Tell that black s**t that you are much better than him' – were recorded by Spanish TV cameras and a whole lorry-load of denials and apologies were offered. Aragonés was subsequently fined £2,000 but appealed – and won.

TREVOR FRANCIS

Let's make one thing clear, Trevor Francis is no racist, conman or gamesmanship exponent. But he can be a fiery character, as Crystal Palace goalkeeper Alex Kolinko found out to his cost. When Bradford took the lead against Palace at Selhurst Park in August 2002, Francis was outraged to see his reserve goalkeeper laughing on the bench behind him, so belted the Latvian on the back of the head. Palace equalised to get a point, Francis was fined and warned by the FA, and Kolinko stopped laughing.

PAOLO DI CANIO

Let's put aside, if that's possible, the fact that Di Canio is a self-proclaimed fascist 'but not racist' and wrote in his autobiography that Benito Mussolini was 'deeply misunderstood'. Even allowing for his colourful views, he could've still been a fine football manager. Except he wasn't.

Di Canio wanted his players to train all the time. But they didn't. And when players stepped out of line, Di Canio was happy to correct their behaviour. At Swindon, striker Leon Clarke was coming off the pitch after running his legs off in a 3-1 League Cup defeat to Southampton in 2011 when the fitness trainer told him he'd be running again in training the following day.

As Clarke walked past Di Canio, the forward was caught by pitch-side microphones saying: 'You telling me I'm going to run again tomorrow? F*** that!'

Di Canio grabbed the player by the shirt, inviting him to come down the players' tunnel but Clarke initially refused. Eventually, the pair made their way down the tunnel and an almighty scuffle ensued with screaming, shouting and grappling. Clarke returned to the pitch shortly after and refused to enter the dressing room, leaving the stadium in his kit. He never played for Swindon again.

The red mist descends again.

Di Canio's methods worked – to an extent – as he achieved promotion with Swindon, but their former chief executive Nick Watkins described Di Canio's style as 'management by hand grenade. Paolo would chuck a hand grenade and I would do the repair work at the end, like the Red Cross.' At Sunderland, his luck ran out as senior players rebelled against his draconian ways and he was ousted after only 12 matches in charge.

KENNY LANGFORD

In a drama worthy of a *Breaking Bad* storyline, North West Counties Premier League side AFC Darwen's manager Kenny Langford left the club after he was jailed for four and a half years for conspiracy to supply cannabis. Langford and his two sons were said to have flooded the Lancashire town of Darwen with cannabis. Det. Insp. Mark Vaughton said: 'Between them, the Langfords and their associates have blighted Darwen and the surrounding areas for too long, flaunting their criminal wealth.'

All of which makes Trevor Francis clipping Alex Kolinko around the ear seem a little bit playground.

MALKY MACKAY

Mackay endured a tempestuous reign as Cardiff manager working under controversial chairman Vincent Tan. But the er, excrement, really hit the fan when some confidential text messages that were exchanged between Mackay and his head of player recruitment, Iain Moody, were leaked to the press after the Scotsman had left the club.

The messages did Mackay no favours, given they contained racist, sexist, homophobic and anti-Semitic language. But the Football Association decided not to discipline Mackay or Moody as the messages were sent 'with a legitimate expectation of privacy'. He, perhaps wisely, took some time away from football after that.

MISSING MOMENTS

That photograph of Maradona and my friend was so poor that he missed the chance to document the moment he met his idol, and there's now no proof it ever really happened. Which got me thinking about those moments in football when someone has missed something rather important – come back from behind the sofa Stuart Pearce and Chris Waddle, this is a penalty-miss free zone so it's safe to carry on reading.

GOSLING'S GHOST GOAL

It's the 2009 FA Cup. And it's the Merseyside derby. The stakes could not be higher. After a 1-1 draw at Anfield, the replay has produced 117 minutes of stalemate and penalty kicks are just moments away. The nation is holding its breath. Suddenly, ITV cut to an unexpected ad break and millions of people furiously, and pointlessly, start punching buttons on their remote control.

Then, just as unexpectedly, Goodison Park returns to the country's screens and it's a scene of joy as Everton players are celebrating, and their fans are going wild. Turns out that while the country was being treated to a look at Tic Tacs and Volkswagens, Everton's 19-year-old substitute Dan Gosling had struck a stunning winner.

ITV apologised profusely for the technical error while Gosling was forced to fork out for the club's DVD of the match. Possibly.

The moment far too many of us missed.

AMERICAN SCREAM

But for all its apologising and promises, it seems that the message hadn't quite got through to someone at ITV if their coverage of England's opening 2010 World Cup match against the USA the following year is anything to go by.

This time, only three minutes had been played when viewers watching on ITV's HD channel were taken away to a Hyundai ad (what is it with these cars?) only to return to see England celebrating what would turn out to be the greatest moment of their World Cup – Steven Gerrard giving them an early lead.

'Apologies for those watching in HD,' said presenter Adrian Chiles at half time. 'I believe there was some interruption in your coverage.'

Just a bit! I should point out here that I am in no way gloating. It is a broadcaster's worst nightmare to miss something crucial and I would not wish it upon anyone.

WHITE HART PAIN

And to complete the hat-trick of TV cock-ups, it's over to 2016's highly anticipated North London derby between Spurs and Arsenal at White Hart Lane. With both teams in contention for the Premier League title, there was potentially more at stake than in any derby ever ever ever. Hyped up enough?

In a rare example of a game living up to its billing, the teams shared four goals, Arsenal were reduced to ten men and, as the game headed into stoppage time, the outcome of the match was still up for grabs. And then BT Sport's feed was lost so everyone's screens went blank for a minute. No big deal. It was only stoppage time. On this occasion, there hadn't been any goals, and pictures returned for the last kicks of the game with sound eventually following. A power outage was blamed and the obligatory apologies followed.

KAMMY'S RED MISSED

Down at Fratton Park in April 2010, not a great deal was happening in a goalless affair between Portsmouth and Blackburn – not a lot that is, except a red card for Anthony Vanden Borre of the home team. The only problem was that Sky Sports reporter Chris Kamara had failed to notice. Here's the full transcript of exactly what happened when Jeff Stelling attempted to ask Kammy for his take on the sending off.

Jeff: We're off to Fratton Park where there's been a red card, but for who Chris Kamara?

Kammy: I don't know Jeff. Has there? I must have missed that. Was there a red card?

Jeff: Have you not been watching? I haven't. I don't know where that's come from. I have no idea what has happened there. What's happened, Chris?

Kammy: I don't know, Jeff! [Laughs] I don't know. The rain must have got in my eyes, Jeff!

The videprinter on the bottom of the screen then shows that Anthony Vanden Borre has been sent off for Portsmouth.

Jeff: Chris, Chris! Let me tell you, according to our sources Anthony Vanden Borre's been sent off for a second bookable offence. Get your fingers and count up the number of Portsmouth players who are on the field.

Kammy: No, you're right. I saw him go off, but I thought they were bringing a sub on, Jeff! [laughs]

Jeff: As professional as ever Kammy...

Kammy: Still 0-0!

WANDERING WOLF

Fans can often get caught in traffic and miss the beginning or all of a match – but it rarely happens to players.

Back in 2008, Wolves defender Richard Stearman set off from his Harborough home to make the 60-mile journey for a midweek home game against Swansea. Unfortunately for Stearman, heavy traffic due to snow meant that he never made it to Molineux in time and manager Mick McCarthy was forced to make a late change to his starting line-up. Fortunately for Stearman, his team-mates did the business for him and they won 2-1.

HALF-TIME HANGING

Footballers stuck in traffic are a bit like London buses. You wait half a book for one, and then two come along at once. Leyton Orient striker Darius Henderson was delayed by a traffic accident and turned up 45 minutes late for his side's home game against Port Vale in 2015.

He was named on the bench but wasn't needed as his side ran out 3-1 winners, although that didn't stop the club's, er, charismatic owner Francesco Becchetti (who later in the year would run on to the pitch to kick assistant manager Andy Hessenthaler in the backside after a home *win*) deciding to publicly criticise his player for being late – via the Brisbane Road PA announcer at half time.

Alongside all the fans' birthdays, anniversaries and half-time scores, the O's PA man Phill Othen also had to tell Henderson he'd been a very naughty boy. After the game, Othen said: 'I was told to announce the president was very angry that he was 45 minutes late. I was perplexed, but I did my duty. It's probably the strangest announcement I've ever made.'

FLIGHT OF FANCY

Travelling to games was always going to be difficult for a team from the Channel Islands, but Guernsey's arrival on the non-League scene went smoothly enough – until they turned up at the local airport for a flight to Gatwick to play Carshalton Athletic in 2014.

Club secretary Mark Le Tissier (yes, he's Matt's brother) had forgotten that he'd booked the 'Green Lions' onto a 7am departure, so when they turned up for an 8.30am departure they had missed their flight, and couldn't make it to the mainland in time for the game. 'It was totally my error,' said Le Tiss. 'Being half-term, all the flights were booked and we couldn't get on another one.'

BROWNED OFF

Staying with flights missed, Celtic's Scott Brown also missed one for bizarre reasons following the Bhoys' 2-2 Europa League draw with Red Bull Salzburg in Austria.

Brown, who scored Celtic's second goal in the 2014 tie, was one of the players randomly chosen to provide a urine sample for a drugs test after the game. But after an all-action performance in which he sweated buckets, Brown could not produce a sample in time to make it to the airport for the team's flight home and was forced to spend the night in Austria with Celtic physio Tim Williamson. Eventually, nature took its course and Brown was a wee free man. Sorry.

BEST 'TIL LAST

Sir Matt Busby and his Manchester United team were waiting at the station in Manchester for their train to London to play Chelsea one Saturday morning in 1971 – the man they were waiting for was George Best. But he never showed up.

The team made their way down to the capital, and were followed by Best, although the flamboyant footballer was not heading to Stamford Bridge. He had other business to attend to in London. While his team-mates were battling to a 2-1 win, Bestie was in Islington with gorgeous young actress Sinead Cusack, who would later marry actor Jeremy Irons. Best's actions prompted a media circus as the press descended on Cusack's property and the couple were holed up in there for four days.

It turned out that Best, as only he could, had decided he wasn't in a fit state to play for United but that he should still honour his planned rendezvous with Miss Cusack, who was utterly bewildered that a date would lead to a siege situation where the couple ended up watching the outside of the flat they were inside on TV, such was the huge media interest in the story. And there was you thinking that media over-reactions only happened in the 21st century.

10 RELATIVELY OBSCURE 90s PREMIER LEAGUE FOOTBALLERS

Writing about watching the likes of Reggie Blinker and Orlando Trustfull at Hillsborough got me reminiscing about some of the more obscure names and faces who graced top-flight stadia in the Premier League's embryonic years. How many of this lot do you remember?

FABIAN DE FREITAS

The striker played a starring role in the 1995 play-off final to help Bolton into the Premier League and also turned out for West Brom.

STEFAN SCHNOOR

The German defender joined Derby from Hamburg in 1998 and stuck around at Pride Park until the turn of the century.

SIEB DIJKSTRA

Blink and you missed the Dutch goalkeeper who made 11 appearances for QPR in the mid-90s.

ULRICH VAN GOBBEL

A cult hero at The Dell where the one-man Dutch defending unit played for Southampton in the 1996-97 season.

Mr Van Gobbel does it for the Saints.

CLINT MARCELLE

The Trinidad & Tobago striker was a Barnsley crowd favourite in their only Premier League season of 1997-98.

WILLIAM PRUNIER

The Frenchman joined Manchester United from Bordeaux initially on trial but was thrust into the first team after an injury crisis – he lasted only two matches, the second of which was a nightmare 4-1 defeat to Spurs.

HUGO PORFÍRIO

The Portuguese winger enjoyed two 90s loan spells at West Ham and Nottingham Forest before heading back to sunnier climes.

PONTUS KÅMARK

The excellently named defender went from a third place finish with Sweden at the 1994 World Cup to a four-year spell at Leicester City.

NAJWAN GHRAYIB

The Israeli-Arab defender played five games for Aston Villa right at the end of the century – and with a transfer fee of £1 million that worked out at £200,000 per game.

NIKODIMOS PAPAVASILIOU

The first Cypriot to play Premier League football, turned out seven times in midfield for Newcastle in 1993-94. Commentators were delighted it didn't work out for him.

MILTON NÚÑEZ

Signed from PAOK Salonika in 1999 by manager Peter Reid, the striker was only 5ft 5in, leading to rumours that the gaffer had got the wrong man from the Greek club. He came, no one saw him, he left.

In honour of the great Maradona, it seems only fitting to conclude this chapter with a #SouthAmericanXI. Remember these are all made up of your social media suggestions over the last few years so don't get mad, get punning. And before you moan, I am aware that some of these are stretching 'South America' a little bit.

#SouthAmericanXI

Team Name: Inca Milan
Reserves: Nottingham RainForest
Stadium: Reeboca
Management Team: Levein Da Vida Loca
Villas Boas Constrictor
Pre-match Entertainment: Bolivia Newton-John

First Team:
Freidel Castro (Cuba not in South America but too good to leave out)

Chile Sagnol
Rory Delapagos
UruGuay Demel

Andes Limpar
CopacaBannan (c)
Lee Guacamole (I know it's Mexican)
Tierra Del Figo

Michu Picchu
Bolivier Peru
VenezueLuaLua

Subs:
PinoShay Given
Lima Ridgewell
Brazilian Petrov
FalkLandon Donovan
Regi Blinca Trail
Fajita Crouch

I always enjoy going on *Countdown* as a guest on dictionary corner. What's not to like? You get to sit next to Susie Dent, you can't actually lose, you don't have to embarrass yourself on the numbers game, and it doesn't matter if you could stare at the conundrum for two days without being able to see that TIFFEROID can be re-arranged into FORTIFIED.

Mrs Walker doesn't think that other TV shows bring out the best in me. She might have a point. I think she feels that my natural competitiveness gets the better of me. I would like to

Dictionary corner with the magnificent Lady Dent.

argue my case, but a quick look at the evidence suggests the case for the defence doesn't look particularly impressive:

A Question of Sport – got over-excited – lost by a point
Celebrity Mastermind – came second by a single point after getting a question I knew wrong
A Question of Sport again – on a run in the final on the buzzer round – got the team ahead – jumped in – got it wrong – deducted two points – lose by a point again

I have since won on *QoS*, but let's not allow that to get in the way of a good story.

I have also been on *Celebrity Pointless* on two occasions and gone home in the first round both times. The first occasion was entirely my fault. I was on with Charlotte Jackson, from Sky Sports News, who is now Charlotte Coleman. Alexander Armstrong announced that the first category would be 'Berries'. For the three people on the planet who haven't watched *Pointless*, the idea is to find the answers selected by the fewest people out of the 100 they asked. The more obscure the better, and if it's not mentioned by anyone... it is Pointless.

'Loganberry' popped in my head, as did 'Elderberry'. Not only did I have a solid first choice, I had a back-up. Some fella from *EastEnders* was the first to guess. 'Loganberry,' he said. There was a mild 'ooh' from the audience. I was down to one obscure berry. 'Elderberry,' came the second answer. I was in big trouble. Charlotte was next and tentatively went with 'Gooseberry'. From memory, 66 people had said the same as Charlotte so we were already on a sticky wicket.

Trev from Trev and Simon came out of nowhere with 'Cowberry', which was pointless and after one more guess I was up next. Imagine desperately trying to think of rare berries and having absolutely nothing in your head. I was left to wander down the well-known path and suggested 'Raspberry', knowing we were heading for an early bath. The audience sniggered, Richard Osman looked slightly disappointed and Xander revealed that 88 people had also said raspberry.

Charlotte looked at me and said: 'You had a cranberry juice in the green room about ten minutes ago!' She was right, but sadly my berry knowledge had let us down and we left the studio with our tails firmly between our legs. When the show eventually went out on telly, I got 1007 tweets telling me what an idiot I was and about another thousand suggesting alternative berry choices.

My second appearance on the show was for the episode they showed on FA Cup final day. This one also ended early, but I'm delighted to say it wasn't my fault. I was on with Mark Lawrenson and we were taking on several other football pundits and presenters. The first question asked us to name a country that starts with the letter A, T, L or S. Lawrenson whispered 'Trinidad & Tobago' to me. I responded with a hushed: 'Yep, but ssssh. We're not allowed to confer' and felt confident that we had this one in the bag. There was to be no repeat of Berrygate here.

The fella on the left is getting an atlas for Christmas. #Alaska

Safe in the knowledge that Lawro had a banker, I set about digging through what I could remember of the Commonwealth Games. I toyed with 'St Kitts and Nevis', but couldn't remember if it was actually a country. The other teams had gone for 'Azerbaijan' and 'Albania'. We were up next.

Alexander Armstrong: So, Mark. We are looking for a country starting with the letter A, L, T or S. What have you got?
Lawro: I'm going to go with Alaska.
Crowd: *GASP*
Trevor Sinclair: *JAW DROP*
Kevin Kilbane: *SNIGGER*
Me: *Face of fury* followed by 'That is a state. A state.'

Armstrong was a little confused. Of all the pundits I have worked with, Lawro is perhaps the most well-travelled, so I've got to say I was surprised at the size of his faux pas. The host continued with the rigmarole, even though we all knew what was happening. 'Let's have a look to see if it's right.' A big red cross appeared on the board and I was once again on the early train home.

When that one was shown on Cup final day, 'Alaska' was trending on Twitter for about two hours. Every now and again, I'll get a flurry of 'Raspberry?' tweets, which normally indicates that somewhere in the world our episode is being replayed.

I should point out that Lawro's *Pointless* debacle originally went out on the same day he called Steven Pienaar 'Steven Penis' live on *Match of the Day*. It wasn't his finest Saturday.

So in summary: *Countdown*, good. *Pointless*, bad. Alaska is definitely not the right answer.

THE EIGHT MOST OBSCURE COUNTRIES TO BE REPRESENTED IN THE PREMIER LEAGUE

I toyed with the idea of suggesting St Kitts and Nevis as a country beginning with S, and it turns out I would have been right. I know that now, because the two-island country in the West Indies has produced a Premier League player – and it's not the only relatively minor nation to have representation in England's top division, as this handy list will show you.

BOBBY BOWRY (ST KITTS AND NEVIS)

The striker played for Crystal Palace in the first-ever Premier League season and scored his only goal in a 1-0 win over Aston Villa.

SHELTON MARTIS (CURAÇOA)

The West Brom defender graced the top flight for one season and is a Curaçoan – the country only came into being in 2010 and was part of the former Dutch Antilles in the Caribbean.

Shelton Martis proudly representing the good people of Curaçoa.

GUNNAR NIELSEN (FAROE ISLANDS)

Goalkeeper Nielsen was the first Faroese Premier League player when he came on as a substitute for Shay Given for Manchester City against Arsenal in 2010. Just in case you didn't know, the Faroes lie halfway between Denmark and Iceland.

PELÉ (CAPE VERDE)

Not *that* Pelé, or The Romford Pelé, or even Abedi Pele, but simply Pelé (or Pedro Miguel Cardoso Monteiro to his parents), who turned out for West Brom in the Premier League and won 11 caps for Cape Verde.

GAËL BIGIRIMANA (BURUNDI)

The midfielder from the central African nation that's one of the five poorest countries on earth made 13 appearances for Newcastle during the 2012-13 season, after signing for £1 million from Coventry.

KEVIN BETSY (SEYCHELLES)

He was a lower-league journeyman, but he made one appearance for Fulham in the Premier League in 2001. A decade later, Betsy won the first of seven caps for Indian Ocean island Seychelles.

STÉPHANE SESSÈGNON (BENIN)

The attacking midfielder played for both Sunderland and West Brom in the top flight and was once voted the best-ever player in the history of West African country Benin.

BERTRAND TRAORÉ (BURKINA FASO)

Benin's neighbouring country is Burkina Faso, from where Bertrand Traoré originates. He scored a few goals for Chelsea in 2015-16 before heading out on loan to Vitesse Arnhem of Holland, which is a small, flat country in western Europe.

A QUESTION OF SPORT

I had mixed success on the famous BBC quiz show. Everyone is always quick to point the finger so why don't you test yourself on these, then test your mates.

1. As of 2016, only seven players have Premier League winners' medals with two different teams. Name the lot.
2. How many of the 12 players who have missed penalties for England in major tournament shoot-outs can you name?
3. Which seven Dutch players have scored Premier League hat-tricks?
4. Who is the only player to win the FA Cup at the old Wembley, the new Wembley and the Millennium Stadium?
5. Who is the only player to have scored in a Champions League final, FA Cup final, UEFA Cup final and a League Cup final?
6. Who is the only player to have scored in the Glasgow, Merseyside and Manchester derbies?
7. Derby only won one match in their record-low points tally in the 2007-08 Premier League season – who did they beat?
8. Which three Robertos have managed FA Cup winning clubs?
9. Which three car brands have sponsored Coventry City's shirts?
10. Only one Premier League season has featured a top six without a London club. Which season and what was the top six?

Answers

1. Robert Huth (Chelsea and Leicester), Gaël Clichy (Arsenal and Manchester City), Nicolas Anelka (Arsenal and Chelsea), Ashley Cole (Arsenal and Chelsea), Kolo Touré (Arsenal and Manchester City), Henning Berg (Manchester United and Blackburn) and Carlos Tevez (Manchester United and Manchester City)
2. Stuart Pearce, Chris Waddle (Germany 1990), Gareth Southgate (Germany 1996), Paul Ince, David Batty (Argentina 1998), David Beckham, Darius Vassell (Portugal 2004), Frank Lampard, Steven Gerrard, Jamie Carragher (Portugal 2006), Ashley Young, Ashley Cole (Italy 2012)
3. Robin van Persie, Dennis Bergkamp, Ruud van Nistelrooy, Jimmy Floyd Hasselbaink, Marc Overmars, Dirk Kuyt and Georginio Wijnaldum (who scored four v Norwich in 2015)
4. Patrick Vieira (Arsenal 1998, 2002, 2004 and Manchester City 2011)
5. Steven Gerrard
6. Andrei Kanchelskis
7. Newcastle United
8. Mancini (Manchester City 2011), Di Matteo (Chelsea 2012) and Martínez (Wigan 2013)
9. Talbot, Peugeot and Subaru
10. 1994-95 – Blackburn, Manchester United, Nottingham Forest, Liverpool, Leeds, Newcastle (Spurs were seventh)

This entire chapter seems to be pointing towards a TV show-themed XI. I would be a fool to disappoint so here goes… Your #TVShowXI.

#TVShowXI

Team name: Lille Or No Lille
Reserves: Diff'rent Stokes
Stadium: Dr Who Camp
Management Team:
Some Mothers Do Avram, Klopp Gear, Celebrity Bruce

First Team:
Only Kruls And Horses

Last Of The Summer Clyne
Mysterious Cities Of Bould
Through The Keown

CSI Diame
Cash In The Matic
McCall The Midwife (c)
Million Pound Diop

Rooneyversity Challenge
Bodger & Baggio
Bargain Huntelaar

Subs:

Match Of De Gea
Quedrue Do You Think You Are
Downton Xavi
Super Nani
Absolutely Fabregas

Cabaye Got News For You
Who Wants To Be A Willianaire
Call My Duff
N'Gog Barry Avoid
The Soldados

John Motson has perhaps one of the most famous coats in the all the land. Ever since he stood in a blizzard at Wycombe in 1990, protected only by the sheepskin, there has been a strange fascination with his outer garments. I must confess that when I introduce him on *Football Focus* and then turn to the screen to chat, I am always disappointed to see him wearing something other than the famous coat. It usually comes out at the start of October and disappears sometime in April, giving us seven months to glory in its magnificence.

I don't know about you, but I have never owned a sheepskin. I put one on once in a charity shop in Sheffield, but the best way I can describe it would be to imagine Gandalf trying on Bilbo Baggins' waistcoat. At one point I thought I might never get out of it and had to call for assistance from an elderly gentleman admiring the china figurines in a nearby aisle.

The coat is part of Motty's thing. He gets almost universal love for it and yet the same cannot be said for a little number I chose to wear for a couple of FA Cup games in the 2015-16 season. It was a lovely, full-length camel number, and I remember vividly the first time I put it on in our house. I was checking myself out in the living-room mirror as Mrs Walker and the kids arrived back from school. Our eight-year-old ran in to offer me one of her Tudor biscuits baked with lavender. As she held out her paper plate and said 'Would you like one, Daddy?' she clocked the coat.

'Is that Granddad's?' she said, a little startled.

In order to fully appreciate the significance of this question, you need to realise that my dad is well known for his horrific choice of overcoats. Despite that underwhelming start, I wasn't about to be dissuaded by the opinion of just one eight-year-old – especially when she was rocking a pair of dungarees on top of floral leggings! Perhaps Mrs Walker, who was following close behind, would have a more positive offering?

'Love, what do you think of this?' I asked in a tone that suggested I wasn't perhaps 100 per cent convinced and required a modicum of reassurance.

'Hmmm... are you actually wearing it outside?' wasn't exactly what I was looking for, but I have developed a thick skin when it comes to clothing and I ploughed on and wore it to Derby County v Manchester United in the fourth round of the FA Cup. We were live at the iPro Stadium on a Friday night, and I was pitchside with Paul Ince.

As I arrived that night, Robbie Savage – part of our studio line-up – was already there. I took his comment of 'Very nice clobber, Daniel. I've just got one of those' as a resounding compliment, but maybe it should have come more as a word of warning... Robbie was sporting white jeans at the time. As I walked down to the side of the pitch to conduct the pre-match interviews, one of the stewards called out 'All right, Rodders!' and another offered 'Evening, Arthur'. I acknowledged their high-class #banter with a smile and ignored the fact that they were both wearing luminous orange numbers that were 19 sizes too big for them.

We've got some half price black tights, miles and miles of carpet tiles...

Once I appeared on TV, the world of social media was awash with coat-based comments, but for every 'what is that?' there were two 'great coat' or 'where did you get that bad boy?' so I left the iPro convinced the camel beauty was worthy of another chance to shine.

That opportunity came in the form of the fourth round replay between Reading and Crystal Palace. I was working on the side of the pitch with Martin Keown and, once again, one of my pre-match duties was to interview the managers. Alan Pardew was first up.

'That's a brave one,' he said as he walked into our little room. It was about to get worse. Brian McDermott was next. This is how the interview went. The start and the end were the important bits:

Me: Brian, thanks for talking to us so close to kick off. Reading have had great success in this competition in recent seasons. What is the secret?
Brian: Well... [laughter] I'm so sorry but I can't take you seriously in that coat. You look like you should be in *Only Fools and Horses*.
The interview continued for a few minutes and then...
Me: Brian, all the best tonight. Thanks for talking to us.
Brian: Thanks, Rodders [laughs again, shakes hands, walks off giggling].

Within 30 seconds 'Rodders' was trending on Twitter. Gary Lineker was asking Ian Wright in the studio if he thought I looked more like Rodney or Del Boy, and my wife sent me a text which simply said 'Told you #Rodders'.

As I walked back around the pitch to the live position with Martin Keown, 'Bonnet de douche Daniel, bonnet de douche' was hollered at me from the terraces and one of my best mates sent me a picture of a handful of mange tout.

I still get asked about the coat regularly and one day soon it will come out again – as soon as I can shift this boot load of hooky Rolex watches.

THE EVOLUTION OF THE GAFFER'S COAT

While my statement overcoat may take a while to slip into most football people's matchday wardrobes, there are many other layers which have become synonymous with football for a whole host of reasons. Dear readers, I give you my definitive guide to a manager's get-up.

THE TRACKSUIT

When England won the World Cup in 1966, Sir Alf Ramsey sported an all-blue tracksuit with a Three Lions motif on the crest. Simple and extremely effective.

THE SUIT

The 1973 FA Cup final saw a clash of managerial styles as Don Revie's Leeds took on Bob Stokoe's unfancied Sunderland. While Stokoe remained in tracksuit throughout (confusingly paired with an overcoat and smart shoes), Revie showed a glimpse of things to come with a suit and tie. But it was the tracksuit that won the day.

CLOUGHIE'S TRACKSUIT

Not to be confused with the ordinary tracksuit above, Brian Clough made his football casuals his own. The Derby and Forest manager did things his own way on and off the touchline, and his green sweatshirt became particularly iconic.

THE SHEEPSKIN

As mentioned above, commentator John Motson made it famous, appearing at football grounds across the country clad in his trademark number, but it was Malcolm Allison who really blazed a trail for the coat by donning a camel sheepskin with a fedora hat every fortnight at Selhurst Park when he was Crystal Palace manager.

The coat is one thing, the hat is next level.

THE TRAINING COAT

This late 80s/early 90s addition to the football manager's winter wardrobe was to dominate the technical area for a decade – even before the dotted white lines of said area had been painted on to the sides of pitches. Warm and sporty, the training coats also featured the initial letters of the managers on the breast, just in case we forgot who Alex Ferguson or Ron Atkinson were.

THE TRENCHCOAT

José Mourinho broke the managerial mould in many ways, not least in the sartorial stakes as he brought a touch of class to the touchline not seen since Malcolm Allison's days. His grey Armani trenchcoat epitomised his first spell at Chelsea from 2004-07. With it on, Chelsea and Mourinho were simply unbeatable, although it did provoke the opposition fans' chant of 'Your coat's from Matalan'.

THE LEATHER JACKET

As rare as a Gary Lineker yellow card, occasionally continental types may be seen in a leather jacket while furiously chain smoking their way through a match – until Paul Jewell made it a regular sight in English stadia while he was managing Wigan. Never one to shy away from the limelight, Phil Brown took it one stage further than Jewell by wearing a leather number complete with fur collar. Thankfully, that particular trend ended there. It was a one-match-only number.

THE OVERCOAT

As Barcelona and then Bayern Munich manager, Pep Guardiola brought a new, easy-on-the-eye feel to dugouts all over Spain and Germany. He paired a simple, dark overcoat with a V-neck grey jumper on a white shirt and tie to create the impression of a multi-layered tactical genius.

THE GILET

Robbie Savage may have worn it underneath his suit to much derision, but that was nothing compared to the stick that Spurs boss Tim Sherwood took for wearing a gilet on the touchline. When Sherwood took over at Aston Villa, he appeared at his first press conference without the offending item, only for a wisecrack from a journalist asking for the gilet's whereabouts. 'F****** hell, I thought it would be two seconds before I heard a gilet joke,' replied Sherwood. 'It was one!'

THE TIGHT TROUSERS

We are straying slightly off topic here, but there needs to be a mention of Zinedine Zidane's keks. Twice in the Champions League in 2016 the occasion proved too much for his unbelievably tight trousers. He failed to learn his lesson from the tie with Wolfsburg, where he ripped his trousers in the groinal area. In the next round, he opted for another pair of spray-ons and once again he was left with a significant area of visible pant after a little over-exuberance.

FOOTBALL NICKNAMES THAT AREN'T BAZZA, WAZZA OR GAZZA

We all love a nickname, don't we? Whether it's simply adding an 'ee' sound to the end of a name, like 'Wrighty', or just a shortened form of a normal name with Barry becoming Baz and so on. There are no bounds to our creativity! But mentioning Paul Ince above, known as The Guvnor (although I think he gave himself that moniker), got me pondering the best nicknames in football.

FITZ HALL – ONESIZE

It was Oldham fans rather than any of his team-mates who came up with the belting idea of calling the player Onesize – if you don't get it, try saying his nickname followed by his full name.

ROBERTO BAGGIO – THE DIVINE PONYTAIL

Or, as they say in Italy, Il Divino Codino. For younger viewers, he was amazing and had a ponytail. OK?

OLE GUNNAR SOLSKJAER – THE BABY-FACED ASSASSIN

This one doesn't require a great deal of explanation, other than Ole never used to kill people, he just scored a lot of goals.

ANDONI GOIKOETXEA – THE BUTCHER OF BILBAO

Any player with a nickname like that demands to be feared, and the Spanish centre-back lived up to his hype.

NICOLAS ANELKA – LE SULK

Take one moody, young French striker, add a French word for 'the' and sprinkle with a childish word for being stroppy, and there you have the perfect nickname for the long-faced forward.

JAVIER HERNÁNDEZ – CHICHARITO

Javier was known as The Little Pea because his father – also named Javier – was known as the pea (Chicaro) due to his green eyes. It remains to be seen if his son will have to be called 'The Really Little Pea'.

LEV YASHIN – THE BLACK SPIDER

The legendary Russian goalkeeper always wore black and was such a useful shot-stopper, that it was almost like he had eight limbs.

FRANZ BECKENBAUER – DER KAISER

Captain, talisman, leader. Enough said.

NORMAN 'BITE YER LEGS' HUNTER

The Leeds defender was not actually a dog, as his nickname might suggest, but he was a pretty fearsome opponent nevertheless.

STUART PEARCE – PSYCHO

Just in case the penny hasn't dropped, look up Psycho in the dictionary and one of the definitions is almost certainly 'Stuart Pearce's Euro 96 penalty shoot-out celebration v Spain'.

Psycho goes psycho back in 1996.

GILLES DE BILDE – BOB

Sheffield Wednesday fans decided the best way to make their new Belgian international striker feel at home would be to give him a nickname that made him sound like the children's TV character that fixes stuff. Can we fix it? Yes we can!

GORDON DURIE – JUKEBOX

The former Chelsea and Spurs striker's nickname derives from the name of an old TV programme where critics would decide whether new music was any good or not. Its name? Jukebox Jury. Nickname gold.

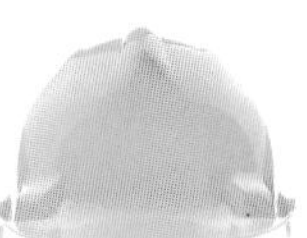

FATHERS AND SONS

So it seems I'm quite similar to my father in terms of our choice of overcoats, although I still maintain that my camel number was up there with anything you might see on the Paris or Milan catwalks. Anyway, this seems like as good a time as any to look at football's best father-and-son combos – with or without jackets.

THE MALDINIS

When Cesare Maldini lifted the European Cup as captain of AC Milan, his son Paolo had not even been born. In fact, Cesare and Mrs Maldini had not even thought about him. Forty years later, Paolo repeated exactly what his father had done to create a formidable father-and-son double.

THE CLOUGHS

Cloughie Senior was a goal-glutty (just made that up, think I got away with it) striker for Middlesbrough and Sunderland before his career was cut short by injury. He went on to become the absurdly successful manager of Derby County and Nottingham Forest, winning back-to-back European Cups with the latter. Cloughie gave his son Nigel his debut at Forest and he went on to have a successful career as a striker, also scoring goals for Liverpool and England before managing Burton Albion to the brink of the Football League. He then followed in his father's footsteps as Derby boss. That didn't go quite as well, but Clough returned to Burton (after spending 18 months at Sheffield United), who were by then a League 1 club, and led them into the Championship.

THE GUDJOHNSENS

Now here's a thing. We've all played on the same pitch as our fathers – usually in the park or the back garden when we were nippers. Arnór and Eidur Gudjohnsen did exactly the same thing, except their park was the national stadium in Tallinn and the match was a full international between Iceland and Estonia. Technically, they didn't play at the same time, because Eidur actually came on as a sub to replace his father (a prolific striker like his son) during Iceland's 3-0 win, but let's not allow that to spoil a unique father-and-son moment.

THE WITCHES

The who? Bear with me. Juan Ramón Verón and Juan Sebastián Verón are father and son. Ramón was known as *La Bruja* (witch) during his playing days, in which he won three Copa Libertadores with Argentine side Estudiantes. So, naturally, Sebastián became known as La Brujita (little witch) when he started playing, and although his career took him to Europe, he returned to Argentina and also won a Copa Libertadores with Estudiantes, just like daddy witch.

THE SCHMEICHELS

Once upon a time, Peter Schmeichel was the Manchester United goalkeeper helping them dominate the early years of the Premier League with his all-action, big-hearted, massive-handed displays. During this era, the *Match of the Day* cameras caught Peter having a kickabout in the Old Trafford tunnel with a little blond mini-me

What a picture. It took a while but Schmeichel Junior has now followed in his dad's footsteps.

wearing a tiny version of his dad's goalie jersey – this was Kasper. About two decades later, the fairytale was complete as young Kasper had grown up into his own version of the all-action, big-hearted, massive-handed goalkeeper and helped Leicester City to win the unlikeliest Premier League of all.

THE JOHNSONS

For years, Gary Johnson was a successful manager in his own right with decent spells in charge of Yeovil and Bristol City, even twice employing his son Lee as a player. But it all changed in 2012 when young Lee entered the managerial game and suddenly the pair were in charge of teams in the same division, Gary at Yeovil (his second spell) and Lee at Oldham. They met in neighbouring technical areas in April 2013 when son bested father, as Lee's Oldham earned a crucial 1-0 win in their fight against relegation.

THE DJORKAEFFS

We all know about Youri, the French striker who helped his country win the World Cup in 1998 and the European Championships in 2000, but we may not have known that his father, Jean, was a decent defender who won 48 caps for France and also played in the 1966 World Cup – but they didn't win that one.

THE FERGUSONS

Darren Ferguson was a half-decent footballer, with spells at Manchester United, Wolves and Wrexham. But it was at Peterborough, first as player-manager, then as manager, that Fergie really made his managerial mark by guiding the club to successive promotions. He then left for a year, during which time they were relegated, and returned to win another promotion in the League 1 play-off final at Old Trafford. It was there, I'm reliably informed, that Darren's father Sir Alex was also quite a good manager.

Now, we did a #ClothingXI in *The Thronkersaurus* (my first book, which is still available in all good bargain buckets), so even though it would fit nicely here I think we'll go for something that requires an excellent outfit instead. Ladies and gentlemen, I give you, the #WrestlingXI...

#WrestlingXI

Team Name: Million Dollar Mansfield Town
Reserves: Ken Shamrock Rovers
Manager: Chokeslam Allardyce

First Team:
Legion Of Poom

Half Nelsen
Jaap Slam
Mexes Tornado
Figure 4 Lescott

Giant Fayestacks
Macho Man Robbie Savage
Dungataker (c)

Ravishing Rick Ruud Van Nistlerooy
Chamakhdown
Messi The Body Ventura

Subs:
Ince McMahon
Stone Cold Charlie Austin
The Big Shola Ameobi

CHINESE KARAOKE AND MASSIVE BEARS

I would like to take you to China. I went there a few years back to make a documentary for ITV. Things have changed quite a bit at Edgeley Park over the years, but back at the beginning of the century, Stockport County were a forward-thinking Championship side. In a bid to 'open up lines of finance and support', they had taken over a Chinese Second Division side and renamed them Stockport Tiger Star. County had also recruited former Chelsea boy John Hollins to manage the team in the northern industrial city of Shenyang. If you're wondering where exactly that is, I have included a handy map.

I was travelling with a cameraman called Bob. Bob was a biker. A hairy biker. Unlike the famous pair of hairy bikers, Bob wasn't a good chef but he was an excellent cameraman. Bob was about 5ft 6in and had a beard down to his sternum; I was 6ft 6in and largely hairless. Together we looked a little bit like a freak show, and anywhere we went in China we attracted a crowd. People stroked Bob's beard and wanted their picture taken with the freakily tall pasty bloke.

Turn right at Inner Mongolia and carry straight on 'til you reach a giant pin.

Sadly, our comical appearance was responsible for some unwanted attention at Chinese customs. Our entire kit was confiscated by the officials and – despite having all the correct paperwork – we had to grease a few palms to get it released. Once the cameras were safely back in our hands, it was off to a rather large restaurant to meet the chairman of Stockport's new best friends. There were two rooms laid aside for us. Bob and I were in room two, the head honchos were next door and we were sat around a table with 12 seats. Bob and I were the only two who spoke a word of English.

For about two hours it was like an elaborate game of charades. Despite being able to communicate only via a combination of pointing, smiling, random hand gestures and rudimentary noises, we were all getting along rather well. At about 11pm, the fella who was hosting the table uttered a word that everybody understood: 'karaoke'! He circled his finger around everyone at the table, intimating that no one would escape the rather battered microphone that was pulled out of an ornate box in the corner of the room. Bob turned to me, looking rather terrified: 'I can't sing a note. You'll have to take one for the team here, Dan.'

Our Chinese hosts were rattling through their favourite numbers. Bob and I clapped along, but none of them sounded familiar. Eventually, the book made its way round to me. I flicked through several pages of Mandarin text searching for something familiar. At the bottom of the penultimate page I saw 'Thomas Jones – Delilah'. Not exactly the greatest choice, but I pointed it out to the fella who was in charge of the machine and he looked at me with deep confusion. I was handed the microphone and, after several minutes of CD sifting, the words 'I saw the light on the night that I passed by her window' appeared on the screen and I was off.

At times like this, I feel it's important to give it your all. My effort levels were slightly higher than the levels of appreciation. On the rare occasions that I opened my eyes, I saw ten blank faces staring at me and one heavily bearded clown giggling away in the corner. No one joined in at the chorus, not even Bob. At the end there was an awkwardly sparse round of applause and I was quickly followed by the next singer who went down like Elvis Presley on a comeback tour. This incident has severely dented my karaoke confidence.

The final few days of our trip were taken up with a tournament in the port city of Yingkou. By this time the Stockport County players were longing for some home comforts. They asked the hotel chef if he could make them spaghetti bolognese as their pre-match meal. The chef looked a little confused, so our fixer explained to him that it was meat in tomato sauce served with pasta. About two hours later the meal arrived – tinned macaroni cheese, tomato ketchup and deep-fried chicken feet!

Most of them played the final on an empty stomach in front of a crowd of 60,000 people who had been specially bused in. The vast majority of the crowd were still in their school uniform. However, County had a secret weapon on their side, something to completely distract the partisan crowd and eventually win them over. A 6ft bear called Vernon.

The crowd was quite hostile towards the visitors until Stockport County's mascot – Vernon Bear – came out to loosen up. The initial reaction was total silence, followed by occasional laughter and full-on furry enjoyment. I know we are used to giant swans, horses, bees and various other animals tweaking bottoms, falling over and warming up supporters, but for the crowd in Yingkou, this was a completely new experience.

They couldn't get enough of Vernon and it was hard to hear the game over the sound of uncontrollable laughter every time Vernon rubbed his stomach, bumped into an official or pretended to eat a football. The giant bear was milking the attention and got a standing ovation both at half time and the end of the game. I would estimate that 93 per cent of the audience were so engrossed in Vernon's antics that they were unaware their team lost the final 2-1 to the bear's boys.

THE CRAZY WORLD OF FOOTBALL MASCOTS

They're furry, have weirdly oversized heads and are usually dressed in your team's colours – I'm not talking about that freak giant striker your manager just signed from non-League. I am of course referring to the football mascot, loved by all except perhaps some slightly frightened toddlers who can't work out why people are laughing at an enormous shrimp. Stockport's Vernon Bear took China by storm, and this selection of the wackiest football mascots also made a splash.

PARTICK-ULARLY PETRIFYING

Somebody at Partick Thistle thought it would be a good idea to let Turner Prize-nominated artist David Shrigley come up with a new design for the club's mascot. When Kingsley was finally unveiled at Firhill Stadium, there couldn't have been a single person left who still thought the experiment had been a success. The mascot seemed to be a spikey yellow sunshine on long legs, with a face straight out of a Freddie Kruger film.

Shrigley's idea was for a mascot who would intimidate opponents and there was no doubt Kingsley's unusual spiked features would do just that. The problem was that Kingsley would also intimidate Partick, their fans and pretty much anyone who ever set eyes on the ghastly creature.

DOROMPA STOMPER

The idea of family-friendly, shiny, happy mascots must also have been lost on the powers that be at FC Tokyo, whose Tokyo Dorompa is not a mascot to be messed with. While others walk around the perimeter of football stadia high-fiving kids and giving away unwanted stuff from the club shop, Dorompa stands angrily at pitchside karate-chopping blocks, and any stray kids who get in his way. OK, the last bit was not strictly speaking true.

ROBBIE SEES RED

With his big, smiling face and friendly eyes, Bury mascot Robbie the Bobby looks like the kind of furry thing you'd invite to your kid's party. But that would be a big mistake. In 2001, Robbie made history by managing to get himself sent off three times. First, he mooned at Stoke City fans and followed that up by ripping the ears off Peterborough's rabbit mascot. But he saved his best until last when he and Cardiff's Bartley the Bluebird had a full-scale fight which had to be broken up by stewards – but only after Robbie had removed Bartley's head.

NICE ONE CYRIL

Swansea City's Cyril the Swan was once fined £1,000 for a pitch invasion, but he saved his best work for when the Swans faced Millwall and their mascot Zampa the Lion. Cyril took Zampa's head off and kicked it into a bewildered crowd – that one *really* confused the children.

LONE WOLF ATTACK

The uninspiringly named Wolves mascot Wolfie proved to be considerably livelier than his name suggested when Wanderers played Bristol City at Molineux in 2000. City had brought along their three pigs (no idea why they had pigs, the Robins' mascot is now, fittingly, a Robin called Scrumpy) and Wolfie could not resist staying true to type and having a go at the pigs. After much huffing and puffing, a fist fight broke out but was broken up by stewards.

GOING GREEN

This is Yeovil Town's Jolly Green Giant. Now I know you might be thinking this is another David Shrigley production, but the Giant is completely unrelated to Partick's Kingsley. It would seem that the Jolly Green Giant must have been inspired by a terrifying vision from someone who went to the circus once too often as a child and started having clown nightmares. Either that, or every day in Yeovil is St Patrick's Day.

CHADDY THE BADDIE

Oldham's mascot Chaddy may have won the Mascot Grand National twice, but he's also got a bit of previous. When Oldham played Blackpool, Chaddy got a bit upset with the Bloomfield Bear during the game and pulled off his opposite number's boots before chucking them into the crowd.

MASCOTS OBSERVING MINUTE'S SILENCES

There's nothing funny about a minute's silence – unless of course you're wearing a great big oversized furry suit and are pretending to look solemn even though you have an enormous, open-mouthed smile on your face below a pair of beaming eyes. Someone much cleverer than me has made a tumblr site which consists solely of pictures of mascots joining in with sporting minute's silences. Here's a couple of my favourites:

WHY STOCKPORT TIGER STAR IS A RELATIVELY NORMAL FOOTBALL TEAM NAME

We've had unusual team name endings elsewhere, but what about the plain peculiar team names, not too dissimilar to Stockport Tiger Star? Well, let's have a look, shall we?

TOTAL NETWORK SOLUTIONS FC

The Welsh Premier League side, made up of a merger between Oswestry Town and Llansantffraid FC, became known as Total Network Solutions, or TNS, when they were sponsored to the tune of £250,000 by a local IT and communications firm. However, when British Telecom bought the company, it ceased to exist, so the club changed their name to The New Saints, which conveniently could also be shortened to TNS. That does mean that Jeff Stelling can no longer say 'they'll be dancing in the streets of Total Network Solutions tonight', which is a massive disappointment.

FOTBALLAGET FART

Another schoolboys' favourite, this Norwegian lower-division team are based in Vang in the north of the country. Their name literally means football team speed.

INSURANCE MANAGEMENT BEARS

The Bahamas club was set up with a grant from an insurance company, hence their corporate yet extremely family-friendly name.

DINAMO BENDER

The Belarus second-tier side represent the town of Bender, where the pub crawls must be the stuff of legend.

Stop it. That's Benjamin Tan from the Asian Football Federation.

SEMEN PADANG

Comical if you're British with a juvenile sense of humour, but not so much if you're a follower of Indonesian football, where Padang ply their trade. Semen is actually the name of an Indonesian cement producer, while Padang is the place where the team are from. It makes sense.

KALAMAZOO OUTRAGE

Don't worry, I haven't momentarily taken leave of my senses and just started making these up. The Outrage were a US team (franchise, American readers) playing in the lower echelons of the country's football pyramid. And they hailed from the Michigan town of... you guessed it, Kalamazoo.

TLOKWENG NAUGHTY BOYS

The Botswana Premier League side are based in Tlokweng, which is a village adjacent to the Botswana capital Gaborone. This book is more educational than Wikipedia.

BIG BULLETS FC

The Malawi club are based in Blantyre. Founded in 1967, the club was adopted by the country's president Bakili Muluzi, who modestly renamed them Bakili Bullets instead.

HOUSE OF DREAD

Trinidad & Tobago boasts teams with great names including Joe Public, the team owned by disgraced former FIFA vice-president Jack Warner, and the brilliant House of Dread.

CAPE COAST MYSTERIOUS DWARFS

The Ghanaian club based on the Cape Coast have two names. One is Mysterious Dwarfs, the other is Ebusua Dwarfs. I've always called them the former.

WHY DO STOKE SING 'DELILAH', AND OTHER CLUB ANTHEMS EXPLAINED

My Chinese hosts may not have appreciated my stirring rendition of 'Delilah' (are there any other ways to sing that song apart from stirringly?), but I can imagine tens of thousands of folk in The Potteries may have given me a standing ovation or, better still, joined in. But why on earth do all those Stokies sing that Tom Jones song? And why are they always blowing bubbles at West Ham? And, while I'm here, do fish ever sleep? No, hang on, I can't answer that last one.

STOKE CITY – DELILAH

It's now impossible for Stoke to play a match without at least one rendition of the Tom Jones hit 'Delilah' by their fans – it's close to being a FIFA law. There is no clear reason why Stoke fans sing 'Delilah', as the lyrics are not connected with the club in any way. Legend has it that, back in the 80s, fans were enjoying a drink or two in a pub after an away match at Derby when police asked them to refrain from singing anything with swear words. At roughly the same time, 'Delilah' was playing on the jukebox so the Stoke fans started to sing that instead. And to this day they've never stopped.

MANCHESTER CITY – BLUE MOON

The song that is synonymous with Manchester City has its football roots in a different north-west club – Crewe Alexandra. Their fans often chanted 'Blue Moon' during Alex games in the 80s way before anyone at Maine Road had thought of it. Then, during an away game at Liverpool in the 1989-90 season, City fans, who had been held back at Anfield by police after the final whistle, started singing 'Blue Moon'. It quickly caught on and was a City fans staple by the end of the season.

LIVERPOOL – YOU'LL NEVER WALK ALONE

When Gerry Marsden handed a tape of 'You'll Never Walk Alone' to Liverpool manager Bill Shankly in 1963, neither of the men could ever have imagined the impact that song would go on to make. Shankly was said to be very impressed with the song's motivational qualities, and at a time when terrace chants were becoming increasingly heard at grounds across the country, the Liverpool song took off. Other clubs like Celtic also adopted it, but with the Shankly Gates at Anfield carrying an inscription of the name of the anthem, it will always be associated with Liverpool.

NEWCASTLE UNITED – BLAYDON RACES

An anthem that is pure Geordie was written, appropriately, by Geordie Ridley in 1862. The song celebrates the popular race meeting and fair held at Blaydon, a Gateshead town, and charts the four-mile journey from Newcastle to the racecourse venue. The song lived on through to the next century and was always chanted at St James' Park. Other teams stole the tune and adapted the words to suit their own needs (Exhibit A: Manchester United's 'Busby Aces'), but Blaydon Races will always belong to Newcastle.

LEEDS UNITED – LEEDS! LEEDS! LEEDS!

The song you may well know as 'Marching on Together' is actually called 'Leeds! Leeds! Leeds!' It was written specially for the club and was the B side to the Leeds 1972 FA Cup final song imaginatively titled 'Leeds United' (younger readers, records used to have two sides, A and B, with different song(s) on each). The club's fans decided the B side was far better than the A, and it wasn't long before Elland Road was filled with renditions of that song. Eventually, the club started to play it before every home match and the anthem was born.

WEST HAM UNITED – I'M FOREVER BLOWING BUBBLES

In London's East End music halls of the 20s, 'I'm Forever Blowing Bubbles' was one of many popular songs. As a result, it was one of the tunes that the Beckton Gas Works Band would play at Upton Park before matches. You would assume the rest is history, but there is actually a fair amount of debate as to why Hammers fans still sing it.

Other than fans picking up the song from the band and music halls, there is another story about a former Hammer youth teamer called Will Murray, whose curly hair closely resembled the child's in an advert for Pear's Soap Bubbles. Murray was then nicknamed Bubbles, and the chant soon followed. Other football anoraks, sorry historians, point to a match between West Ham and Swansea when Welsh fans aired the song and it was then adopted by West Ham supporters. Whatever the reason, it's catchy, it's moving, and it's here to stay.

SHEFFIELD UNITED – GREASY CHIP BUTTY

One of the most stirring terrace anthems in British football, Blades fans took John Denver's 'Annie's Song' and rewrote the lyrics as a tribute to Sheffield. It was much copied by fans of other northern clubs, but remains a Blades original. If you've always wondered what the words were, here they are:

You fill up my senses
Like a gallon of Magnet
Like a packet of Woodbines
Like a good pinch of snuff
Like a night out in Sheffield
Like a greasy chip butty
Like Sheffield United
Come fill me again!
Na Na Na Na Na Naaaaa, oooh!

BIRMINGHAM CITY – KEEP RIGHT ON TO THE END OF THE ROAD

Birmingham's anthem is a song which has its roots in Scotland and was written during the First World War by Sir Harry Lauder. After hearing his son had died in battle, Lauder channelled his grief into writing a tribute song. 'Keep Right on to the End of the Road' became popular in Scotland after the war and finally arrived in Birmingham years later via the Blues Scottish winger Alex Govan.

During the club's run to the 1956 FA Cup final, Govan taught the song to his teammates and it quickly caught on among the fans, too – the story goes that when the team bus arrived at Highbury for the quarter-final against Arsenal, the Blues team were singing the song to the fans who were waiting to greet them. And the rest is history.

BRISTOL ROVERS – GOODNIGHT IRENE

We have to go back to 1951 to trace the origins of Rovers fans' obsession with this American folk song. Trailing 1-0 to Plymouth Argyle, Rovers were taunted by their rivals singing 'Goodnight

Irene', but The Gas turned the game on its head and eventually ran out 3-1 winners. At that point, their fans returned the compliment to Plymouth by singing 'Goodnight Argyle', and a club anthem was born.

NORWICH CITY – ON THE BALL, CITY

Norwich believe their anthem is the oldest football song still in use today – and it's hard to argue. 'On The Ball' was written in the 19th century and first chanted in support of local Norfolk teams Norwich Teachers and CEYMS. When the Canaries were formed in 1902, they also used the song and more than a century later it seems to have stuck. Here's the chorus in original Victorian English:

Kick it off, throw it in, have a little scrimmage,
Keep it low, a splendid rush, bravo, win or die;
On the ball, City, never mind the danger,
Steady on, now's your chance,
Hurrah! We've scored a goal

I challenge you to find another chant with 'scrimmage', 'bravo' and 'hurrah' in it. Dream trio.

CARDIFF CITY – I'LL BE THERE

Also ancient is the anthem still chanted by Cardiff City fans that dates back to the time of the 1926 General Strike. At that time, the song united the mining communities of South Wales and was often heard at Cardiff games, as much as it would have been on picket lines. It was passed down through the generations and, even though the mines have long since shut, Bluebirds fans still chant 'I'll Be There' which starts like this:

When the coal comes from the Rhondda,
And the water's running fine,
With my little pick and shovel,
I'll be there
I'll be there, I'll be there
With my little pick and shovel,
I'll be there

HIBERNIAN – SUNSHINE ON LEITH

Up there with 'You'll Never Walk Alone' in terms of its stirring qualities, The Proclaimers track is always sung on special occasions by the Hibees fans. It's a moving song about loss, redemption and hope, and there wasn't a dry eye in the house as 40,000 Hibs fans chanted it together when the club finally won the Scottish Cup in May 2016, putting to bed a 114-year wait to land the trophy. If ever a club anthem fitted the moment, this was it. Here are the opening verses from the song:

My heart was broken, my heart was broken
Sorrow sorrow sorrow sorrow
My heart was broken, my heart was broken

You saw it,
You claimed it
You touched it,
You saved it

My tears are drying, my tears are drying
Thank you thank you thank you thank you
My tears are drying, my tears are drying

We had a great night at the Euros in Paris in 2016, which started as a meal and developed naturally into a late-night karaoke session where I was in charge of the music system. Alan Shearer, Rio Ferdinand, Kevin Kilbane, Danny Murphy and Jermaine Jenas were all present. I detail their song choices in a later chapter (A Low Blow). Neil Lennon had just taken the job at Hibernian and was constantly pestering for a bit of 'Sunshine on Leith'. Eventually we relented and he did a decent job.

And with that, I need to take a lie down because I've come over all emotional. While I do that, and talking Hibs, why don't you have a little look at the #ScottishXI. Serious shortage of defenders so we're having to play a few midfielders out of position...

#ScottishXI

Team Name: Hull Of Kintyre
Reserves: Bayern Bru
Stadium: Och Aye The Nou Camp

Management Team: Ole Gunner Saltire, Steve The Bruce

First Team:
Cullen Spink

Bould Lang Syne
Graham Sporrans
Joey Tartan

See You Jimmy Bullard
HooteNani
Lionel Nessie
El Haggis Diouf

Hadrian Mutu
Och Aye The Nugent (c)
HolyRuud Van Thistlerooy

Subs:
Ali Al Rab C Nesbitt
Deep Fried OverMars Ba
Bonnie Prince Charlie Austin

'Parlez-vous Anglais, monsieur?'

'Yes... a little.'

'Good. Thierry Henry is coming here and we'd like to get him through security quickly. There will be lots of people. Is that OK?'

'THIERRY HENRY? HENRY?' he said, with obvious excitement.

'Yes.'

'Here?'

'Yes... he is working for the BBC today, but has to come in the media entrance. He will be here in five minutes. *Cinq minutes*.'

The security guard at the Stade de France sprinted off to tell his boss they had a VVIP on the horizon. They were ready. It was a good job because as he turned up for the opening game of Euro 2016 between France and Romania, he was followed down the street by huge swathes of fellow Frenchmen and women all desperate for a glance of the Parisian or one of those terrible on-the-run selfies that you look at later and wonder why you bothered.

The fella on the gate played a blinder and within a flash Thierry and his people were inside the confines of the Stade de

France. Then began a long series of photographs with virtually every security guard between us and the media centre. In the end, the rest of us gave up and allowed Henry and his agent to make the ponderous journey.

Thierry is an approachable superstar. He seems to understand where he has come from and where he is now. When he arrived at the BBC base at the Eiffel Tower fan zone, he went round and shook the hand of everyone at their desks – around 30 people in total. He did the same the next day and the day after that.

At the Stade de France as we walked out to our position to cover the game for Radio 5 Live, he looked strangely impressed: 'I have never seen it from up before. I was with the French squad from the time I was a teenager – this is one of the few games I will watch as a fan. As a kid growing up in Paris this was impossible. There is no way I could have ever dreamed of watching a game

Decided to go for the rare 'shoulder grip and point double'. Think I got away with it.

like this. Football has opened so many doors for me.' Henry wasn't the only French hero covering the game. Robert Pirès was at the side of the pitch working for French TV, Christian Karembeu was 50 yards from us and as Henry was waving to him, in strolled Bixente Lizarazu.

When they saw each other there were no words necessary. All that was needed was a look and a nod. A nod that recognised all they had achieved together. A nod that took them back to the

World Cup of 1998 and the European Championship that followed two years later. A nod that acknowledged how they had brought a disparate nation together. Amazingly, in the 12 months after the summer of 1998, support for the National Front in France had more than halved. The leader of that party, Jean-Marie Le Pen, talked about the mixed team to attack it and that same team took on the world and won.

As we covered the game, Henry boiled with enthusiasm, shouting 'No way' when the referee awarded a penalty to Romania and jumped out of his seat when Dimitri Payet somehow conjured up a magical moment right at the end to deliver the three points.

He was working alongside Danny Mills, in the 5 Live commentary box, and at one point I reminded them of a famous incident involving the pair at Highbury from the 2003-04 season, where Henry was pinned in a corner by Mills only to produce a cheeky nutmeg and then scamper away. In Paris, more than a decade on, Mills claimed that the ball was in fact out of play. This photo of the pair of them was taken at the precise moment and captures Henry's reaction beautifully. I think you can see he didn't quite agree.

The following day, still beaming from a French victory, we were working together again in the BBC studio on the Albania v Switzerland game. Again he shook hands with everyone in the

office on arrival, and about 20 minutes before we were on air we were talking things through in the studio. I remembered that the previous evening there had been some discussion as to whether we should be calling France's new hero Dimitri 'Payet' or Dimitri 'Payay'. Patrice Evra had thrown a significant spanner in the works by calling him 'Payay' in his post-match interview. Henry said: 'Let me sort this out,' and picked up his phone.

'Who are you calling?' I perhaps foolishly asked.

'The man himself,' replied Thierry. Payet picked up immediately and talked at length with Henry about the game, the goal, the importance of family and then a brief goodbye. 'In France it can be either,' said Henry, 'but he is definitely "Payet". He said: "Don't listen to Patrice, he hasn't got a clue."' It helps to be connected.

The French sadly failed to do the business in the final, but they did take part in a game that provided one of my highlights of the tournament. Their semi-final in Marseille saw them take on the Germans. I was presenting at the side of the pitch with local legend Chris Waddle – they still love him in that part of France, but I didn't realise how much until that night.

As we were making our way down to the side of the pitch, we were stopped by a burly security guard who told us the whole stadium was in lockdown because the French president was about to arrive. I told him we had to get to the side of the pitch to do a bit of live TV, but the answer was a flat 'no'. I tried all possible tactics for ten minutes, but he resolutely ignored every approach. Eventually, I went for the name drop and mentioned that I was working with Chris Waddle. 'Waddle?' said the guard. 'Waddle?' He blurted out again with the second syllable sounding like something you ring in a church tower. I pointed at Chris and again repeated 'Waddle' to the now excited guard. The door opened and, despite the imminent arrival of François Hollande, we were escorted to the side of the pitch. A valuable lesson for us all: if in doubt, drop the Waddle.

THE FOOTBALL NAMES WE ALWAYS GET WRONG

Just like the whole 'Payet'/'Payay' thing, there are certain team and player names in football that most people are pronouncing wrong. I know this is all a bit anal, but stay with me on this one. It's not just the beautiful game that throws up tough names. Djamolidine Abdoujaparov, the Tashkent terror, was my favourite cyclist growing up and I used to love it when Srinivasarghavan Venkataraghavan used to umpire cricket Tests in the 1990s. Everyone was also delighted that he was happy to be called Umpire Venkat.

In order to avoid a massive loss of credibility in your social circle, I've come up with a handy list below of the correct way to say some of the slightly trickier football ones.

RUUD GULLIT

In the 80s, it was fashionable to pronounce the Dutchman's surname as if you were referring to the tube that takes your food down to your stomach. The correct way to say it, of course, is Ruud Hool-it with the 'Hoo' sounding like the 'ch' in the Scottish Loch. It's very complicated.

BASLE

Life was a lot easier when the Swiss team weren't so good that they were in European competition every season. At the last count, there are around 398 different ways of saying the team's name, but let's go with the BBC pronunciation unit's, which is Baa-zuhl, with the first syllable like the Baa in 'Baa Baa Black Sheep'.

JUVENTUS

Big Ron Atkinson used to call them Joo-ventus with a hard J, but everyone knows that the team should actually be called Yoo-ventus.

OLE GUNNAR SOLSKJAER

In Norwegian, the 'skj' actually makes a 'sh' sound, so we should actually all be saying Ole Gunnar Solshar as Barry Davies tried to do for years while everyone else ridiculed him. I think the late Tony Gubba once went for 'SOL-SHIRE-RAR' but that didn't catch on either.

WOJCIECH SZCZĘSNY

The former Arsenal goalkeeper was a Scrabble player's dream (even though you can't use names in the game, but you get the idea) but a commentator's nightmare. The correct way to say the Polish keeper's name is 'Voy-check Sh-chez-nee', with the 'ch' pronounced hard as in 'chair'.

ILKAY GÜNDOĞAN

The man who joined Manchester City from Borussia Dortmund can trip you up easily with both first and second names. The way to say it is 'El-ki Gun-do-han'.

MESUT ÖZIL

You may well call him whatever you like by now, but the correct way to do it is actually 'May-zut Ert-sil'. Got it? At the Euros one of the commentators on 5 Live had been reliably informed you had to pronounce it 'OO-zil' with the 'oo' like 'shoe'. Someone had a word with him at half time and he went back to the more conventional method. If you ever fancy a laugh then just pop down to a pub outside the Emirates on a match day and earwig some fans who will give you 734 different variations.

KIM KÄLLSTRÖM

Things aren't quite what they seem with the Swedish player. Why couldn't he just have an easy name like his compatriot Zlatan Ibrahimović? Kim's second name has a hard 'ch' pronunciation at the beginning so it's Kim 'Chel-strum'.

EDEN HAZARD

Nothing to do with the biblical garden or an obstruction in the road, the Belgian's name is pronounced 'E-den Az-are' with the 'E' like the beginning of 'elephant'.

JAKUB BŁASZCZYKOWSKI

Calm down, take a deep breath – we can do this. The Polish winger can be broken down into six bite-size syllables to leave you plenty of time to concentrate on not getting Lewandowski wrong. 'Ya-koob Blash-chi-kov-ski' is the way to do it, with the 'chi' another hard 'ch' like 'chair'. If you practise it you can dazzle you pals with it.

What a goal… from… from… the magnificent number 16 there!

KEVIN DE BRUYNE

One of the gems of the Belgian golden generation is not so straightforward for our tongues. The way he says it, and therefore the way we should probably try to as well, is 'Kevin de Brer-ner'. I remember interviewing Trevor Sinclair on the day De Bruyne signed and between us we used six variations in about two and a half minutes.

ATLÉTICO MADRID

An easy one. It isn't 'Athletico'. And that's all you really have to remember. There's no 'h' after the 't' so we just say 'Atlético', or 'Atléti' if you're a football hipster.

JOSÉ MOURINHO

I shouldn't really have to tell you this, but there are still people out there who say The Special One's first name with an 'H' sound instead of a hard 'J' sound – it should be 'Jo-say' Mourinho, and never 'Ho-say', OK?

SPANISH STADIA

This all depends on how you want your friends to look at you. Technically we should be calling Barcelona's ground the 'Camp Now' and Real Madrid play at the 'Berna-bay-ou'. Feel free to try it, but you will be like the kid who walks smugly out of his GSCE oral exam.

FOOTBALL FAIRYTALES

As Thierry told me, when he was a young boy growing up in Paris, it was impossible for him to dream about playing football for his country – it wasn't even a dream, just impossible. But he made the impossible possible, which rarely happens in life, never mind football. And that got me scratching my head about those other fairytale moments in football when the impossible also became possible.

THE VARDY PARTY

If you'd told Jamie Vardy in May 2012 that the Conference Premier player would be playing, and scoring, for England four years later at the European Championships off the back of winning the Premier League with Leicester and finishing as the club's leading scorer, he'd have laughed in your face. If you'd then told him that a book would be written about his extraordinary journey and a Hollywood film would be hot on its heels, he'd probably have got a bit aggro with you for taking the mick.

THE BOYS DON GOOD

In 1977, Wimbledon were still a non-League side. Eleven years later, they won the FA Cup with a Wembley victory over Liverpool, the most successful English club side of all time. It's hard to explain just how unlikely that achievement was, even more so when you consider that just six years before the final, the Dons were still a Fourth Division team. Three promotions in four seasons changed all that and the rest, including that Lawrie Sanchez header, is history.

GREAT DANES

It's hard to believe now, but the European Championships of 1992 had only eight teams participating: two groups of four, the winners and runners-up of each group then playing in the semi-finals. It was very much a quality over quantity tournament and was the last of its kind. As one of the top European nations at the time,

Yugoslavia were expected to do well, especially with the likes of Dragan Stojković, Dejan Savićević and Siniša Mihajlović in the squad. But when war broke out in the Balkans on the eve of the tournament, Yugoslavia were suspended and Denmark were invited to take their place on 30 May, just 11 days before the start of the tournament. Once the Danes had managed to round up their players from various Southern European beaches and holiday resorts, they arrived at the tournament with little expected of them – after all, they were there literally to make up the numbers. But in one of the most extraordinarily unlikely football victories, Denmark used the lack of expectation to squeeze through the group, then win their semi-final on penalties against defending champions Netherlands, before beating Germany in the final to complete their fairytale.

GREEK GODS

The only thing more impressive than Denmark's success occurred 12 years later in Portugal. This time, there were 16 teams competing in the Euros, making Greece's achievement in winning the whole shebang even more extraordinary – although it should be pointed out that they had a little bit more time to prep than Denmark. Sour-grapes merchants would point to the fact that Otto Rehhagel's side weren't the prettiest to watch and took advantage of a brief vaccuum among Europe's traditional football powerhouses, but that would be cruel. Nobody gave Greece a prayer at the start of the tournament, even when they beat hosts Portugal 1-0 in their opening game. And that continued to be the case as they made their way through to the final where they did the same job on the hosts to become continental champions.

KINGS OF THE CASTEL

Castel di Sangro is a hamlet in the Abruzzo area of Italy which is home to around 6,000 people. It's a tiny place, and not the kind that should have a football team playing to any kind of level other than Sunday morning kickabouts. Yet, against all the odds, the town's team rose through the Italian football pyramid and made their way right up to Serie B, the professional second division just below the mighty Serie A. The amazing story was documented in a great book by American author Joe McGinnis, which I would highly recommend you to read – but only once you've finished this one.

FOREST ON FIRE

It's hard to over-emphasise just how utterly incredible Brian Clough's achievements at Nottingham Forest were in the late 70s, but I'll try. Forest were an average Second Division side when Clough took the reins. Yet within a season they were promoted to the top flight which they won at the first time of asking – a Leicester-esque feat. But Clough's Forest took it to a whole new level when they took Europe by storm in 1978-79 to land the European Cup, but that wasn't even the pinnacle. The cherry on the icing on the cake was the successful defence of the enormous trophy the following season when Forest became kings of Europe again. Stupendous.

CLASS IN A GLASS

For all your Forests, Greeces and Denmarks (even though none of these things can be pluralised) for my money, the greatest football fairytale moment happened at Brunton Park, Carlisle, in 1999. It was a moment so astonishingly Roy of the Rovers that it's hard to believe that it really happened.

Carlisle were about to be relegated out of the Football League to the obscurity of non-League nomadic status. It was deep into stoppage time and they needed a goal to beat Plymouth to stay up. With seconds remaining, the Cumbrians won a corner and goalkeeper Jimmy Glass, on loan from Swindon and playing his third and final game for the club, sprinted to the Argyle penalty area. The corner was met by Scott Dobie's head, but visiting keeper James Dungey managed to parry the ball as far as his opposite number, who slammed a fine half-volley into the net – cue bedlam. Glass was swamped by team-mates, the terraces emptied and the pitch was a scene of pure, uncensored joy. Even Hans Christian Andersen couldn't have come up with that one.

PLUCKED FROM OBSCURITY – FOOTBALL'S MOST RANDOM RISES

As all West Hams fans will gleefully tell anyone who will listen, nobody outside of France had heard of Dimitri Payet before he arrived in London in 2015. But that all changed as Payet left his calling card at every Premier League ground in an amazing breakthrough season in English football. At the age of 28, who could have imagined that happening? And the same can be said for these players who all made surprisingly rapid transformations after spending time in the football wilderness.

GARDENING LEAVE

A few years ago, if you were a Wycombe Wanderers fan and you fancied a drink at Adams Park before the game, the chances are it would have been poured by huge barman Jason Mooney. The 6ft 9in Northern Irishman was also a gardener, but he had to put all the weeding and pint-pulling to one side when the club handed him a contract to become their goalkeeper – his previous experience was playing seventh-tier football in Northern Ireland. But, coming from the club that pulled the Roy Essandoh Ceefax rabbit out of the hat, it's hardly surprising.

RECORD-BREAKING REJECT

When he was a teenager, Miroslav Klose attended a football training camp which didn't go according to plan. 'I was sent home on the first day with the following: "You'd be better off learning a better job because you'll never have a career as a footballer."' He took the advice on board and became a carpenter, a trade which he practised until he was 21. At that point, Kaiserslautern offered Klose a chance to play professional football, a decision which turned out to be a fairly good one, as the carpenter ended up becoming Germany's record international goalscorer.

SOUPED-UP CAMPBELL

DJ Campbell may sound like the kind of name you might see on a flyer about a banging new club night somewhere or other, but in fact it was just the name of a delivery van driver – until he was 23, that is. At that stage, courier Campbell was a part-time poacher for non-League Yeading until Brentford took a chance on him. Within a year, he was in the Premier League playing for Birmingham City and stayed in the top flight with QPR, giving football writers everywhere the chance to come up with even more puns about the striker 'delivering the goods'.

DJ loves to get defenders in a spin. Sorry.

GREENWICH GOAL MACHINE

When the prison doors slammed shut on a 21-year-old south London plasterer, he decided it was time for change. It was only a two-week stretch for driving without tax or insurance, but it was enough to make sure this young man would never fall foul of the law again. Shortly after, the striker who had been rejected by Southend and Brighton and was turning out for Greenwich Borough in his spare time was offered the chance of a lifetime by Crystal Palace manager Steve Coppell. In exchange for a set of weights, Palace secured the services of Mr Ian Wright, who took a while to adjust to pro football, but then spent the rest of his career making up for lost time by breaking goalscoring records for fun.

OUR MAN IN GERMANY

In 2011, when German giants Bayern Munich announced they had signed 18-year-old English wonderkid Dale Jennings, the rest of the world replied in unison 'Who?' Jennings had been on Liverpool's books at the age of 15, but was released and spent a year out of football before joining Tranmere and playing in League 1. Suddenly, Munich came calling and were so keen that they sent Dietmar Hamann to Jennings' house to convince him to make the move across Europe. Sadly for Dale, it didn't work out in Germany and he returned to the UK to play for Barnsley and then MK Dons.

TOTO'S GOLDEN SUMMER

Salvatore Schillaci wasn't a complete unknown before the Italia 90 World Cup, as he had spent the season before at Juventus, scoring more than 20 times after having only played in Serie B previously. But he had never played international football until March 1990, so it was still a major surprise to see him named in Italy's World Cup squad. The first two group games saw 'Toto' Schillaci used as a substitute, scoring in the first against Austria, but he then started every subsequent game and helped Italy to a third-place finish, winning the Golden Boot in the process thanks to his six goals. He made only eight further appearances for the Azzurri after that World Cup, highlighting what an incredible rise his had been.

DOYLE'S ROYAL REIGN

In 2005, Kevin Doyle was plying his trade as a striker for Cork City in Ireland and was just about known to some of the locals in the south-west of the country. Just over a year later, Doyle was a name on the lips of football fans around the world thanks to his and Reading's exploits in the Premier League. Signed by Steve Coppell – who has previous when it comes to the plucking out of obscurity – Doyle helped the Royals win promotion from the Championship and then carried on terrorising defences in the top flight, netting 13 times as Reading finished in an amazing eighth place in their debut Premier League campaign.

Some of the names on the list came from humble beginnings and went on to get paid vast sums of dosh. I think all this calls for a #FinancialXI. Here we go...

Team name: Borussia MunchenCashBack
Reserves: TSB Eindhoven
Stadium: Royal Bank of Spotland
Manager: Ian Woan Shark

First Team:
Poom & Bust

Fiscal Chimbonda
ATM Capoue
John Arne Visa

Stephane ReCessignon
Nikkei Butt
Show Me The Mane (c)
BackAnders Limpar

Dividend' Gog
Brit Assombawonga
Quantitative Griezmann

Subs:
Jens Lehmann
HSBCdorf
Andre I.O.Yew

AFGHANISTAN

Of all the cup competitions I've covered over the years, one of the most incredible experiences came in Afghanistan back in 2013. We were flying out there to do some filming at Camp Bastion and hosting a game between British troops and the Afghan National Guard.

'Don't really think I'm sleeping,' was the text message I received from Kevin Kilbane at 00:45 on the morning of our flight. 'I was. Thanks Kev,' was my reply, knowing that the alarm was set for 02:55 in order to get to Brize Norton to fly to Cyprus and then on to Afghanistan.

We were off to film a *Football Focus* special with the British armed forces, shoot another show for BBC World and record a Christmas Day show for Radio 5 Live. John Hartson was the other pundit who accepted the offer to come on the trip within

That Apache behind us is worth the same as a decent footballer... £40 million.

approximately four seconds of picking up his phone. 'When I was diagnosed with testicular cancer, I got hundreds of letters from troops in Afghanistan,' he told me. 'This is my chance to say thanks in person. I'm in.'

On our flight was Brigadier Neil Marshall, who was pivotal in the training of the Afghan national forces in Kabul. He spends much of his time training high-ranking officers. 'One of the first things I tell them is to make sure they never underestimate the importance of football in a soldier's life.'

That is certainly something we discovered from the moment the journey started. The troops on the plane were asking Kevin and John about their predictions for the season and also had some friendly warnings about the task ahead: 'When we fly into Bastion you'll have to put your body armour on and they'll turn all the lights off.'

'Sounds like an Old Firm game,' replied Mr Hartson, who scored 110 goals for Celtic and quite a few against Rangers – but he doesn't like to talk about it.

We arrived in Afghanistan in the early hours of a freezing morning. Our schedule was a hectic one. We had two TV shows and a one-hour radio documentary to record in a day and a half. We also discovered that a VVIP was arriving later that day. The then PM, David Cameron, was choppering in to watch a training session we were putting on.

I remember I started our pre-recorded show with the following introduction: 'Welcome to *Football Focus*. We have a slightly different show for you this week. We are in Camp Bastion for Christmas with Kevin Kilbane and John Hartson. We'll talk to these two in a moment, but first I need to introduce this man. The prime minister is also here now... don't take this the wrong way but... what are you doing here?'

The game itself was a huge success. Kev showed off his silky skills, Big John pushed a few people around, almost hit the PM with a stray shot but much fun was had by all on one of the worst pitches known to man. It did, however, end as most football adventures on foreign soil do: an Englishman missed a penalty.

Everywhere we went was that love of football. Hartson was asked to autograph countless Celtic, West Ham and Arsenal shirts. Kilbane ran out of signed pictures. While we were being shown around an Apache helicopter by Captain Nick Nugent, one of the engineers shouted out: 'Have you guys heard the news about AVB?' (Mr Villas-Boas had been sacked from his job at Spurs.)

The vast majority of the Afghan guards spoke little or no English but could reel off the names of most players in the Premier League. This is a conversation I had with one of them, called Antaz:

Me: You like football?
Antaz: *Enthusiastic thumbs up and nod*
Me: Have you heard of Crawley Town? [More in hope than anything else]
Antaz: *Deeply blank expression*
Me: Arsenal? Chelsea? Manchester United?
Antaz: [With a huge smile] Rooney! Rooney! [Pointing at me]
'He wants to know if you've met Rooney,' said the interpreter.
Me: Yes! [Big smile and thumbs up]
Antaz: Cantona?
Me: Yes.
Antaz: Henry?
Me: Yes.
Antaz: Van Persie?
Me: Yes, and him.

What followed was about five minutes of Antaz running me through players he knew, wanting to know if I'd met them. As much as I was enjoying our chat, we had to move on so I asked Antaz if he'd heard of Jason Dozzell or Ian Woan. Sadly his knowledge of Premier League footballers didn't extend to the halcyon days of the 1990s and he quickly lost interest.

We had no trophy to give out, so the victors in our Camp Cup game received an Xbox that we had brought out with us. The game that came free with it was *Call of Duty*, which seemed a bit weird so I threw in a fresh *FIFA*, too.

The trip was a real eye opener into life in a war zone and the enduring love of football. What struck us all was the warmth of the welcome and the resilience of those who used to call Camp Bastion home for four, six or sometimes nine months at a time.

I also left with a little cup of my own. They ran a competition in the mess tent to see who could eat the most profiteroles after a main meal. If I remember correctly, the record stood at about 27 but I dug deep and took it well into the thirties. I regretted it later and I'm not sure Big John and Super Kev enjoyed being in the same tent as me that night, but that mark will take some beating.

FOOTBALL RECORDS THAT WILL PROBABLY NEVER BE BROKEN

As I munched down on profiterole #35, it occurred to me that what myself, Big John, Big Kev and the assembled masses at Camp Bastion were witnessing was not just the setting of a record, but the hitting of a mark that may well never be beaten. Alongside my profiterole exploits, what are the extraordinary football records which, all things being equal, have no chance whatsoever of being broken, I hear you ask? The answers are right here.

WINNING THE EUROPEAN CUP FIVE TIMES IN A ROW

Real Madrid's achievement of winning five consecutive European Cups (which were also the first five) is never going to be repeated. No club has even managed to retain the trophy since AC Milan in 1989 and 1990, so five in a row in this era of football is completely unthinkable.

13 GOALS SCORED IN ONE WORLD CUP

In 1958, France's Just Fontaine scored a ridiculous 13 goals during the tournament – and his country didn't even win it. To put it into context, when Spain won the World Cup in 2010 the entire team scored eight goals. Fontaine's record is Just never going to be beaten. See what I did there?

1311 MINUTES WITHOUT CONCEDING A GOAL

In the 2008-09 Premier League season, Manchester United goalkeeper Edwin van der Sar managed to play for an astonishing 1311 minutes without anyone troubling his onion bag. If you're struggling with the scale of the maths, that's 14 games in a row! The run started on 8 November 2008 after Samir Nasri had bagged for Arsenal, and lasted until a van der Sar mistake led to Peter Lovenkrands scoring for Newcastle. That was on 4 March the following year.

173,850 PEOPLE ATTEND A FOOTBALL MATCH

Given the current era of all-seater stadia and strict ticket policies, there is very little chance of an arena being built that could hold almost 200,000 people and therefore the attendance at the Uruguay v Brazil 1950 World Cup match at the Maracana will never be surpassed. This was the game that Brazil sensationally lost 2-1, giving Uruguay the trophy (it was a final four group that tournament). Brazil's white shirts were subsequently replaced by some yellow ones that you might be more familiar with.

149-GOAL WINNING MARGIN

It's a bit of a farce, but the 2002 Madagascan championship play-off between AS Adema and SO l'Emyrne ended with a final score of 149-0. l'Emyrne were protesting at the poor refereeing in their previous match and so decided to pass back from every kick off and score own goal after own goal as their bemused opponents looked on.

14 PLAYERS USED ALL SEASON TO WIN THE ENGLISH TOP DIVISION

It might be hard to believe in this era of 30- or 40-player Premier League squads, but Aston Villa managed to win the 1981 First Division with just 14 players used in total throughout the season. Come to think of it, it's probably harder to believe that Aston Villa won the top flight. These days, of course, teams will name more than 14 players in their match day squads alone.

SCORING 9 (NINE) GOALS IN ONE FA CUP TIE

Bournemouth striker Ted MacDougall holds an extraordinary FA Cup record that has as much chance of being broken as I have of being the next England manager (I am available). When the Cherries thrashed Margate 11-0 in a 1971 FA Cup tie, MacDougall helped himself to nine goals. Impressive and greedy in equal measure.

106 LEAGUE GAMES UNBEATEN

Arsenal's Invincibles thought they were something very special when they won the league without losing a game and extended their total unbeaten league run to 49 games. But that suddenly sounds decidedly average when compared to the 1980s legends of the Steaua Bucharest team who dominated Romanian football with five straight league titles, which included a 106-game undefeated run (and a 1986 European Cup win, too).

29 LEAGUE WINS IN A ROW

Staying unbeaten is one thing, but winning every single match is something quite different. Between the end of 1971 and the beginning of 1973, Benfica managed to win 29 games in a row, which is a European record. Dinamo Zagreb did 28 in 2006-07, and Celtic did 25 in 2003-04, both of which are amazing – but they're not quite 29.

140-SECOND HAT-TRICK BY A SUBSTITUTE

Bournemouth were 3-0 up against Wrexham in 2004 and cruising to victory when James Hayter came on as an 84th-minute substitute. Two minutes later, he scored his first and precisely two minutes and 20 seconds after that he had completed a hat-trick, much to the amazement of everyone – especially his parents and brother who had left the game in the 82nd minute to catch a ferry back to the

Isle of Wight as they didn't think Hayter would see any action. Instead, his family listened to his exploits in the car: 'We heard a cheer just as we were getting in the car and we turned on the radio and found out James had come on and scored,' said brother Ben. 'Then he got the second one and we were starting to regret leaving early and we could not believe it when he scored again. I am delighted for James, but we are all gutted that we missed it.'

IN LOVING MEMORY OF THE OLD-FASHIONED BIG TARGET MAN

Spending time with Big John made me realise I was in the company of one of a dying breed – the old-fashioned target man. When I grew up, almost every team had one, but the game has changed to such an extent that there are only a handful of those old battering rams playing top-flight football today. Fear not, as this little trip down memory lane will help revive an almost lost art and show that it still exists to a degree today.

MICK HARFORD

HEIGHT: 6ft 4in
WEIGHT: 12st 9lb
GOALS: 233
GOOD TOUCH FOR A BIG MAN? Harford could play, but scored more than his fair share of headed goals, too. The former Lincoln and Luton target man knew what he was there for.
FOOTBALLER OR BOXER? Harford was very handy and never shied away from a scrap. Just ask pretty much any defender he played against. He would've made a terrifying super middleweight in the mould of Joe Calzaghe but with more attitude.

JAN KOLLER

HEIGHT: 6ft 8in
WEIGHT: 15st 11lb
GOALS: 255
GOOD TOUCH FOR A BIG MAN? It is unclear whether the huge Czech, who first trained as a goalkeeper, ever touched the ball with his feet – ongoing research has proved inconclusive. But his record speaks for itself.
FOOTBALLER OR BOXER? Koller would have made a fantastic massive boxer in the mould of Ivan Drago from *Rocky IV* or even Nikolai Valuev, the real-life 7ft Russian fighter. I always like to imagine that one day I'll remake *The Princess Bride* and ask Jan Koller to be Fezzik (originally played by André the Giant). I have suggested to Tony Pulis that he could be recast as Vizzini. He walked off.

EMILE HESKEY

HEIGHT: 6ft 2in
WEIGHT: 12st 9lb
GOALS: 164 (and counting)
GOOD TOUCH FOR A BIG MAN? At his peak, Heskey was way more than a battering ram. He had quick feet and the intelligence to gain Sven-Göran Eriksson's trust as a key member of his England team for several years. He may at times have had a head like a 50 pence piece, but ask Michael Owen if he liked playing with him.
FOOTBALLER OR BOXER? Not the type of big man to throw his weight around in a destructive way, Heskey was always a footballer first.

DUNCAN FERGUSON

HEIGHT: 6ft 4in
WEIGHT: 13st 5lb
GOALS: 124
GOOD TOUCH FOR A BIG MAN? Big Dunc could mostly do what he wanted on the pitch because most opponents were terrified of his menacing reputation. Which was completely justified. Having said that, he had a left foot that was far more impressive than his left fist.

FOOTBALLER OR BOXER? Sparred with Wayne Rooney when they played together at Everton, and knocked out a couple of burglars who picked the wrong house to break into – would've been very much at home in the ring, like a heavyweight Ricky Hatton.

BILLY WHITEHURST

HEIGHT: 6ft
WEIGHT: In his words 'I weren't fat, the kit was too small'
GOALS: 99
GOOD TOUCH FOR A BIG MAN? Yes. In short, you don't say anything derogatory about the former Hull and Oxford striker or he'll come looking for you. He is one of the best footballers ever.
FOOTBALLER OR BOXER? Whitehurst was born to fight. The true connoisseur's choice as the hardest footballer ever to play the game. I was once talking to Sir Alex Ferguson about hard men and I threw Billy's name out there. Fergie tapped me on the shoulder and said: 'Yes lad. They don't come any tougher than Whitehurst.' There are many stories, but one involves Billy playing for Oxford against Nottingham Forest ten days after a pub fight which left him with 30 stitches to a facial wound. During the game, Forest keeper Steve Sutton accidentally punched him in the face, reopening the wound. With half his cheek hanging off, Whitehurst had his face stapled – yes, literally – at half time before re-emerging for the second half and playing the whole game, pausing only to occasionally wipe the blood away. Yikes.

NIALL QUINN

HEIGHT: 6ft 4in
WEIGHT: 13st
GOALS: 190
GOOD TOUCH FOR A BIG MAN? Former Arsenal, Manchester City and Sunderland hero was a massive pain in the neck for defenders thanks to his robust approach to the game. Never pretty to watch but very effective and also an incredibly nice man with excellent disco pants.
FOOTBALLER OR BOXER? Given the story elsewhere in this book about Quinn splitting Steve McMahon's nose in a boxing ring, he might

have fancied himself as a Steve Collins type of fighter, but he was far more genteel than that story and his size would indicate.

PETER CROUCH

HEIGHT: 6ft 7in
WEIGHT: 11st 11lb
GOALS: 205 (and counting)
GOOD TOUCH FOR A BIG MAN? If there's one thing you have to say about Peter Crouch it's that he does indeed have a good touch for a big man. In fact, there's now a new FA by-law which means we have to say that when discussing Crouch. I love the fact that Umbro had to make a special England kit for him to cater for his 'unusual dimensions'.
FOOTBALLER OR BOXER? Wouldn't last ten seconds in a boxing ring. Big reach advantage but, with more than 200 goals, stick to the football Crouchy. By the way, did I mention that he's got a very good touch for a big man?

ANDY CARROLL

HEIGHT: 6ft 3in
WEIGHT: 12st 4lb
GOALS: 68 (and counting)
GOOD TOUCH FOR A BIG MAN? Still plying his trade and still terrorising defences. His head is his weapon, his feet are a luxury.
FOOTBALLER OR BOXER? That hair wouldn't be allowed in any Queensberry rules ring and Carroll has never really scrapped on the pitch. A footballer through and through.

ADEBAYO AKINFENWA

HEIGHT: 5ft 11in
WEIGHT: 16st
GOALS: 159 (and counting)
GOOD TOUCH FOR A BIG MAN? Bayo is a lower division legend who can mix it with the best, as Liverpool found out when they visited Wimbledon in the FA Cup in early 2015 and he scored (although the Dons lost). I was once at a dinner with him. He ate his dinner, my dinner and finished off the fella's next to us who had

just popped to the bog. He also asked for extra chicken. It was impressive to watch. The man likes chicken.
FOOTBALLER OR BOXER? Bayo has his own 'Beast Mode' brand and, you won't be surprised, is fond of the weights room (he can bench press 200kg), but that doesn't necessarily translate to the boxing ring. Let's just say that the official 'strongest man in football' (according to the *FIFA* console game) can look after himself (and chickens).

CARSTEN JANCKER

HEIGHT: 6ft 4in
WEIGHT: 14st 9lb
GOALS: 97
GOOD TOUCH FOR A BIG MAN? Jancker seemed to have the ability to extend his legs in a similar way to Inspector Gadget or Dhalsim from *Street Fighter*. He was surprisingly poor in the air for a man his size, but his game was all about power and strength.
FOOTBALLER OR BOXER? With his shaved head and huge presence, he looked like a player you wouldn't push in front of in the kebab queue, but he never really got involved in anything untoward on the pitch. This big man was a footballer.

THE EVOLUTION OF FOOTBALL COMPUTER GAMES

As a kid, when my friends and I were finally called back into our houses after endless games of Wembley, headers and volleys (60 seconds) or 'three 'n ' in', there were a few computer games to keep us entertained but things have changed immeasurably. When I gave the boys at Camp Bastion a copy of *FIFA*, my mind wandered back to those days of really shambolic digital football games which I absolutely loved. Here's how we got from then to now.

CHAMPIONSHIP SOCCER (ATARI, 1981)

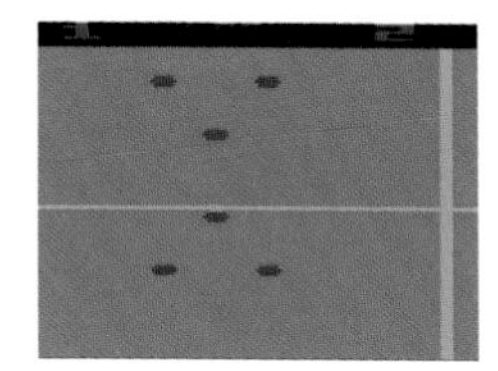

GAMING EXPERIENCE: The first serious console football game, and possibly the worst representation of what football actually was, given that it was three-a-side. Despite all that, the thrill of the crowd noise when scoring a goal was hairs-on-the-back-of-the-neck-pricklingly awesome.

REALISM FACTOR: Atari took the spaceship from *Space Invaders*, put a weird pair of flippers on it and decided that was a footballer. Teams were either red or blue, which in fairness most football teams are, and goals were greeted by some insane firework fan celebrations. In short, spot on.

FOOTBALL MANAGER (SINCLAIR ZX SPECTRUM, 1982)

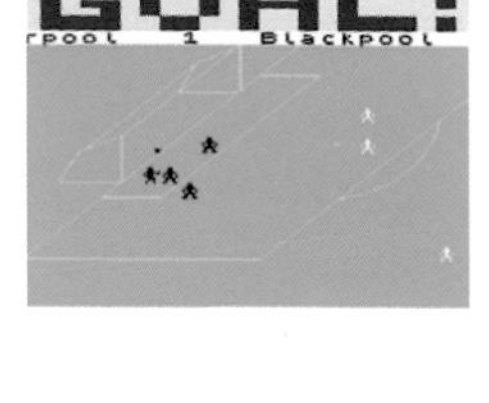

GAMING EXPERIENCE: The first football management simulation game was as addictive as anything out there now – you were the gaffer! It had all the English teams and leagues! Amazing!

REALISM FACTOR: You might as well have been managing a professional football club as this game literally took up all your time.

SOCCER (NINTENDO, 1987)

GAMING EXPERIENCE: Light years better than the early Atari effort, it featured little players flickering around the screen, the ability to choose which country you wanted to play as, and the skill level. On top of that, half times featured some pink-clad cheerleaders doing a dance. Way ahead of its time.

REALISM FACTOR: I can't remember ever playing football and having to listen to an irritating Nintendo soundtrack throughout. Also, I still have an issue with the words 'Goal In' that appeared when you bagged! Who on earth decided that was a good idea? I'll tell you… a moron. 'Goal' would have sufficed. But now I'm being picky.

KICK OFF (AMIGA/ATARI, 1989)

GAMING EXPERIENCE: A revolutionary aerial view made this game extremely popular, plus it was much faster and therefore more playable than anything that had gone before.

REALISM FACTOR: Quality crowd noises for goals and the kind of zippy one-touch passing that you always imagined your team played until you turned up to watch them. Not far off the real thing at all.

CHAMPIONSHIP MANAGER (PC, 1992)

GAMING EXPERIENCE: Written by Paul and Oliver Collyer, this management simulation took the gaffer game to the next level with everything from team selection dilemmas, to dealing with player demands and contract negotiations. Other than the annoying background music, it was near perfect. It was a massive time stealer, though, and millions of people suffered at the hands of the 'just one more game' curse. My mate showed me how to write your own player into the game. I created 'Dave Longface' and gave him unbelievable stats. He was eventually sold to Barcelona for £62 million but not before winning the Champions League back-to-back with Wolves! Don't ask.
REALISM FACTOR: There is no doubt about it, then Liverpool manager Graeme Souness couldn't have found his task any tougher had he been playing this superb game.

SENSIBLE SOCCER (AMIGA, ATARI, SEGA, 1993)

GAMING EXPERIENCE: We are stepping on hallowed turf here. At the time this was computer perfection. More aerial action, a huge choice of teams and incredibly catchy start-up music. This was the rival that *Kick Off* did not want. Yes, you could score from just inside the halfway line by quickly pulling back on the joystick every time without fail, but there was so much love about this bad boy.
REALISM FACTOR: Playing 90 minutes of this seemed to be as draining as playing 90 minutes of the real thing. I would estimate that between the age of 12 and 16 I spent almost three entire years playing this and wore out 207 Zip Sticks.

FIFA (SNES, SEGA, 1994)

GAMING EXPERIENCE: The original in the EA Sports gaming behemoth, this one changed everything, offering players the view of a pitch that you tend to see now on the telly. There were constant crowd noises, too, and pleasing thudding noises every time you passed or booted the ball forwards. *FIFA* would go on to add proper commentary, teams and ever more realistic players thanks to a rather expensive official licence.

REALISM FACTOR: If you weren't watching the early days of the Premier League, you were definitely playing *FIFA* because it was the next best thing.

INTERNATIONAL SUPERSTAR SOCCER (SNES, 1994)

GAMING EXPERIENCE: Wow! The players just got taller and more lifelike, even celebrating their goals with knee slides and the like. There was even a commentator, well a voice, who yelled 'Goooooooooal!' whenever you scored. Quality.

REALISM FACTOR: Arguably, as U2 were singing back then, even better than the real thing.

PRO EVOLUTION SOCCER (PS2, 2001)

GAMING EXPERIENCE: Woah! Somebody made football games much harder. Previously it had all been about goals, goals, goals. *Pro Evo* came along and made it slightly trickier to score. This was revolutionary.

REALISM FACTOR: Like football itself, *Pro Evo* divided the football gaming fraternity with people taking one side or the other – you were either a *FIFA* or *Pro Evo* player and once you'd chosen, you couldn't switch. *PES* was for the purist, those who thought they were decent footballers. I was always a *FIFA* man. While working on the Key 103 breakfast show in Manchester, I once made an outrageous claim that there was no one who could defeat me on a football game. Lots of people claimed I was an idiot and it turned out they were right. The other presenters organised for *PES* world champion Clare to come in and she humiliated me live on air. I think I could have given her a good game on *FIFA* but she was 8-0 up at half time. It remains a career low point. Up there with when an 11-year-old beat me at chess in nine seconds.

I feel that the only team XI that can do the business here is a #ComputerXI so here it is...

#ComputerXI

Team Name: Fontpellier
Reserves: USB Eindhoven
Stadium: Comic Sans Siro
Manager: Qwerty Vogts
Owner: Times New Roman Abramovich

First Team:
iPaddy Kenny

Desktop Maicon
Abdoulaye WiFaye
MSN Thome

Giovanni MS Dos Santos
Kaboul Holt Petit
MouseMatt LeTissier
Wes Yahoolahan

Marouane Chamacbook
Shift Key Kuqi
Peter Modemwingie

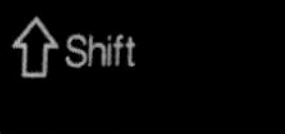

Subs:
Anti-Virus Niemi
Rory Delaptop
Wiki Lambert
Dexter Capslock
Jan Vennegoor of Hyperlink

CUP FINAL DAY

The day of the FA Cup final has always been an epic one. I used to love watching seemingly endless pictures of the coaches arriving, with Des Lynam weaving his broadcasting magic over the top. Now it is my privilege to be involved in that build-up. The 2016 final between Crystal Palace and Manchester United was the 13th I've covered. It's one of the longest working days I have, but also one of the best. Here it is from start to finish:

06:50 Alarm goes off. Press snooze.

06:52 Alarm number 2 goes off. Realise I have to get up so drag myself out of bed and into the shower.

06:58 Pre-match shave. Need a smooth face to take me all the way through to potentially extra time and penalties, which could be about 9pm.

07:05 Start going through my notes for *Football Focus*. Read through the scripted sections and flick through the morning's paper to see if there are any juicy headlines.

07:30 Call from *BBC Breakfast* checking that I'm still OK to go on the sofa with Mike Bushell at the side of the pitch at 8:30. I'm asked if I can make sure I bring Phil Neville with me. Phil has probably already been up for hours running somewhere.

07:45 Throw on outfit number 1 and pop downstairs for some scrambled egg. The hotel corridor honks of chemical cleaner. Someone had a big night.

07:58 Stroll through reception. Phil has been up for hours. 'You joining me for a power breakfast, big boy?' I ask. 'I'll have mine afterwards, Daniel. No need to rush.' Unfortunately I don't have that luxury.

08:01 Spot the *Football Focus* editor Matt halfway through a full English and join him for some powdered egg followed closely by half a bowl of Rice Krispies and a glass of orange juice.

08:10 Leave the hotel with Mr Neville to make our way to Wembley via the West Gate. 'Morning fellas,' says Mike on reception. He checks our bags and we make our way to pitchside after stopping in the production office for a chocolate Hobnob – first of the day.

08:25 Meet the magical Mike Bushell and take our seats on the *BBC Breakfast* sofa for the day's first bit of live telly. Phil tells the story about how his dad took him out of school to watch the 1990 FA Cup final replay, where Manchester United beat Crystal Palace by a single goal. Phil missed a history exam for it but, as he told the nation: 'You don't need to know about the Battle of Waterloo when you're chasing Marc Overmars.'

08:38 Hobnob number 2.

08:40 Record a little Facebook Live video from the side of the pitch. All of a sudden 11,000 people are watching me test out the surface with my brogue. Anne from Stafford says 'I love you' in the comments section. 'Rascal shoes' says Rajid, while Pete opts for 'F%?€ off you s5€?#}€'. I show the phone to Phil. 'Pete's a good lad, isn't he?'

08:59 Hobnob numbers 3 + 4. Find a watermelon with 'FA CUP' carved into it. Someone got up very early and has a sharp knife.

09:00 Matt joins us in the broadcasting truck to watch the pieces for *Football Focus*. We've got Alan Pardew, Wayne Rooney, Yannick Bolassie, Alan Stubbs on the Scottish Cup final and a magic trick from Jamie Raven that I still cannot get my head around.

09:40 Call home to say 'hi' to the kids while eating Hobnob number 5. They are watching *The Descendants* and have minimal interest in the FA Cup final. Our little five-year-old tells me he has dog poo on his foot.

10:00 Kevin Kilbane turns up. He's our second guest on *Focus*, alongside Phil Neville. I offer Kev a Hobnob. He declines. I eat it (number 6).

10:10 We run through the rest of the technicals for the show, checking camera positions, lights and access. There's an elaborate bit that involves walking from right under the stadium to the mouth of the tunnel. It seems to work.

10:40 Groundsman Carl is painting the lines on the side of the pitch. He is fully in the zone. I record a little Facebook live video with him. Within 20 seconds, Pete is back in the comments section reminding everyone that he's not my biggest fan. The rehearsal continues.

11:50 We are allowed onto the precious Wembley turf to film the opening sequence to *Football Focus* using the spider cam – the funky one that floats above the pitch. It's the closest I'll ever get to *The Matrix* in my life.

11:55 Final pre-*Focus* Hobnob and we get ready for the start of the show.

12:07 Fella turns up with the FA Cup trophy. He's a big lad called Mo. We plonk it in place between me and the pundits and we're ready to go.

12:10 *Run titles* Show goes perfectly apart from the seven full-volume rehearsals of the national anthem and having to bin off Tinie Tempah, who asked for a selfie with us as we were sprinting to the Royal Box. I made sure I grabbed him afterwards. More from Mr Tempah later.

13:00 Focus ends. Last one of the season. Hugs and Hobnobs all round (we're well into double figures).

13:10 Quick lunch and then a chat through my *Match of the Day* jobs with Richard, who is editing that show. My role is pitchside presenter and Manchester United interviewer. Gabby Logan is looking after Crystal Palace. Richard talks me through the meticulous pre-match timings and how it is essential that I release Sir Alex Ferguson and Steve Coppell (who are taking the trophy out onto the pitch) at 17:17 exactly so we don't delay kick off.

14:00 I walk into the production office and Ruud Gullit is FaceTiming professional golfer Andrew 'Beef' Johnston. Beef has become something of a full-time legend in the sporting world but – while speaking to Ruud – he is playing at the Irish Open. Ruud insists that I show him my swing. Gary Lineker is in the background, fully clothed, going through the plan for the match. Before I leave I ask Ruud if he's got any Dutch insight on Louis van Gaal as I'm due to interview him in a couple of hours. He laughs (worrying) and tells me to ask LVG about the 'cow chasing the rabbit'. 'Will he get it?' I ask tentatively. 'Are you stitching me up?' He insists it's a well-known Dutch saying and that LVG will 'love it'.

14:15 Pitchside again. This time with Alan Shearer. We are filming a little ten-minute interview about Euro 96 for *BBC Breakfast*. He says the crucial thing about taking penalties is to make your mind up early and NEVER change it – just like he said in the foreword. We reminisce about 'Football Coming Home' and decide that Baddiel & Skinner should be knighted.

14:30 Film a live continuity link with Phil Neville in between FA Cup *Question of Sport* and FA Cup *Pointless*. Phil is on BBC 5 Live and is still sprinting down the steps with ten seconds to go. He jumps in, grabs a microphone and never once takes a deep breath during the next five minutes of TV #athlete.

15:30 Change into *MOTD* outfit. Eat half a pack of fun-sized Mars Bars and head to the tunnel. Next job is interviewing Louis van Gaal. He has already refused to speak to me in the build-up to the game because of a question I asked him at the semi-final. We've had a few run-ins throughout the season, but I'm armed with questions – including that one for Ruud – and ready for action.

15:55 Michael Carrick arrives first, so we do the interview at pitchside and then I have to leg it down the other end of the pitch to do the team news.

16:15 Biscuit break. One of the floor managers has a box of Fox's Crunch Creams. This is not one of the healthiest days of my life.

16:32 LVG exits the dressing room and heads our way. He looks to be in a good mood. He doesn't hear my first question. Not sure if he's pretending or his notoriously bad ear is playing up. We restart the interview. It's all going well until I throw in Ruud's 'cow and rabbit' thing. He says something about 'that's what happens when you spend two years in a studio'. I thank him. The end.

16:45 It's starting to become clear that there might be a timing issue. People are frantically running around in the tunnel. Alan Pardew comes down to ask me what time 'Abide With Me' is on. He wants to make sure he's there for that. I tell him it's scheduled for 17:19 but who knows?

17:10 Fergie and Steve Coppell turn up. Tinie Tempah has a selfie with them and I talk them through what will happen, while the floor manager tries to locate the FA Cup for them to carry out onto the pitch. Time is pressing on.

17:15 The issue seems to be that a massive pitch flag has taken eight rather than three minutes to be unfurled. Gary says: 'Dan is at pitchside with two men who remember 1990 very well...' and I introduce our two former managers and we chat for about two minutes. Sadly, when I let them go to take the trophy onto the pitch – as instructed – they are told to wait. That flag is still on the pitch! We all stand like lemons in the tunnel for another three minutes. Tinie Tempah is behind us limbering up.

17:20 This has totally messed up my long-planned link of handing from Sir Alex to the live music. 'And now from a man renowned for his rage to a fella with a Tinie Tempah' doesn't really work after a five-minute delay. The kick-off is definitely going to be put back. Tinie makes his way out onto the pitch, but it's all becoming a little awkward. Months of meticulous planning is going out of the window. Throw in an almost mute national anthem and you have the build-up from hell. The poor girl singing 'God Save The Queen' couldn't hear a thing and it was only after a rabid man shouted 'Just sing!!!' a few times that she picked up for the last few words.

17:35 The game kicks off. Manchester United win. We watched it from behind the dugout eating biscuits. It's amazing how many Custard Creams you can get through in 120 minutes. At full time we had an elaborate plan to get as many interviews as possible. Our tactic was for Gabby to find Wayne Rooney, floor manager John to get [winning goal hero Jesse] Lingard, producer Mike to rally Carrick or David de Gea, while I concentrated on LVG. It worked seamlessly. The boss took a bit of persuading: 'Talk to the players, there are eighteen of them.'

'I've already grabbed four of them. The fans want to hear from you. Give me two minutes and I promise to be nice.'

He laughed out loud but thankfully agreed. He gave me two minutes and told us how he'd now won a domestic cup in Germany, Holland, Spain and England. It was his last live interview as Manchester United manager.

20:00 Post-game Toffee Crisp and a quick run back to the hotel for an end-of-season farewell to everyone before the Euros. I saw Ruud giggling as I entered. We shared some Bombay mix and laughed about cows and rabbits. He tells me I should have used 'pulling a monkey out of your sleeve' instead as 'the Dutch love that'. I resolve never to take pre-interview advice from Ruud again. I shake a few hands and head for the long trip back to Sheffield.

01:00 M1 is closed.

01:30 Diversion is closed.

02:32 Open the door to Chateau Walker. One final biscuit. My wife has left a Garibaldi by the stairs. She knows. Off to bed to count cows or Dutch rabbits. A long day but a beauty.

THE FOOTBALL TRADITIONS YOU NEVER STOPPED TO THINK EXISTED

I'm all for football traditions like singing 'Abide With Me' before the FA Cup final. These are moments that are steeped in history and connect us with football's great heritage and all those amazing memories from years gone by. That's all fine. But there are many other weird football traditions that have crept into the game as stealthily as James Bond on the trail of a Russian assassin. They're almost like a whole new set of rules which everyone adheres to but nobody really knows why. Confused? You will be.

NO SUBS BEFORE CORNERS

Whether you play Sunday league or Champions League, never ever make a substitution before a corner which you are defending. If you are defending a throw-in from roughly the same place as a corner, that's not a problem – throw on a sub, make a double change if you like, go crazy. But never before a corner. Why? Who knows.

GIVING THE OTHER TEAM THE BALL

There aren't any situations where you would give your opponent the ball on purpose – except when one of their players gets injured and the internationally agreed gesture of goodwill is to return the ball to the team of the injured player when play restarts. At that point, those in attendance must also burst into spontaneous applause.

WHEN TO BLOW FOR FULL TIME

We're never privy to referees' meetings where they discuss things like awarding a penalty to the other team if you realise you've given a soft one at the other end. And that's why we can't be certain, but we can take a pretty good guess that referees are only allowed to blow the full-time whistle when the ball is safely in the middle third of the pitch.

Textbook legal shielding from Aaron Ramsey.

WHEN OBSTRUCTION IS ALLOWED

During a match, a player is not allowed to stand in an opponent's path to prevent them from getting to the ball, as that is an obstruction and a free kick. But from the 88th minute until the end of stoppage time, that is a perfectly legal tactic by the team in the ascendancy as long as it takes place within five square metres of the losing team's corner flag.

WHEN VIOLENCE IS ALLOWED

As a sub-clause to the tradition above, in this situation, the losing team are allowed to do whatever they like to the player from the winning team who is shielding the ball, including kicking, raking studs or shoving – all of which would usually be yellow- or red-card offences at any other point in the game.

PHYSIOS MUST SPRINT

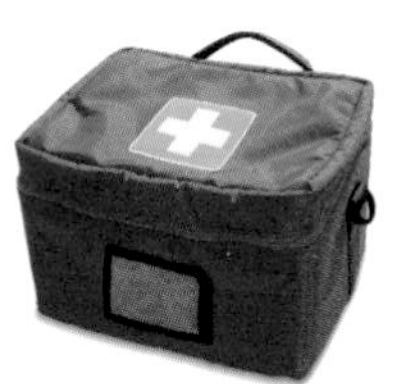

Some 99.99 per cent of injuries on a football pitch are not life threatening, but nevertheless, when a physio is required on the pitch to assess an injury they must sprint as quickly as possible to the stricken player as if his life really did depend on it.

MANAGERS COVERING MOUTHS

A manager is not allowed to discuss anything with his players or coaching staff in the technical area without covering his mouth, just in case anybody tries to lip read what he's saying or, worse still, he's being tailed by the FBI for his mafia connections. This now extends to players on the pitch passing instructions to each other from the bench – always cover your mouth when speaking.

HOW TO WATCH A PENALTY SHOOT-OUT

Players are allowed to watch their team-mates take part in a penalty shoot-out, but only if they stand in the centre circle in a single line, with their arms around each other.

TIME ADDED ON

No matter what has happened during the first half of a match, even if there were no injury breaks, goals or substitutions, the referee must still add on a minute at the end of the 45. Similarly, the amount of added time at the end of the second half has to be a minimum of three minutes, regardless of what has actually happened on the pitch.

HOW TO BE A GOALKEEPER

If a keeper makes a spectacular save, he is not allowed to acknowledge any of his team-mates who come to congratulate him. Instead, he has to either shout at them or gesticulate about what they should be doing next, like marking from the subsequent corner, for example. If he smiles he will be instantly substituted.

THE NOT SO MAGNIFICENT SEVEN FINALS

Working at 13 cup finals, not to mention watching countless others, has taught me that just because it's a final doesn't necessarily mean that the quality of the match is going to live up to the occasion. And, let's be honest, there have been some absolute stinkers over the years – not every final can be Real Madrid 7 Eintracht Frankfurt 3. Here's my take on the most unmemorable showpieces.

1994 WORLD CUP FINAL

SCORE: Brazil 0 Italy 0 – Brazil win on penalties

WHAT WENT WRONG: To suit European audiences, the game was played in the searing afternoon heat of Pasadena, California, and 94,000 fans (as well as countless others around the world) had to suffer their way through a drab goalless draw.

HIGHLIGHT: The penalties. The world watched as Roberto Baggio ballooned his over the bar. The divine ponytail momentarily lost his magic.

2003 CHAMPIONS LEAGUE FINAL

SCORE: AC Milan 0 Juventus 0 – Milan win on penalties

WHAT WENT WRONG: Both teams deciding that their gameplan was not to lose ensured this was 120 minutes of pain. Even the penalties were poor, with only five out of ten scored. I was at this one and the guy next to me disappeared for 20 minutes to get a steak slice in the second half. When he came back he asked me what had happened. Nothing had happened.

HIGHLIGHT: Andriy Shevchenko scoring an offside goal. Yawn.

1977 LEAGUE CUP FINAL

SCORE: Aston Villa 0 Everton 0

WHAT WENT WRONG: The backpass rule was yet to be invented and both teams took full advantage. There wasn't a serious shot on goal for the entire game, and two replays were necessary before the shackles were removed and Everton won 3-2.

HIGHLIGHT: The half-time cuppa.

2008 FA CUP FINAL

SCORE: Portsmouth 1 Cardiff 0

WHAT WENT WRONG: As brilliant as it was for Championship side Cardiff to reach the final, they couldn't quite believe they were there and failed to really take part in the match.

HIGHLIGHT: Kanu's goal, making him the oldest person to ever score in the FA Cup final at the age of 68.

It's not a red card... it's an arrestable offence.

2010 WORLD CUP FINAL

SCORE: Spain 1 Holland 0

WHAT WENT WRONG: Spain tiki-taka'd their way around the pitch for about 116 minutes while the world fell asleep, before finally deciding to score a goal and put everyone out of their misery.

HIGHLIGHT: Nigel de Jong karate kicking Xabi Alonso in the chest but only receiving a yellow card (one of 14 in the match) from England's finest referee, Howard Webb.

1990 WORLD CUP FINAL

SCORE: Germany 1 Argentina 0

WHAT WENT WRONG: Argentina had spoiled their way to the final and tried to do the same against Germany. It almost worked, but Andy Brehme's penalty five minutes from time foiled their cunning plan.

HIGHLIGHT: Argentina finishing with nine men and Diego Maradona crying at the final whistle.

1986 EUROPEAN CUP FINAL

SCORE: Steaua Bucharest 0 Barcelona 0 – Steaua win on penalties

WHAT WENT WRONG: Even El Tel Venables couldn't prevent his Barça side from doing as little as their Romanian opponents for 120 minutes. Then, the worst penalty shoot-out in history saw no fewer than six kicks missed, including all four of Barça's, meaning Steaua won the shoot-out 2-0. Pathetic.

HIGHLIGHT: Midway through the second half, a bird flew into the stadium. Then it flew out again.

FOOTBALL'S MOST FEROCIOUS FALLOUTS

With Mr Van Gaal refusing to speak to me since the semi-final, I was pleased he was happy to talk on the big day. But that was just a very minor spat compared to some of the stupendously petty and spectacular fallings-out football has witnessed between team-mates, managers and players. All of which have been great fun for us to watch from the sidelines.

ANDY COLE v TEDDY SHERINGHAM

Despite playing together for Manchester United, and both scoring a ridiculous number of goals in that time too, Cole and Sheringham reportedly never uttered a word to each other throughout. Their fallout dated back to Cole's England debut in 1995 against Uruguay, when he came on as a substitute at Wembley, replacing Sheringham. 'I walked on to the pitch, 60,000 or so watching,' said Cole. 'Sheringham is coming off. I expect a brief handshake, a "Good luck, Coley." I am ready to shake. He snubs me. He actively snubs me, for no reason I was ever aware of then or since. He walks off. I don't even know the bloke so he can't have any issue with me. I was embarrassed. I was confused. And there you have it. From that moment on, I knew Sheringham was not for me.'

DAVID BATTY v GRAEME LE SAUX

The Blackburn pair were in action in Moscow for Rovers' Champions League dead rubber against Spartak. Early in the game, they went for the same loose ball and collided with each other. No big deal, these things happen on a football pitch. Except it was a big deal. Batty squared up to Le Saux, words were exchanged and, in the blink of an eye, Le Saux threw a punch at his team-mate. The match was still going on as Tim Sherwood stepped in to break up the fight. Blackburn lost 3-0 and Le Saux headed to A&E: 'I swung at him, connected and knew immediately that I had broken my left hand. I am not a fighter. I hadn't closed my fist properly. I was in a lot of pain, which just made me feel more ridiculous.'

ALEX FERGUSON v ROY KEANE

For at least a decade, the pair were like father and son, united in their desire to succeed and win everything. But, as Keane's career was coming into its twilight, the atmosphere changed. In 2005, Keane conducted a notorious interview on MUTV following a defeat at Sunderland, in which he laid into some of his team-mates. Ferguson made sure the interview was pulled and their relationship was never the same again. After a falling out with coach Carlos Queiroz, in which Keane questioned the Portuguese man's loyalty and even had a go at Ferguson in front of the entire squad, he was on his way out of Old Trafford. The spat continued with both men having a gentle dig in their autobiographies and many other forms of media, too. This one is set to run and run.

JACK CHARLTON v BOBBY CHARLTON

England's World Cup winning brothers had a falling out over comments Jack made about Bobby's wife Norma and haven't been in close contact for some time. After Norma herself struggled to get on with the Charltons' mother Cissie, Jack publicly criticised her, driving a huge rift between he and Bobby. 'Jack came out in the newspapers saying things about my wife that were absolutely disgraceful,' said Bobby. 'My brother made a big mistake. I don't understand why he did it. He couldn't have possibly known her and said what he said. I was astonished.' Sadly, the pair are civil if they meet in public, but that's about it.

DAVID MOYES v WAYNE ROONEY

Moyes was fiercely protective of his young charge as Rooney shot to fame as a teenager at Goodison Park, but the youngster made clear in his autobiography that he left Everton because he felt that Moyes was 'overbearing, just wanting to control people'. Rooney also claimed in his book that a breakdown of trust around the time of his transfer had also disappointed him – and the pair then went to court over those comments, with Moyes winning damages after proving that he had not leaked details of a private conversation between the pair to newspapers. Both Moyes and Rooney agreed to move on, which was just as well, as they ended up back in their manager/player relationship again at Old Trafford a few years later, although that didn't last too long.

RUUD GULLIT v ALAN SHEARER

When Ruud Gullit was Newcastle manager, he decided to up the stakes in his power struggle with the club's star player Alan Shearer by dropping him, along with Duncan Ferguson, for the club's huge derby at home to Sunderland. It wasn't a decision that went well for him, as the Toon lost the game 2-1 and Gullit resigned the next day, but not before Ferguson had kicked the manager's door off its hinges at the training ground. Relations between Gullit and Shearer remained frosty, but when they were both employed by the BBC years later to provide punditry, they started to see the funny side of it, especially when people like Gary Lineker would set Gullit up with questions like: 'Have you ever dropped your star player, Ruud?' They now get on very well and Shearer has dropped a few perfectly timed comedy barbs in Ruud's direction.

OLIVER KAHN v JENS LEHMANN

Two fiercely proud German men, both with massive personalities, vying for only one goalkeeping position in the national team – what could possibly go wrong? Up until 2004, Kahn was the German keeper, but when Jürgen Klinsmann took over as national coach, he eventually installed Lehmann as his preferred choice and the keepers fell out. Lots of public sniping followed, with Lehmann claiming Kahn was too intense, while Kahn, even in retirement, mocked Lehmann for losing his place in the Arsenal team to Manuel Almunia, and later suggested it might be time for the keeper to retire. Nice.

KIERON DYER v LEE BOWYER

Back in Newcastle, the Geordies were losing at home to Aston Villa in 2005 and Bowyer came short for a pass from Dyer, but Dyer chose to give the ball to another team-mate. Five minutes later, the same thing happened. 'You never pass to me,' said Bowyer,

according to Dyer, who claims he replied: 'The reason I don't pass to you is because you're s***, basically.' Bowyer started raining blows on Dyer who responded in kind and, incredibly, the pair were both sent off. They wanted to carry on scrapping in the tunnel and dressing room, but were kept apart by the large, but sensitive, hands of the club's masseurs.

MAURO ICARDI v MAXI LÓPEZ

Once, the Argentinian pair were Sampdoria team-mates. Then, Wanda Nara happened and the pair became bitter enemies. López was married to Nara and the couple had three children together. But the pair divorced and, before Icardi could say 'Would you mind if…' he was dating his mate's ex-wife and *they* then got married the following year. López was miffed, but not as miffed as he was when he saw a picture of Icardi's new tattoo on which were the names of *his own* three children! The Argentinians continued to play in Italy, but López refused to shake his nemesis's hand when his Torino side faced Icardi's Inter. Another one that might last a while.

Inspired by some of those rather childish football spats I think the best way to polish things off here would be a #BabyXI. Here we go…

#BabyXI

Team Name: Burnley Learning Centre
Reserves: Pramathinaikos
Stadium: Gas and Airsome Park
Management Team: Koochy Koochy Koeman, Kindergarten Klopp, Laudrup The Duff, Buggy Freedman

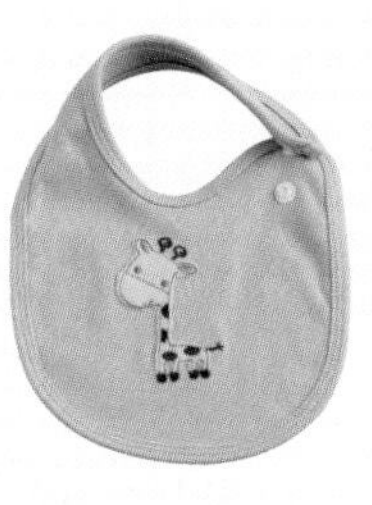

First Team:
One Vorm Every Minute

Twinkle Twinkle Little Vlaar
EmbRio Ferdinand
Kieron Bibbs

Umbilical Cord Makalele
Steven N'Onesie
Pampers Bouba Diop
Chris Swaddle

Rock-a-bye-Bebe
Nappies Cisse
3am Feed Malbranque (c)

Subs:
MMRson Boyce
Victor Moses Basket
Sudocremi Moses
Tony Potty

FERGIE, SUE, KLOPP AND TRACEY TOO

A question I often get asked is: 'What is the most surreal situation you have found yourself in over the years?' When I sit down and think about it, there are quite a few 'how did this happen?' moments. I have always felt very privileged to do this job, and it puts me in some amazing places with some amazing people.

In 2015 I was asked by Sir Alex Ferguson to host a few events with him after the publication of his latest book on the art of management. One of them was at the beautiful Bridgewater Hall in Manchester. The place was a complete sell-out, with over 2,000 tickets gone in just a couple of minutes. Fergie asked me to get there a few hours before kick-off and when I arrived I got dragged into his dressing room.

We cracked open a packet of crisps and briefly went through the plan for the evening. We still had a few hours to kill but Sir Alex had a plan. He glanced at his watch and rubbed his hands together. 'It's time,' he said, as he picked up the remote control for the TV. 'I love this,' he chuckled as he switched on BBC2. *Eggheads*! He is something of an addict and he's quite tasty at it.

So when you ask me for surreal moments, eating crisps with the most successful manager in the history of football while he shouts, 'Albatross! It's an albatross!' at the TV is right up there. The

question was 'The Gooney is a species of which bird?' in case you were interested.

When you see Sir Alex with his old players now, there is an unbelievable bond between them – even most of the ones he fell out with. It takes a special manager to be able to create that sort of connection, and it's also something that I've witnessed from Jürgen Klopp – first at Borussia Dortmund and most recently at Liverpool.

I went to go and see the big German boss a few months after he arrived at Anfield and his impact was obvious. The lady on reception at the Melwood training ground smiled when she said his name, and you could see his care and attention when he broke off to talk to some of his injured players. It's a small thing, but he shook the hand of, and said 'hello' to, each and every member of our camera crew.

We wandered into his huge office overlooking the pitch. The walls were plastered with reminders of the club's glorious past and, by his desk, mementoes from Dortmund – a watch, a book about what makes managers great, an English dictionary and a pair of wacky glasses – a present from an unnamed player with a sense of humour according to the manager.

Over the course of our 45 minutes with him, he was engaging, exciting, passionate, funny and dismissive of any criticism levelled at either his players or the club – a club he seemed to understand very well, even though he'd only been there a few months.

We met again in slightly more, shall we say, confined circumstances at Liverpool's FA Cup third round tie against Exeter City. One of the things I love when a big team goes to a minnow in the FA Cup is the clash of cultures. Premier League teams are used to space, service and a perfect pitch. You don't get two of those at Exeter, but you can't fault the middle one.

I got there about four hours before kick-off and – along with floor manager Mark Price – decided to scope out the facilities. The tunnel was thin, the dressing rooms pokey and the interview room was... well... non-existent. The plan was to use the tea room at the end of the tunnel next to the referee's office.

I'll do my best to describe the room to you. It was about two metres square with a sink on one wall, cupboards and an urn on another and the door in the middle of a third. The final wall was plastered with the FA Cup board which has all the sponsors' names on it – that's what your interviewee stands in front of.

We wedged our camera into the tiny floor space, but about two hours before kick-off Sue and Tracey turned up. This was their domain and they were understandably unhappy. There was an awkward ten minutes of trying to work out how we would all fit in. In the end, we settled on a plan. We would wedge in a corner, they could brew in behind and when Klopp turned up for his pre-match interview, Sue and Tracey would turn the kettles off and stand tight to the kitchen cupboards about 70cm away from the Liverpool manager, who would be explaining why he was playing so many youngsters in the competition.

The plan was working perfectly. Half the Exeter team came in for their customary pre-match hot drink and the immaculately dressed manager, Paul Tisdale, found the whole thing very comical.

About 90 minutes before the kick-off, the Liverpool team started filing into the dressing room. I was waiting in the tiny tunnel, keen to give Klopp a heads-up about what was about to happen. 'Hello again,' he said as he rounded the corner with press officer in tow, 'where are we doing this?' I explained that this was going to be a slightly unusual pre-match chat and asked him if he was up for a bit of fun at the end. 'Of course,' he said with a smile. I pointed him in the direction of Sue and Tracey's miniature football fiefdom.

We all squeezed in and Gary Lineker handed down to us for the interview to start. The first couple of questions were all about the team selection, the occasion and the pitch. The German was a bit worried. As promised, I left the fun to the end...

'And before we let you go... have you ever been interviewed in a tea room before?'

'No,' said Klopp, laughing as the camera panned round to show the cupboards and a sea of crockery. 'I see they have quite a collection of cups,' said the German. I made a pointless comment about the FA Cup and, as the camera continued to pan, I introduced the Liverpool manager to Sue and Tracey. There was hardly enough room for them to lift their arms to wave, but it was a beautiful moment as Herr Klopp requested a black coffee. As I thanked him and the interview ended, he hung around for a few minutes, sipping away and chatting to the two star-struck tea ladies.

He must have enjoyed it, because he came back after the thrilling 2-2 draw for another black coffee. He complained again about the pitch and then signed off in style.

'Jürgen, appreciate your time. Thanks for talking to us.'

'Yes... I had to,' and with that he walked off to start the long journey home. Sue and Tracey found it all very funny.

THE 14 WORST MANAGERIAL EXCUSES OF ALL TIME

Other than excelling at *Eggheads*, Fergie was a serious Dugout Don. However, like many of the great gaffers, he was never afraid to offer reasons for his team not winning, some might call them excuses – and his most famous one features here.

PLAYING GAMES

When Real Madrid lost to Real Betis, putting their La Liga title hopes in danger, José Mourinho was quick to point out that his side were handicapped by that horrible football demon – the fixture list. Despite each team having to play all the other teams in the league home and away, Mourinho was convinced that the fixtures were just not quite fair enough. 'It's obvious that other teams are controlling the calendar,' he said. 'They are laughing behind my back.'

THE LAW OF THE SOD

When Louis van Gaal's struggling Manchester United team lost 2-1 to unfancied Danish outfit FC Midtjylland in the first leg of a Europa League tie in 2016, the man they call LVG was asked for his explanation of United's poor performance, to which he shrugged his shoulders and said, 'Murphy's law.' Unsurprisingly, he was out at the end of the season.

NOT SO SUPER MAC

Huddersfield manager Malcolm MacDonald was at a loss to explain how his side could possibly have ended up on the losing side to Manchester City. We've all been at games like that where one team dominates, but they don't get the rub of the green and then get caught out by a sucker punch. 'Before City scored we could have been three-nil up,' said a frustrated MacDonald. 'We were playing so well I turned to my physio and said: "I think I'll have a cigar – if we keep this up we'll get double figures."'

Yes, it can be such a frustrating game at times. And the final score on that particular afternoon? Manchester City 10 Huddersfield 1.

SEEING REDS

Millwall manager Keith Stevens had a novel explanation for the reason behind the Lions' awful disciplinary problems one season. The south-east London club had suffered no fewer than ten red cards in one campaign, but Stevens was convinced that he knew the root cause of the issue: 'Of the ten sendings-off, nine have been different players, so it proves we're unlucky.'

GIVEN THE SLIP

When Plymouth literally slipped to a 2-1 home defeat to Cambridge after defender Peter Hartley fell over to gift the visitors a winner, Pilgrims manager Derek Adams knew exactly where to point the finger of blame. 'It was an algae on the pitch, it has to be treated and hopefully that will be sorted in the week,' he said. 'That is the reason [for Hartley's slip].'

A GREY DAY

A perennial favourite in everyone's random excuse generator, Alex Ferguson stunned United fans and all sane people with his reason for his team's 6-3 shellacking by Southampton in 1996. United were playing in grey in the first half, but Fergie made them change their kit at half time. 'The players don't like the grey strip,' he said. 'They find it difficult to pick each other out. We had to change the strip.' And that change of kit helped United go from being 3-0 behind to losing 6-3.

POCH'S PITCH

Tottenham were on a poor run. Three defeats in five matches in October 2014 had put pressure on new manager Mauricio Pochettino, but luckily he knew what the problem was so Spurs fans could rest easy. It was the size of the White Hart Lane pitch, of course. 'Our style means we need a bigger space to play because we play a positional game,' he said. Well that's OK, then.

YOU'RE NOT SINGING ANYMORE

There was no doubt why Millwall had lost 1-0 to Leeds in a Championship match, according to the Lions manager Ian Holloway – it was all down to the fans. Not enough of them, to be precise because, due to trouble at previous games between the clubs, only 200 Millwall fans were allowed in to Elland Road. 'We couldn't get the volume of noise from our fans that we got in our last game,' said Ollie. 'Who knows, when we had momentum in the second half, that might have got us a goal and the point we deserved.'

TALKING BALLS

When Stevenage played Newcastle in the 1998 FA Cup fourth round, the match was played with plenty bubbling beneath the surface following a public spat between the clubs in the build-up to the game. Newcastle asked the non-Leaguers to switch the game to St James' Park, but Stevenage refused to be bullied and the game was staged at their ramshackle Broadhall Way home.

And that might be why, when Stevenage earned a famous 1-1 draw against the might of Alan Shearer and co, Toon manager Kenny Dalglish complained that 'the balls were too bouncy'.

SOCK IT TO 'EM

They're not strictly speaking managers, but we'll call them the exceptions that make the rule (along with the next couple) as Christian Panucci and Francesco Totti excelled after the Euro 2004 0-0 draw between Italy and Denmark. Totti said that his boots were the problem as 'it was like having your feet on boiling sand', while Panucci thought the blame lay with his socks: 'The thread that these socks were made with is too rough,' he pleaded.

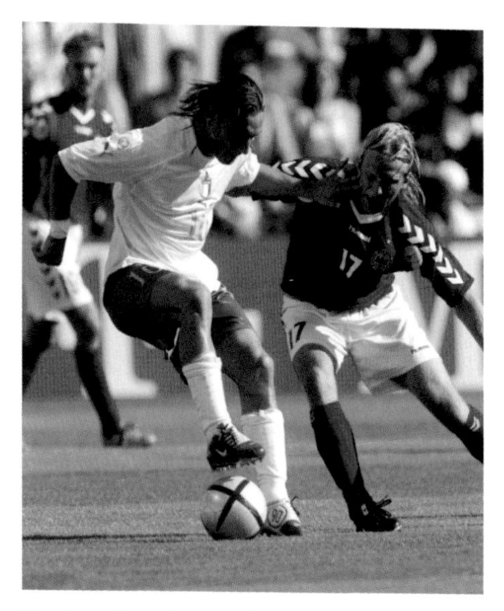

Feet on fire... but not in a good way.

SHIRTING THE ISSUE

On a similar theme, Liverpool's Emlyn Hughes was understandably upset after his side lost 2-1 to Arsenal in the 1971 FA Cup final. The Anfield club were wearing a new wool kit on a balmy May day in 'that London', and it was obvious that it put them at a disadvantage. 'We lost the FA Cup final because our kits were too heavy for such a hot day,' said Hughes.

A FROG STANDARD STORY

Ukraine were thrashed 4-0 by Spain at the 2006 World Cup, so there wasn't a great deal anyone could offer in terms of an excuse – they were beaten fair and square. Except they weren't, of course, because it was all the frogs' fault, according to defender Vladyslav Vashchuk. 'Because of the frogs' croaking, we hardly got a wink of sleep,' he said. 'We all agreed that we would take some sticks and go and hunt them.' Perhaps thinking about the Spain game might have been a wiser choice.

COLD PRESS

A manager can blame himself, he can blame the players and he can sometimes even blame the fans – but that's about it, isn't it? No, because Alan Pardew blamed the media. As Newcastle struggled towards the end of the 2013-14 season, he lashed out at the local press: 'I don't actually think the local media in the north east helped us this week,' he said. 'They whipped it up for whatever reason. I know one or two have been banned from the stadium and they probably use that as a bit of an agenda. Which is a bit of shame for us, because we want them to support us.' But Pards had probably bitten off more than he could chew because newspapers, like the *Newcastle Chronicle*'s 'Sunday Sun', can do things like this.

SUNDAY Sun

HOWEY
MEDIOCRITY IS NOT ENOUGH FOR TOON

CRICKET: BORTHWICK AIMING TO IMPROVE WITH BAT

WE'RE SO SORRY

SUNDAY Sun APOLOGY

As Pardew blames the local Press for fans' anger after disastrous form in 2014, your Sunday Sun would like to apologise for losing 3-0 to Sunderland, 4-0 to Manchester United, 4-0 to Southampton, 4-0 to Spurs, 3-0 to Chelsea, 3-0 to Everton, 2-0 to Man City, 1-0 to Fulham, 1-0 to Stoke, 1-0 to West Brom and 2-1 to Cardiff ...oh, and for headbutting David Meyler too

STOKE CITY 1 NEWCASTLE 0 – PAGES 100, 101, 102 & 103

The story of our season

Karanka hails star man Dimi

BOYS WILL BE BOYS

It's only right to start and end this section with The Special One, who came up with a new entry into the (as yet unwritten) *Book of Great Football Excuses* after Real Madrid had lost a cup match away to Barcelona. 'There were no ball boys in the second half,' he said, adding that it was 'something typical of small teams'.

THE FUNNIEST FOLK IN FOOTBALL

Seeing those wacky glasses in Klopp's office reminded me that there are some footballers who have a sense of humour that goes way beyond a comedy gift or deep-heat in their team-mates' undercrackers. This lot are slightly more sophisticated.

PETER CROUCH

GAG: The robot dance was good but not as good as this:
Interviewer: 'What would you be if you weren't a footballer?'
Crouch: 'A virgin.'
COMEDY RATING: ☺☺☺☺

JIMMY BULLARD

GAG: Too many to mention, but best of all was his goal celebration mimicking Phil Brown's on-pitch half-time team talk for Hull at Manchester City.
COMEDY RATING: ☺☺☺☺☺

A lecture from Jimmy. I'm sure the boss saw the funny side.

IAN HOLLOWAY

GAG: The one-man quote machine went down this particular road when asked about his team's performance: 'To put it in gentleman's terms, if you've been out for a night and you're looking for a young lady and you pull one, some weeks they're good looking and some weeks they're not the best. Our performance today would have been not the best-looking bird, but at least we got her in the taxi. She weren't the best-looking lady we ended up taking home, but she was very pleasant and very nice, so thanks very much, let's have a coffee.'
COMEDY RATING: ☺☺☺

GEORGE BEST

GAG: All about the attitude on and off the pitch: 'I spent a lot of money on booze, birds and fast cars. The rest I squandered.'
COMEDY RATING: ☺☺☺☺

BRIAN CLOUGH

GAG: A career full of legendary one-liners including: 'They say Rome wasn't built in a day – but I wasn't on that particular job.'
COMEDY RATING: ☺☺☺☺

MARIO BALOTELLI

GAG: His coup de grâce was scoring in the Manchester derby, two days after letting off fireworks which set fire to his bathroom, and then revealing a t-shirt which read 'Why Always Me?'
COMEDY RATING: ☺☺☺

MORITZ VOLZ

GAG: The funniest German alive, the former Fulham player is obsessed with *Baywatch* and David Hasselhoff, and once managed to lock himself in his own toilet.
COMEDY RATING: ☺☺☺☺

PHIL JONES

GAG: No idea about his sense of humour, but his inadvertently ridiculous facial expressions while he plays have created a comedy genre of their own.
COMEDY RATING: ☺☺☺

RIO FERDINAND

GAG: One of the first footballers to embrace social media with good humour, he also had his own 2006 TV show, *Rio's World Cup Wind-ups*, in which he 'merked' his team-mates to great comedic effect.
COMEDY RATING: ☺☺☺

EMMANUEL FRIMPONG

GAG: Another social media star, the former Arsenal player signed for Barnsley and wrote on Twitter 'How am I gonna draw girls now?' before swiftly deleting his tweet.
COMEDY RATING: ☺☺☺

MANAGERS WHO COLLECT TROPHIES* LIKE THE REST OF US COLLECT FOOTBALL STICKERS**

Most supporters dream of winning a single trophy at any point in their lifetime. That's the truth of being a football fan for so many of us. So, when you read this utterly outrageous list of success enjoyed by some of the game's most astonishingly talented managers, including the most successful of all, Fergie, spare a thought for those of us who have never tasted even one moment of silverware-tinged glory – and then applaud these greedy beasts who were clearly never taught to share when they were kids.

BOB PAISLEY

CLUB(S): Liverpool

TROPHIES WON: 6 Leagues, 3 European Cups, 1 UEFA Cup, 3 Domestic Cups

SWAG BAG TROPHY HAUL: 13

PEP GUARDIOLA

CLUB(S): Barcelona, Bayern Munich

TROPHIES WON: 6 Leagues, 2 European Cups, 4 Domestic Cups, 3 Club World Cups

SWAG BAG TROPHY HAUL: 15

ERNST HAPPEL

CLUB(S): ADO Den Haag, Feyenoord, Club Brugge, Standard Liège, Hamburg, FC Swarovski Tirol

TROPHIES WON: 8 Leagues, 2 European Cups, 5 Domestic Cups

SWAG BAG TROPHY HAUL: 15

UDO LATTEK

CLUB(S): Bayern Munich, Borussia Mönchengladbach, Barcelona

TROPHIES WON: 8 Leagues, 1 European Cup, 1 European Cup Winners' Cup, 1 UEFA Cup, 4 Domestic Cups

SWAG BAG TROPHY HAUL: 15

OTTMAR HITZFELD

CLUB(S): FC Aarau, Grasshoppers, Borussia Dortmund, Bayern Munich

TROPHIES WON: 9 Leagues, 2 European Cups, 6 Domestic Cups

SWAG BAG TROPHY HAUL: 17

JOSÉ MOURINHO

CLUB(S): Porto, Chelsea, Inter Milan, Real Madrid

TROPHIES WON: 8 Leagues, 2 European Cups, 1 UEFA Cup, 7 Domestic Cups

SWAG BAG TROPHY HAUL: 18

GIOVANNI TRAPATTONI

CLUB(S): Juventus, Inter Milan, Bayern Munich, Benfica, Red Bull Salzburg

TROPHIES WON: 10 Leagues, 1 European Cup, 3 UEFA Cups, 1 European Cup Winners' Cup, 3 Domestic Cups

SWAG BAG TROPHY HAUL: 18

WALTER SMITH

CLUB(S): Glasgow Rangers

TROPHIES WON: 10 Leagues, 11 Domestic Cups

SWAG BAG TROPHY HAUL: 21

MIRCEA LUCESCU

CLUB(S): Dinamo Bucharest, Rapid Bucharest, Galatasaray, Beşiktaş, Shakhtar Donetsk

TROPHIES WON: 12 Leagues, 1 UEFA Cup, 9 Domestic Cups

SWAG BAG TROPHY HAUL: 22

VALERIY LOBANOVSKYI

CLUB(S): Dinamo Kiev

TROPHIES WON: 12 Leagues, 2 European Cup Winners' Cups, 9 Domestic Cups

SWAG BAG TROPHY HAUL: 23

JOCK STEIN

CLUB(S): Dunfermline Athletic, Celtic
TROPHIES WON: 10 Leagues, 1 European Cup, 15 Domestic Cups
SWAG BAG TROPHY HAUL: 26

BILL STRUTH

CLUB(S): Glasgow Rangers
TROPHIES WON: 18 Leagues, 12 Domestic Cups
SWAG BAG TROPHY HAUL: 30

WILLIE MALEY

CLUB(S): Celtic
TROPHIES WON: 16 Leagues, 14 Domestic Cups
SWAG BAG TROPHY HAUL: 30

ALEX FERGUSON

CLUB(S): Aberdeen, Manchester United
TROPHIES WON: 16 Leagues, 2 European Cups, 2 European Cup Winners' Cups, 1 Club World Cup, 14 Domestic Cups
SWAG BAG TROPHY HAUL: 35

**All stats correct as of the end of 2015-16 season. Super Cups do not count*

***Admittedly, we do collect more football stickers than any of this lot's trophy haul, but please allow the poetic licence*

When I wrote my first book, a bloke came up to me in Sainsbury's and said 'My wife was reading your book the other day and says it would be much better if there were some cartoons in it.' I'm taking that as a compliment whatever you're thinking, but just to show that I do listen, here is the #Cartoon&ComicXI.

#Cartoon&ComicXI

Team Name: Peter Panathinaikos
Stadium: Smurf Moor
Management Team: That's All Vogts, Charlie and Zola

First Team:
Beano Zoff

Mysterious Cities Of Bould
He-Man Hreidarsson
Pantsil Mob

Pinky and De Bruyne
Lallanaman
Wily E. Tiote
Dangermoussa Dembele

Teenage Mutant Ninja Birtles (c)
ThunderPlatt
Guti & The Beast

Subs:
Penelope Hislop
Long Song Capoue
Kokémon

BESIDE THE SEEDORF

I ate an awful lot of meat during the 2014 world cup in Brazil. For the six weeks I was in South America I was averaging four Brazilian barbecues a week. The Churrascaria are all over the place but the key is finding someone with the local knowledge to find the best ones out there.

When it came to Rio there was no finer guide than Clarence Seedorf. He was very handy to have around. The Dutchman spent a couple of seasons at Botafogo at the end of his career and is still very much loved in that part of the world.

We asked The C Bomb if he was up for giving us a tour of Rio to put out on the telly during the build up to Brazil's final group game. After some gentle arm twisting he agreed – or at least his people did. As I was settling down to a gigantic piece of ham that night, the word came through that Clarence would meet us outside his hotel at 10am sharp and that we'd have him for a couple of hours.

At 10:15 the next morning there was no sign of Clarence. At 10:23 he appeared briefly, speaking on two mobile phones while simultaneously eating a large slice of mango. I have no idea how this stunning feat of dexterity is possible but he immediately disappeared back into the hotel. Five minutes later one of his people emerged and said 'Clarence will be about ten minutes' and asked if we could set the air con to 24 degrees Celsius. We opted for 23.

A few minutes later – bereft of both phones and mango – Mr Seedorf raced into the back of the car. We all waited slightly nervously to see if he'd notice the car was slightly cooler than expected but he didn't. He grabbed my leg 20 per cent harder than any other human ever has and said 'Come on then, Dan... where am I taking you?'

I explained that we had six locations we'd like to get to and that we'd finish up on the beach before dropping him back at the hotel. 'Not the beach,' said Clarence. 'Have you seen how busy it is?' I glanced across the dual carriageway to the throbbing hive of quasi-nakedness that was Copacabana. If Lola the showgirl was out there, she was surrounded by about one million fellow humans enjoying the sun.

We started to drive around the heaving heart of Rio de Janiero with Clarence pointing out his favourite sights and sounds. I glanced at the air con – 24 degrees – the producer had bottled it. Our first stop was a rooftop 5-a-side pitch with a glorious view across the city. Clarence got a ball out. It was one of those weird moments when you think to yourself: 'I think I might be playing keepy-uppy with the fella who has won the Champions League with three different clubs.' I pulled out a few killer touches and felt I hadn't disgraced myself. 'You have the same touch as a donkey,' said a giggling Seedorf as we left. I remain crushed by this.

The masterful midfielder wanted to head to the lagoon, where we decided to brave a little stroll around with our cameras. Sugarloaf Mountain was in the background and I offered to buy Clarence an ice cream. I thought he might be tempted by the Toffee Crumble but he went for the Brazilian version of a Magnum. The ice cream turned out to be a bad idea. When it's 36 degrees outside, that gives you approximately two minutes to neck the ice cream before it starts melting down your forearm. Clarence is still a massive name – particularly in football-mad Rio – and there was quite a crowd gathering to watch our interview. I needed some time to get rid of some of my increasingly liquid ice cream so asked Seedorf a question that I thought would illicit a long response and then took a massive bite out of my magnum. Unfortunately Clarence didn't read the script and gave a three-word answer requiring a response. I had no other option but to swallow that gigantic lump of ice cream and crack on. It was during Clarence's next answer that the mother of all ice cream headaches kicked in. My wife doesn't believe the condition exists but let me tell you it was up there with the time at middle school when Anthony Sargeant and I decided to neck an entire slush puppy.

Despite the brain freeze, it was a real pleasure to spend a few hours with Clarence outside the studio and as we were driving back to his hotel he stopped the car and said 'Come on then, the beach.' 'I thought you said it would be too crazy,' I responded. 'Let me show

Ipanema beach, perfect for some sunset football.

you what Rio is really like,' said the Dutchman as he skipped across the main road with our cameras trailing in his wake.

Ipanema beach is marginally quieter than Copacabana but it was still heaving, and as soon as Clarence hit the sand it kicked off. There were 30 people around him and by the time we'd got down to the water it was three times that. Autograph hunters, selfie takers, football fans and parents wanting pictures with their none-the-wiser toddlers were everywhere. As we walked back up the beach to the car it was like watching the Brazilian Pied Piper. I still feel a little guilty about the young lad who'd spent much of the day building a giant sandcastle only to see it completely totalled by an army of Seedorfians.

Eventually we got back to the safety of the BBC camera wagon and headed back to Clarence's hotel. 'Is it like that everywhere you go, Clarence?' I asked, sweating profusely after our frantic beach adventure. 'That's why you have to be careful. Imagine that a thousand times over and you have an idea of what it's like to be Neymar at the moment.' We dropped our Dutch guest off, adjusted the air con – because we could – and headed for another Brazilian barbecue.

FOOTBALLERS WITH THE BEST NAMES

I've been thinking long and hard and have come to the conclusion that there aren't many Clarences out there. Clarence Acuna of Columbia used to play for Newcastle and there was a Clarence Beeks in *Trading Places* and Clarence Boddicker was the bad guy from *Robocop* but – as fictional characters – those two don't really count. But there are...

LAUGHTER CHILEMBE – Zambian who played in Zimbabwe for Caps United. Hopefully a happy man.

Surprise Moriri surprised by the very hairy Mr Puyol.

SURPRISE MORIRI – The Mamelodi Sundowns star plays in South Africa – it's a fair guess his parents might not have been trying for a kid.

LYNNEEKER NAKAMUTA PAES DE ALBUQUERQUE – Does his thing in the Brazilian leagues – his parents were big fans of my BBC colleague, apparently.

HAVE-A-LOOK DUBE – Another Zimbabwe-based player who struts his stuff for Njube Sundowns.

DANGER FOURPENCE – Completing the hat-trick of unbelievable names for Caps United – that's quite a collection.

YAGO PIKACHU – Brazilian goalscoring full back was a big Pokémon fan.

NAUGHTY MOKOENA – Played for South Africa. I remember reading an interview with him where his parents said he was actually a well-behaved child.

BEN-HUR MOREIRA PERES – Another Brazilian midfielder, another reference to popular culture (of the past).

MAHATMA GANDHI HEBERPIO MATTOS PIRES – Played for Brazilian second-tier outfit Atlético Goianiense. Seriously.

CREEDENCE CLEARWATER COUTO – His old man Aflanio was a huge fan of the band Creedence Clearwater Revival and burdened his son accordingly.

BONGO CHRIST – Bongo from Congo. Both his names are wonderful. The combination is something very special.

NORMAN CONQUEST – Aussie goalkeeper and a history lesson rolled into one.

JOHNNY MOUSTACHE – Not a cartoon villain, but a Seychelles international.

FOOTBALLERS WHO WOULD HATE THE CHURRASCARIA

Despite everything you would believe about footballers dining on fine meats and even finer women, some of them live a far more saintly lifestyle and even abstain from eating fish or meat, which is unusual in this protein-obsessed sporting age. Here, I present to you a menu of vegetarian footballers who would steer well clear of those Churrascaria. Please be upstanding for the Vegeta-ballers.

JASON ROBERTS

When the former Blackburn striker was playing in the twilight of his career, he used to go vegan throughout the season – and then gorge himself on meat in the summer. Probably.

DANIEL STURRIDGE

Not a total veggie, but the sort of chap who speeds up his recoveries from injury by sprinkling bee pollen into banana smoothies to give himself extra energy.

BOLO ZENDEN

The former Chelsea and Boro star became a strict vegetarian at the age of 19 and stuck to his guns throughout his career.

SIR STANLEY MATTHEWS

The England legend was a famous vegetarian and also refrained from alcohol – that didn't stop him from advertising and enjoying Craven A cigarettes, but those were very different days.

SERGIO AGUERO

The Manchester City goal machine struggles with injuries and in the 2014/15 season he took drastic action to stay fit – he went vegetarian. 'I had to change a lot of things, starting with my food,' he says. 'I needed a healthier way of life and, touch wood, I haven't had any muscle injuries this season.'

NEIL ROBINSON

The former Everton player blazed a trail for non-meat eating footballers of the 70s (he was the only one) and was known as Bananaman because of his pre-match meal of banana on toast. Robinson also ate pasta, rice and beans and made his own tofu and soya milk. 'I was always one of the top three fittest players at all the clubs I played for so there were no issues,' he says .

PHIL JAGIELKA

The Everton and England centre-half stays vegan during the season to give himself a nutritional edge. Unfortunately his over-reliance on vegetables means nobody wants to share a room with Phil...

PHIL NEVILLE

At the age of 37, Neville worked out that it was completely unnecessary to eat meat and described himself as ignorant. 'I thought if I became a vegetarian that would take away a lot of the nutrients that I would require to be a professional footballer and an athlete,' he said. 'I was really ignorant.' Told you.

DEAN HOWELL

Former Crawley and Fleetwood player Dean Howell was so hooked on being a veggie that he set up his own business selling vegan produce called Revolution Foods.

FOREST GREEN

And finally, Forest Green Rovers are the only club in the English four divisions whose stadium catering only serves vegetarian meals. Rovers are owned by Vince Dale who is a strict vegan – his club, his rules.

EVEN MORE MANAGERIAL MELTDOWNS

Everyone loves it when gaffers go ga-ga in a galactic way. Indeed, we touched upon it in a book I may have mentioned before called *The Thronkersaurus*. And now, back by popular demand, here's my selection of all-new interview irrationality. These are the managers who decided to definitely not give a three-word answer like Seedorf did while I was trying to eat my ice cream.

LOOPY LOU

Louis van Gaal may have been widely ridiculed at Manchester United but the Dutchman was more than capable of holding his own, sometimes going way over the top.

When he was Ajax manager he might have just ignored a question from journalist Ted van Leeuwen, but instead Van Gaal chose to reply with quite a lot more than three words:

'Are you really that stupid, Ted van Leeuwen? Are you really that stupid? Didn't I start with telling that I'm here for Ajax? Didn't I start with telling that we have agreements with the players. Then why do you ask this question? Am I that smart or are you that stupid? Because I have an agreement with those players. And who has the right to talk about the players, if the players don't want that. Oh, oh, oh, oh. I thought I explained everything perfectly. And now I am the arrogant a**hole, I'm the authoritative a**hole, but those are all stupid questions!'

STEVE VAN MCCLAREN

The more he spoke, the worse it got. For reasons only he will know, when McClaren was FC Twente manager and he was asked to give his thoughts on the Champions League tie against Arsenal, he proceeded to talk like a Dutch manager speaking English, complete with the 'sh' sound instead of 's' and a lot of umming and erring – which was mimicked in his native England where everyone struggled to understand why the former England boss was pretending to be Dutch.

REINCARNATION

Never mind, three words. He needn't have said anything. But he did. And then some. During an interview with Matt Dickinson from *The Times*, England manager Glenn Hoddle strayed the wrong way down a one-way street and couldn't find a reverse gear as he tried to explain his controversial views on reincarnation and offended all disabled people in the process. Shortly after, he was no longer England manager Glenn Hoddle but just Glenn Hoddle.

NIGEL BURIES HIS HEAD

Leicester manager Nigel Pearson transformed the club's fortunes towards the end of the 2014/15 season when relegation had seemed certain. But that wasn't enough to lighten his mood during a post-match press conference when he wound himself up and became involved in a bizarre exchange with reporter Ian Baker, to whom he later apologised. Here's the full transcript:

Nigel Pearson: The bottom line is what has given us a chance to survive has been the collective spirit we have. To win four games on the spin at any level, but certainly at Premier

League level, is difficult and for the players to have to deal with the amount of criticism and negativity they've had to endure over the course of the season has tested us. Without wanting to talk too much, the players come out with an awful lot of credit for dealing with setbacks and I expect them to deal with tonight's setback as well.

Ian Baker: What criticism are you talking about?

NP: Have you been on holiday for six months? Have you been away for six months?

IB: No, I am just not quite sure what specific criticism you are referring to?

NP: I think you must have either your head in the clouds, or been away on holiday, or reporting on a different team, because if you don't know the answer to that question... Your question is absolutely unbelievable, the fact you do not understand where I am coming from. If you don't know the answer to that question then I think you are an ostrich. Your head must be in the sand. Is your head in the sand? Are you flexible enough to get your head in the sand? My suspicion would be no.

IB: Probably not.

NP: I can, you can't. You can't. Listen, you have been here often enough and for you to ask that question, you are either being very, very silly or you are being absolutely stupid, one of the two because for you to ask that question, I am sorry son, you are daft.

IB: There hasn't been much harsh criticism of the players.

NP: You are wrong. No, you are wrong. You have been in here, I know you have, so don't give that crap with me, please don't give that crap with me. I will smile at you because I can afford to smile at you. Now do you want to ask a different question or do you want to ask it differently. Come on, ask it. Ask it or are you not capable?

IB: I just don't know what you, erm...

NP: [Mimicks Baker's voice] You don't know. What's 'erm'?

IB: I don't know how you've taken that question.

NP: Well you must be very stupid. I'm sorry. [Pearson walks out]

MANNERS MAKETH ROY

You know those moments where you just don't want your phone to ring and wish the earth would swallow you up because you forgot to put it on silent? You know, like when you're at the cinema, a funeral or a Roy Keane press conference. Well, that's *exactly* what happened to one journalist while the Irishman was Ipswich manager in 2009. Here's how it went:

phone rings
Keane: Whose phone is that?
phone continues to ring
Keane: Whose phone is that, that's the second time it has gone off?
Journalist: That's my phone, sorry.
Keane: Why don't you turn it off?
Journalist: I will turn it off in a minute, thought I'd let it ring out.
Keane: Oh right? That's good manners.

PARDEW PAYS THE PENALTY

Crystal Palace boss Alan Pardew was not a happy man after the Eagles had lost 2-1 at home to Liverpool thanks to a dodgy late penalty. And when Geoff Shreeves probed him with one question too many, the Palace manager couldn't contain his frustration:

Pardew: It was a game we should have come away with something, but we didn't. Our subs weren't good. I point the finger at myself. We move on.
Shreeves: Why weren't they good?
Pardew: Let's not get into a debate here and you try to antagonise me. I'm frustrated because I've lost, alright? And I think the penalty's tough, that's what I'm trying to say, and I think you should accept that and let me go back to do the press elsewhere.
Shreeves: No I understand that, I wouldn't be disrespectful to you, Alan.
Pardew: I think you are a little bit but let's just get on with it.

SEVEN MINUTES OF MADNESS

When Southampton beat Chelsea 3-1 to hand the champions their fourth defeat of the 2015/16 season in mid-October, José Mourinho was a man under pressure.

And he cracked with an incredible seven-minute long answer to one post-match TV interview question which included paranoia, conspiracy theories and so many more than three words that we couldn't fit them all in here. It started like this:

'I think you know me, and I think I don't run away from responsibilities.

'I think, first of all, I want to say that because we are in such a bad moment, I think you shouldn't be afraid to be also honest.

'Because when we were at the top, I understand that it is quite a big pleasure, and it is gone.

'But when you are so down, I think it's time to be a little bit honest and to say clearly the referees are afraid to give decisions for Chelsea.'

And it went on and on and on until it finished with José insisting that a penalty that wasn't given when Chelsea were *only* 2-0 down would have changed the game:

'When you are top, you want to see people come down. When people are down, give us a break, and be honest and be loyal with us because the team deserves that and the penalty is clear, and 2-1 is a completely different story.'

SHUT YOUR TRAP

A legendary press conference took place in Germany in 1998 when Italian manager Giovanni Trapattoni lost it with his own Bayern Munich players in a rather spectacular way. His team, including Lothar Mattheus, Oliver Kahn and Mehmet Scholl, had just collapsed to lose three straight games, meaning they were out of title contention. The Trap, in a mixture of broken German and Italian, wasn't best pleased:

'I'm a coach, not an idiot. A coach can see what happens on the field. And these players, two, three of these players, were weak like an empty bottle. Have you seen Wednesday, what team has played Wednesday? Did Mehmet play, or did (Mario) Basler play, or did Trapattoni play?

'These players complain more than they play. You know why no Italian team buys these players? Because they've seen them play too many times. They say, 'These do not play for the Italian champions.' [Thomas] Strunz! Strunz is here two years, and has played ten games, is always injured. How dare Strunz!

'They must respect their other colleagues. I am tired now, the father of these players, defending these players. I always get the blame over these players. One is Mario, the other is Mehmet. I don't mention Strunz, he has only played twenty-five per cent of the games. I have finished.'

RONALDO PHONES IT IN

The start of Euro 2016 was not a happy time for Cristiano Ronaldo as he and his Portugal side struggled to make an impression and limped into the knockout round as the third-placed team – it was all very different by the end of the tournament of course.

After missing a penalty and several other chances in a stalemate with Austria, the pressure was on Ronaldo ahead of Portugal's final group game against Hungary. And when Portuguese reporter Diogo Torres of CMTV thrust a microphone towards The Great One's face and asked him if he was prepared for the match as the team took a waterside stroll on the morning of the game, Ronaldo promptly snatched it out of the journalist's hand and threw it into the adjacent lake. Why use three words when none will do?

There really is only one way to finish off this chapter... All hail the #SeasideXI, with a special mention for our Clarence.

#SeasideXI

Team name: SunBurnley
Reserves: Cockles & Brussels
Stadium: Surf Moor
Management Team: Slip Slap Klopp, LifeGuardiola

First Team:
Ice Cream Van Der Sar

Sun's Out Dunne's Out
Puncheon Jaidi
Paulo Maldingy

Adu Like To Be Beside The Seedorf
Busquets & Spade Elliott (c)
Jay Jay Baywatcha
Camoranesi Golf

Emile Jetski
Peter Odemwaterwingie
Nude Van Nistelrooy

Subs:
Cundy Floss
Paul Gasgroyne
Crabi Alonso
José Boswingball
Jesper Donkeyar

OSSIE AND JOSÉ

Have you ever looked back over your life and wished you had footage of something? These days, people have both pictorial and videographical evidence of virtually everything from birthday parties to toilet visits. When I was at university we were still in the world of wind-on disposal cameras and no one had taken one of those to The York in January 1996. We had gone there to watch Tottenham, led by Gerry Francis, who had failed to make it past Hereford in the third round of the FA Cup and were involved in a replay.

There were some rather boisterous Spurs fans in the pub arguing over whether Chris Armstrong had been a good buy. After a while, they started singing FA Cup songs from years gone by but, I've got to say, the lyrics were all over the place.

My comrade Nathan took it upon himself to inform the lads that they were struggling vocally and that I – he had heard me before – was something of an aficionado when it came to FA Cup songs of the 1980s. The leader of the Spurs pack was having none of it, so challenged me to what I believe is called a 'Chas-&-Dave-Off'. The landlord got involved and offered free drinks to the winner, based on the judgement of the gathered throng.

A microphone was handed to my opponent and he tentatively took to the stage and launched into 'Ossie's Dream'. I'll be honest – it was an average effort. Sixty per cent of the lyrics were all over the shop, there was no elaborate cockney accent and no attempt at 'in dee cup for Tottingham' at the crucial moment. I was next up and confidently grasped the microphone. I went for the full cockney effort, 100 per cent Chas & Dave, every lyric nailed and some real Argentinian flare on Ardiles' killer line.

The crowd went wild and there was even a cry of 'MORE' from a significant proportion of the heaving mass. I was in a Chas & Dave groove, so switched to 1987 and a bit of 'Hotshot Tottenham'. The growing crowd were lapping it up, so to complete the big triple I switched tack a little and opted for the theme tune to *Only Fools and Horses*. I left the stage to a standing ovation. The problem is, I have absolutely no record of this event so you will have to rely entirely on this version of events. If you ever run into Nathan, he can verify things but there were no pictures, no tweets, no vines, no one Facebook Lived it, and it will never appear on Snapchat.

I'll confess that this leaves me somewhat aggrieved. Since the onset of social media, nothing is forgotten. Even tweets that you try to delete are saved somewhere, and there are thousands ready to remind you of your every indiscretion.

Back in June 2013, it was confirmed that José Mourinho would be returning to Stamford Bridge. I tentatively tossed this into the social media abyss...

'Happy to be wrong about Mourinho but I just can't see it being the all-conquering glorious return everyone is predicting.'

Dan Walker
@mrdanwalker

Happy to be wrong about #Mourinho but just can't see it being the all-conquering glorious return everyone is predicting #CFC

03/06/2013, 20:58

It took about 60 seconds for the threats to arrive. Over the next few months, I had all sorts of things sent to me after every Chelsea victory and when they eventually won the title, at least ten people suggested that I consider taking my own life! I was 'happy to be wrong', but all the scoffers went strangely silent when Chelsea under Mourinho began to unravel in the season that followed.

The hugely successful Portuguese manager now has another significant fish to fry, but I spoke to him on a number of occasions during his time at Chelsea. I was at the 'Special One' press conference when he first arrived at Stamford Bridge and at Bolton when his side sealed their first championship in fifty years in 2005.

The final few weeks of his second stint were not so happy, and my last interview with him as Chelsea manager was a rather

prickly affair at the launch of a picture book marking the key moments in his managerial career.

The interview took place at a store in London, and it was clear from the small press conference beforehand that he was in no mood to mess about. Sometimes managers cancel these events when there are difficult questions to answer. Mourinho was facing them head on. Rumours of unrest were dismissed, accusations about tactics and fallouts denied, and the misconduct charges from the Football Association were referred to as 'a disgrace'. He was bullish and brave, but everyone in that room knew his time at Chelsea was coming to an end.

He spent 15 minutes with the written press and was then directed towards our little room at the side. Chelsea were in the midst of the worst title defence in the history of the Premier League, but he was not keen on the finger being pointed in his direction.

When I questioned him, he questioned me. When I asked why the champions had lost so many games, he said: 'I thought you were an intelligent man.' Over years of interviewing the best in the business at close quarters, I am convinced that the job is not only about managing a team but carefully tickling the media. Sometimes it requires a smile, sometimes a quiet word, a well-controlled rant and an occasional bit of outright manipulation. Knowing which buttons to press, what to take in your stride and what to react to is half the battle when the warriors are against the wall. At the peak of his powers, there is none better than José Mourinho, but this was a man who looked like he had lost some of his will to fight.

His words, when written down, sounded convincing, but if you watch that interview back his eyes and body language paint a slightly different picture. We parted with a hand shake and a smile, but it wasn't long before he was in trouble with the FA again, players were throwing bibs at him as they left the pitch and his side were losing to Stoke in the cup, Bournemouth at home and finally and perhaps fittingly, Leicester away. Three days after the humbling by the former Chelsea manager Claudio Ranieri, the sitting Chelsea boss was no more. When it came to Mourinho, blue was no longer the colour. I have never sung that one. No Chas & Dave, no party.

MANAGERS WITH THE MOST CLUBS

José Mourinho has never been afraid of taking on a challenge or three, which is why he's already managed a handful of top clubs. But that's nothing compared to these gaffers, some of whom, as the original quote goes, have had more clubs than Jack Nicklaus.

PHILIPPE TROUSSIER

The Frenchman has so far managed 19 different teams, made up of 12 club sides and seven international outfits. Among the club sides are Kaizer Chiefs and FUS Rabat, while countries include Morocco, Ivory Coast, Burkina Faso, South Africa and Nigeria.

BORA MILUTINOVIĆ

The Serbian coach can trump Troussier with one more national team on his CV, giving him eight countries in total, including Mexico, USA, China, Jamaica and Iraq. He also has seven club sides to his name so far, including Udinese, Veracruz and Al Sadd.

RUDI GUTENDORF

The king of the multi-club managers, the German's 53-year career saw him take charge of a passport-popping 19 international sides and 16 clubs. When he isn't travelling between jobs, Gutendorf's national tenures included Grenada, Venezuela, Antigua, Botswana and Australia, while his club sides featured the likes of Hamburg, Schalke and Real Valladolid.

LEO BEENHAKKER

The prolific Dutchman has 18 managerial jobs on his slate, not to mention one technical director gig at Ujpest. Beenhakker has managed many Dutch clubs, including Go Ahead Eagles and Ajax, while he's also taken charge of Real Madrid (twice) and national jobs including his native Netherlands, Poland and Trinidad & Tobago.

CLAUDIO RANIERI

Everyone's favourite Italian manager has racked up 15 clubs over the years, with Valencia, Atlético Madrid, Napoli, Juventus, Chelsea and Leicester among the impressive names on his CV.

DICK ADVOCAAT

Just the 17 managerial jobs for the man with the same name as the egg-based liqueur popular at Christmas time. He has managed countries including South Korea and his own Netherlands, and clubs ranging from PSV Eindhoven to Sunderland.

NEIL WARNOCK

The English Beenhakker is a name which Warnock has never gone by, but that doesn't mean he hasn't managed a bag full of clubs –

all in England. It started with Gainsborough Trinity in 1980 and since then he has taken care of a total of 14 teams, including Leeds, Sheffield United and QPR.

TOMMY DOCHERTY

The man about whom the Jack Nicklaus gag was made 'only' managed 13 teams in a career spanning almost 30 years. The Doc started at Chelsea and also took in the likes of Manchester United, Aston Villa, Porto, Sydney Olympic and the Scottish national side during his memorable career.

GUUS HIDDINK

The man who masterminded South Korea's path to the World Cup semi-finals in 2002 has presided over 12 teams in total. He's always on standby when Roman Abramovich comes calling after he's wielded the axe at Chelsea. Hiddink has also been in charge of Real Madrid, had two spells at PSV and led the Australian, Russian and Turkish national teams as well as his own Netherlands side twice.

MICKY ADAMS

Another double-figure doyen of the English lower leagues, Adams could yet surpass most on this list as he started so young as player-manager of Fulham, Swansea and then Brentford, which must be something of a record. Adams has also been in charge of Brighton twice and had spells at clubs including Coventry, Sheffield United and Sligo Rovers.

THE DIRTY DOZEN MANAGERS' NICKNAMES

José Mourinho unintentionally gave himself a nickname for life when he declared he was a special one during his introduction to the British media. His reasoning was strong – he'd just won the Champions League with Porto, which was pretty out of the ordinary. Although it's probably best to let others call you 'special' before you do. Much like this lot of nicknames for gaffers, which were all chosen for them, rather than the other way around – although, ironically, in order to be a manager with a nickname, you do have to be a special one.

EL TEL

From the minute he left England to take charge of Spanish giants Barcelona in 1984, Terry Venables would always be El Tel – even when he returned to Spurs and then coached the national team after Graham Taylor.

THE TRANSLATOR

José Mourinho is so special that he gets two nicknames. After working with Bobby Robson as his interpreter when the late, great gaffer was Barcelona boss, José's remarkable rise up the managerial ranks provoked Barça fans to call him The Translator when he returned to wind them up with Chelsea, Inter Milan and Real Madrid years later.

THE PROFESSOR

It wasn't just his similarity in looks to Professor Yaffle, the ornamental carved wooden bookend from *Bagpuss*, it was also Arsène Wenger's total dedication and commitment to the studying of football that led to this moniker.

THE TINKERMAN

In an age before squad rotation became so common, Chelsea manager Claudio Ranieri used to enjoy shuffling his pack and making changes to his teams from week to week and game to game – even during matches, he'd regularly ensure he used all his subs – as they battled through European, Premier League and domestic cup games. The name 'Tinkerman' seemed to fit nicely.

BIG ____

The exact science of awarding the prefix 'Big' to managers is unknown. A mysterious panel, most probably made up of tabloid newspaper sports editors, meets once a year in a secluded location to decide whether any new gaffers are worthy of the title. To receive the name, managers will usually be tall, perhaps slightly overweight and always imposing figures. Previous recipients of the 'Big' prefix include Big Ron (Atkinson), Big Sam (Allardyce), Big Phil (Scolari), Big Jack (Charlton) and Big Eck (Alex McLeish).

THE WALLY WITH THE BROLLY

Poor, poor Steve McClaren. Facing the biggest match of his career in charge of England, he sensibly decided to watch from the Wembley sidelines under the safety of an umbrella as the rain lashed down. Meanwhile, out on the pitch, England's chances of qualifying for Euro 2008 ended as they lost to Croatia, meaning it was all Steve's fault and he was christened 'The Wally with the Brolly'.

OLD BIG 'ED

Brian Clough was such a one-off manager that there are all manner of names he could have been known by, many of them unprintable. As it was, he was known by most people as Old Big 'Ed because, frankly, he was.

THE BALD EAGLE

A simple refrain based on the fact that former Newcastle, Derby and Portsmouth boss Jim Smith didn't have much hair, but did have a sense of humour.

HARRY 'WHEELER DEALER' REDKNAPP

You could never call him a wheeler dealer to his face because he wouldn't stand for it (see the *Thronkersaurus* book), but thanks to his penchant for using the transfer market, Redknapp became known as something of a market trader type.

DAISY/THE IRON TULIP

Dutch manager Louis van Gaal was known throughout his career as the Iron Tulip due to his Netherlands origins and tough exterior.

But Manchester United players found a new nickname for him, because he used to drive extremely slowly in and out of the club's Carrington training ground to avoid potholes. He quickly became known as Daisy, with reference to the film *Driving Miss Daisy*. That's one of the eight million films with Morgan Freeman in it.

THE ENGINEER

Former Manchester City manager Manuel Pellegrini has an engineering qualification, but is also known for his ability to build football clubs, hence The Engineer.

THE GINGER MOURINHO

Burnley boss Sean Dyche worked wonders with his side to get them to the Premier League twice and (what was left of) his hair was ginger.

FOOTBALLERS WHO ARE MORE INTELLIGENT THAN ME, ACCORDING TO JOSÉ MOURINHO

I may not have been on José's list of bright sparks, but some footballers have let their entire industry down by having proper educational qualifications and making a mockery of the stereotype. Here's a load of beautiful game brainboxes – the big show offs.

THE *COUNTDOWN* KIDS

Several footballers have appeared on tremendous Channel 4 numbers and letters game, *Countdown* – not as celebrity guests on a charity version of the show but as actual clever contestants. I only got as far as Dictionary Corner myself.

Clarke Carlisle managed to win two games, while former Stoke midfielder Neil MacKenzie claimed five wins on his way to a quarter-final. Ex-Norwich player Adrian Coote had less success, going down at the first time of asking, but Matt Le Tissier did himself and his sport proud by winning three games before being unceremoniously dumped out by a maths tutor, who could never have beaten Tim Flowers from 35 yards.

GRAEME LE SAUX

The Chelsea and England superstar gave up studying for his environmental studies degree to become a professional. Le Saux was also ridiculed by some goons because he had the nerve to read the *Guardian*. I have worked with Graeme a lot and he's not only clever, he's also very good.

FRANK LAMPARD

Not only does Frank have 12 GCSEs including an A* in Latin, but he was also tested for his IQ and recorded a score of more than 150, making him one of the most intelligent 0.1 per cent in the country.

BARRY HORNE

The former Everton and Wales international has a chemistry degree from the University of Liverpool, which is impressive enough. But in 2014 he was also appointed the director of football *and* chemistry and physics teacher at a school in Chester.

IAIN DOWIE

The future journeyman striker and manager earned himself a Masters degree in engineering from the University of Hertfordshire and then worked for British Aerospace while playing non-League football, before Luton Town gave him his big break. After more than 30 years in football, Dowie left to become the regional sales manager of a Homebuyers' surveying firm.

SHAKA HISLOP

Those goalkeepers are all a bit mental, aren't they? Not Shaka. The former Newcastle and Portsmouth stopper has a mechanical engineering degree from Howard (at least it sounds a bit like Harvard) University in Washington DC, and also completed an internship at NASA.

DAVID WEATHERALL

Not only did he score the goal which kept Bradford in the Premier League at the end of the 1999-00 season, but the defender also notched four As at A Level, and is the proud owner of a first-class honours degree in chemistry from Sheffield University – the world's finest, I'll have you know. #alumni

GLEN JOHNSON

The former England right back has a tattoo on his forearm which reads 'Tell me I can't and I will show you I can'. By way of living up to that ink, Johnson began studying for a maths degree from the Open University towards the end of his career.

CHRISTIAN BURGESS

The lower division defender has a first-class honours degree in history from Teesside University. But that's not all. His dissertation on German naval expansion prior to the First World War was put forward for a national award.

ROMELU LUKAKU

The burly Belgian striker may not have the degrees and honours of some of his fellow pros, but he is fluent in five different languages, which has to be worth some kind of qualification or award. Lukaku can speak English, French, Dutch, Congolese and Spanish.

PETR ČECH

While we are talking languages – a special mention for Petr Čech, who learns the languages of everyone who plays in the defence in front of him so he can communicate with them all effectively. I think he is currently on six. I asked him once if he'd ever thought about learning Klingon. He understandably walked off.

In the late 20th century, players would be whisked from their FA Cup semi-final victory almost straight into the recording studio, such was the tradition of the cup final song. These days, it's not quite as de rigueur, but let's not let that flagrant flaunting of cup custom dissuade us from a nostalgic look back at the greatest efforts from the heyday of cup final vinyl.

10

Song: 'Go For It, City'
Club: Coventry City, 1987
Sample lyrics:
When you hear the whistle blow,
And you see Big Cyril Go,
Sky Blues Shooting to win,
Go for it, Go for it, City, Go for it, Go for it, City,
Sky Blues, shooting to win
Highest chart position: 61
Victory inspiration: Incredibly, unfancied Coventry beat Spurs 3-2 in a thriller
Jukebox Jury: Great effort for writing an original song, but it lacks that immediate catchy memorable bit that any good cup final song needs
Rating: 3/10

9

Song: 'Good Old Arsenal'
Club: Arsenal, 1971
Sample lyrics:
Good Old Arsenal,
We're proud to say that name,
While we sing this song,
We'll win the game

Highest chart position: 16
Victory inspiration: The words of the song played out as the Gunners won 2-1 to land the club's first Double
Jukebox Jury: Jimmy Hill wrote this first-ever cup final single – it may be a laboured and old-fashioned number, but it caught on with the fans and lasted generations
Rating: 4/10

8

Song: 'Pass and Move'
Club: Liverpool, 1996
Sample lyrics:
Rushie's scored more than all the rest,
Respect to the lad broad upon his chest,
You get cut playing with the Razor,
Sharp like Armani,
Jammo is the saviour

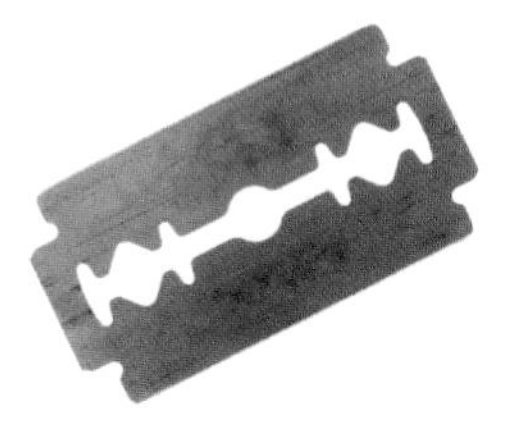

Highest chart position: 4
Victory inspiration: For all the passing and moving, Liverpool lost 1-0 to rivals Manchester United
Jukebox Jury: To borrow inspiration from former England boss Sven-Göran Eriksson, originality is good, but the rest – not so good
Rating: 5/10

7

Song: 'Hot Stuff'
Club: Arsenal, 1998
Sample lyrics:
We're on the march with Arsène's army,
With Tony, Martin, Nigel and Lee,
And vivent les Francais, Remi, Gilles and Patrick,
Et tu es magnifique mon Petit
Highest chart position: 9
Victory inspiration: Did the job as Arsenal won another Double thanks to victory over Newcastle
Jukebox Jury: Top marks for getting some GCSE French into the lyrics, but that was the highlight of an otherwise unmemorable song which wasn't taken up in the stands
Rating: 6/10

6

Song: 'Glad All Over'
Club: Crystal Palace, 1990
Sample lyrics:
You say that you love me (say that you love me),
All of the time (all of the time)
Highest chart position: 50
Victory inspiration: Close but no cigar. Palace took Manchester United to a replay but came away empty-handed
Jukebox Jury: Great song by the Dave Clarke Five, not sure if Palace did it any justice, but their fans certainly did as this was a big terrace tune
Rating: *7/10*

5

Song: 'All Together Now'
Club: Everton, 1995
Sample lyrics:
The spirit's stronger in the blues today,
Gonna play the Everton way.
The Golden Vision, Dixie Dean,
The school of science, by far the greatest team
Highest chart position: 24
Victory inspiration: Everyone was together as Everton stunned Fergie's United 1-0
Jukebox Jury: Not a bad reworking of a classic, and featuring The Farm ensures this one retained credibility
Rating: *8/10*

4

Song: 'Anfield Rap'
Club: Liverpool, 1988
Sample lyrics:
You two scousers are always yapping,
I'm gonna show you some serious rapping,
I come from Jamaica, my name is John Barn-es,
When I do my thing the crowd go bananas
Highest chart position: 3

Victory inspiration: The only Anfield Rap was one on the knuckles for John Aldridge's missed penalty as Liverpool were stunned by Wimbledon
Jukebox Jury: If ever a cup final song falls into the 'so bad it's good' category, this is it. Some shocking outfits worn by the players in the video, too
Rating: 8/10

3

Song: 'Come on You Reds'
Club: Manchester United, 1994
Sample lyrics:
Busby Babes they always made me cry,
Thinking about the teams of years gone by,
Charlton, Edwards, Law and Georgie Best,
We're United – you can keep the rest
Highest chart position: 1
Victory inspiration: A handsome thrashing of Chelsea followed to complete United's first Double
Jukebox Jury: A decent rewrite of Status Quo's 'Burning Bridges' was the first and only cup final song to reach number one in the UK charts. Hard to argue with that
Rating: 8/10

2

Song: 'Tottenham Tottenham'
Club: Spurs with Chas & Dave, 1982
Sample lyrics:
Stevie can't wait to hold the cup again,
Won't be satisfied until it's in his hands,
He'll hold it up for everyone to see it then,
We'll hear the voices of our fans
Highest chart position: 19

Victory inspiration: Spurs claimed their second successive cup with their second successive final replay win
Jukebox Jury: A great follow-up to 'Ossie's Dream' which could have been 'that difficult second cup final record' but was nevertheless a big terrace and chart hit
Rating: 9/10

1

Song: 'Ossie's Dream'
Club: Spurs with Chas & Dave, 1981
Sample lyrics:
We know the enemy will fear us,
In the battle coming up,
They won't even get near us,
We're gonna capture the cup
Highest chart position: 5
Victory inspiration: It took a replay and a Ricky Villa wonder goal, but Spurs got there in the end
Jukebox Jury: The perfect cup final song: catchy, a hit with the fans and performed by Chas & Dave, so there was no over-reliance on players who have no musical ability whatsoever
Rating: 10/10

We've had some wonderful lyrics in this chapter so it seems only fitting that we finish it with a lyrical master, a man who was said to have a vocabulary spanning some 25,000 words. Ladies and gentlemen, boys and girls, please be upstanding for the #ShakespeareXI.

#ShakespeareXI

Team Name: West Hamlet
Stadium: Merry Wives Of Windsor Park
Manager: Alan Bardew

First Team:
2 Enkleman Of Verona

Mid Sonner Kuyts Breen
A Curse On Both Ward Prowses
Comedy Of Berras

Delph Night
Much Edu About Nothing
All's Well That Sidwell
Gallas Fer Boruc, Ayew Him Well (c)

King Weah
2 Noble Klinsmann
Eto'o Brute

Subs:
Is This An Agger I See Before Me?
Toby Or Not Toby Alderweireld
The Bertrand Of Venice
Shall I Compare Thee To A Vaz Te?
Taming Of Giroud

BLACK EYES AND BICYCLE KICKS

I think I can lay claim to the least showbiz black eye in history. The scene was an Oasis concert at Knebworth in the 1990s. I would love to tell you I picked it up during an extreme crowd-surfing incident. I could tell you I got involved in a massive ninja rumble during 'Cigarettes & Alcohol'. If I was really going for it, I could spin a tale about making it onto the stage and then being caught by a stray drumstick during an impromptu guitar solo. None of this happened.

While we were waiting for Oasis to come to the main stage, some of the 250,000-strong crowd started throwing their rubbish in the air. Within a few seconds, everyone was at it. Others started kicking it on the way down. It was like a giant aerial food fight. I thought, perhaps unwisely in hindsight, it was 'time to take this up a notch' and decided to start heading items as they came down.

A sandwich wrapper, a bag of crisps and a half-eaten sausage roll were all dispatched with ease. The same cannot be said for the one litre carton of Ribena that I decided to nut. The carton was unfortunately full, and rather heavier than I anticipated. It certainly wasn't Ribena Light! I woke the next morning to two significant panda eyes. Getting a black eye at Knebworth sounds quite rock 'n' roll. Having it inflicted by a drink popular with under eights? Not so much.

Despite that, Knebworth couldn't ruin what was a simply magnificent summer. The year 1996 was a wonderful time to be alive for any England football fan. I was 18, England were playing well, everyone was singing Baddiel & Skinner and, until 'that penalty shoot-out', it was all going rather well. My German mate Fred (actual name – not short for Friedrich) thinks it's hilarious that we venerate Euro 96 in England when we lost in the semi-finals. He'll never understand.

If I was ever asked to compile a list of my favourite goals, then Alan Shearer's second against the Dutch that summer would definitely make the top five: the little run from Gazza, the beautiful side-foot from Teddy Sheringham and the full-power 'wallop' from my future BBC colleague.

Top of that goal list for me would be a strike from Trevor Sinclair. You may well know the one I am on about. I am so convinced of its quality that when I was asked to take part in a show that was looking at the '50 Greatest Moments In The FA Cup' I made an official complaint after discovering that Trev's belter only came in at number 32!!!

Time to retire on the spot Trev. Simply wonderful.

Let me describe the scene. We're going back to Loftus Road in the 1990s, just a few months after that special summer. QPR are playing Barnsley in an FA Cup fourth round game on 25 January. John Spencer is on the Rangers right and launches a somewhat speculative ball towards the Barnsley penalty area. It's not a great cross. I'm not even sure if it's a cross at all. Sinclair is somewhere near the D. He's shattered. He's run more than normal and is low on energy. In his own words, 'The ball was so high it was coming down with snow on it. I didn't have the energy to control it so decided to just hit it.'

Trevor makes it sound agricultural. What transpired was the greatest overhead kick – and probably goal – in the history of humans. Forget Zlatan against England, Rooney's shin in the Manchester derby or anything you've seen from Jean-Pierre Papin, this was solid gold balletic brilliance.

Trevor, despite being hampered by considerable dreadlocks, leaped, swivelled and unleashed a rare beauty. I've heard some claim it was 30 yards. It was more like 22, but who cares. It was outside the box and he leathered it in. One of the hardest skills in the game made to look simple. If I was Sinclair I'd have walked straight off the pitch and announced my retirement. It does not get any better than that.

The fact that it came in at 32 was a disgrace – one for the Serious Fraud Office to look at. It's been watched about a million times on YouTube and I think I'm responsible for about half of those. I've just watched it again while writing this sentence. Magical. I don't think I'm going too far to suggest it should be Sir Trevor. Maybe I am.

I know you can make arguments about significance, the fact that it was only the fourth round and (sorry Barnsley) question the quality of the opposition, but that's all rubbish. You're all wrong. I was interviewing Pelé once about great goals and afterwards I asked him if he'd heard of the Sinclair Special against Barnsley. He looked a little confused and was ushered away by his people, but I maintain that the great man would have appreciated its class.

Anyway. Feel free to disagree but, for those of you who like this sort of thing and don't mind the fact that it's clearly wrong, here's the Top 10 FA Cup moments from that list of 50.

1. 1999 FA Cup semi-final replay, 14 April 1999
Manchester United 2-1 Arsenal
The one with Giggs' hairy bits.

2. 2006 FA Cup final, 13 May 2006
Liverpool 3-3 West Ham United
The one when everyone forgets that Paul Konchesky scored.

3. 1988 FA Cup final, 14 May 1988
Liverpool 0-1 Wimbledon
The one when the Crazy Gang beat the Culture Club.

4. 1981 FA Cup final replay, 14 May 1981
Tottenham Hotspur 3-2 Manchester City
The one where Villa won the cup but not for Villa.

5. 1972 FA Cup third round replay, 5 February 1972
Hereford United 2-1 Newcastle United, after extra time
The one with a muddy pitch and a Ronny Radford thronker.

6. 1991 FA Cup semi-final, 14 April 1991
Tottenham Hotspur 3-1 Arsenal
The one with Gazza's schoolboy's own stuff.

7. 1973 FA Cup final, 5 May 1973
Sunderland 1-0 Leeds United
The one with the whopping great upset.

8. 1953 FA Cup final, 2 May 1953
Blackpool 4-3 Bolton Wanderers
The one when Stan Mortensen got a hat-trick but the other Stan got the headlines.

9. 1989 FA Cup third round, 7 January 1989
Sutton United 2-1 Coventry City
The one when the top-flight side were dumped out by non-Leaguers.

10. 1990 FA Cup semi-final, 8 April 1990
Crystal Palace 4-3 Liverpool, after extra time
The one when Palace got revenge for 9-0 in the league that season.

So that's the list. A few memories might have been jogged here and a few eyebrows raised. My eyebrows nearly jumped off my head at the positioning of number 32, but I think I've gone on about it long enough now.

THE 34 GREATEST ALTERNATIVE FA CUP MOMENTS

So you've seen that Top 10, but we all know it's wrong. So I thought to myself, this is my book so I'm going to make my own list of the best FA Cup moments where I get to choose who wins. Not only that, I also get to choose the criteria for what goes on the list. So this is my selection of the FA Cup's most bizarre and beautiful moments, with Trevor Sinclair installed back in his rightful place. You may have heard about some of these elsewhere in the book but, just like the real Top 40 where they play all the songs then repeat them again at the end before announcing the No 1, we're going to do it properly.

34. WAYNE ROONEY'S POST-MATCH INTERVIEW *NEW ENTRY*

I grabbed Wayne immediately after Manchester United had beaten Crystal Palace 2-1 after extra time of the 2016 final. Admittedly, it's never easy for a player to talk after a match, especially when they just want to celebrate with their team-mates, but I still had to chuckle to myself when he described the FA Cup final as 'a great advert for the Premier League'.

33. CHELSEA AND DROGBA'S DRESSING-ROOM DANCE *NEW ENTRY*

It's been a while since I listened to the hit parade, so I'm not overly familiar with Donae'o featuring Sarkodie, but I'm sure he/she/they are The Beatles of their time so it was a great moment to see Drogba leading his Chelsea team-mates in throwing some shapes on the dressing-room floor as 'Move To Da Gyal Dem' played following the Blues' 2012 final win over Liverpool.

32. CLOUGH AND VENABLES WALK OUT

Reaching out, touching me, touching you. Beautiful.

When Spurs and Nottingham Forest walked out at Wembley for the 1991 final, they were led by respective managers Terry Venables and Brian Clough. Always one for the big occasion, Cloughie grabbed El Tel's hand. Venables had no choice but to laugh, and the pair walked along hand-in-hand all the way to the middle of the pitch for the team line-ups.

31. SAMMY NELSON'S CUP DRAW DISASTER

The third-round draw is one of the season's most eagerly awaited events and in 2007-08, former Arsenal cup winner Sammy Nelson was invited to help conduct the draw live on TV. All was going well until Sammy pulled out what looked like ball number 24, but he said it was 25. If he had been mistaken, it would have meant Aston Villa were drawn against Manchester United, instead of Middlesbrough. Fans watching the draw complained, the FA investigated, but found no evidence that there had been a cock-up.

30. JACK TINN BEDS THE FA CUP

Pompey manager Jack Tinn was an eccentric type. The man who had worn spats (fabric worn over footwear to protect shoes from mud or rain) as a lucky charm all the way through to the 1939 final where his side beat Wolves 4-1, then took the cup home with him. As that was the last final to be played before war broke out, Tinn kept the trophy under his bed throughout the conflict, making sure it was safe from any German bombs.

29. LAWRO CALLS STEVEN PIENAAR SOMETHING ELSE

On 9 January 2016 it just wasn't Lawro's day. Not only was the episode of *Pointless* aired in which he decided that Alaska was a country, but later that evening he made a bit of a faux pas while appearing on *Match of the Day*. Asked for his views on Everton by presenter Gabby Logan after watching the Toffees beat Dagenham & Redbridge, he said: 'They have got a really good footballing side, but the problem in the last three to four weeks is that they have got in front in games and not really killed the opposition off. Jagielka's back as we saw today, Mirallas, Penis... Pienaar as well.' The right honourable Trevor Sinclair alongside him could barely contain himself while, if you listen really carefully, you can hear a snort from Lady Logan.

28. HORSES FOR COURSES

The fact that the 1970 final between Leeds and Chelsea went ahead at Wembley was hilarious. Watching the footage back now makes it clear that there are park pitches in this country today which are in better condition than Wembley was that day. A week earlier, the Horse of the Year show had been staged on the (apparently not so) hallowed turf, and the pitch had been completely wrecked, with muddy divots everywhere and a passing game virtually impossible. Fittingly, a replay was required so Wembley's blushes were spared and Old Trafford was used.

27. AYLESBURY DUCKS

That waddling duck celebration may not seem all that clever right now, but back in 1994 it was revolutionary and merits a place in any worthy cup history tome.

26. THEY CALL THEM THE WANDERERS

They're not here in their guise as the first-ever cup winners back in 1872. Oh no, that would be too predictable. Wanderers are here because of this delightful team photo, which looks like a bunch of convicts doing some community work on day release and is a thing of real beauty. In 2022, for the cup's 150th anniversary, I would like to see the winners recreate this magical moment.

Wanderers, FA cup winners in 1872. Just look at how much they enjoyed it.

25. THE RODDERS COAT *NEW ENTRY*

Just to prove that I do have a sense of humour about it, at the request of the publisher, I'm putting my own humiliation on this list – yes, my camel coat which went down so well with the Reading manager Brian McDermott is now part of FA Cup history.

24. ROONEY AND CARRICK LIFT THE LID... *NEW ENTRY*

... and promptly drop it into the lower tier. Is it just me, or was the 2016 final a wonderful vintage for the inane? When Wayne Rooney and Michael Carrick lifted the cup they didn't take great care of that famous old lid and hardly noticed when it flew off the top of the trophy and ended up in the section of seating immediately below them. When security guards found it, there was a slight dent in it. Oops.

23. TIM BUZAGLO'S HAT-TRICK

Non-League striker smashes in a second-half hat-trick to help his Woking team win 4-2 at second tier West Brom. It's what the cup is all about.

22. DAN GOSLING BACK WHERE HE BELONGS 

Right here, right now we can right that awful wrong when TV pictures sneaked off for an ad break as young Gosling won the cup replay for Everton against Liverpool. Now, here's the recognition of this as a crazily brilliant cup classic moment.

21. TOMMY SMITH'S PENALTY MISS

Smith actually converted the spot-kick, but in doing so missed out on a load of money. The problem for Tommy was that by taking part in a 1996 Veterans' penalty shoot-out for Liverpool against Manchester United before the main event at Wembley, he inadvertently showed that he wasn't a suitable recipient for incapacity benefit and his payments were subsequently cut by more than £100 per week. Ouch.

20. SPURS SHIRT SHAMBLES

Back to that 1991 final, and half of the Spurs team managed to play the first half wearing the wrong shirts. They didn't have Nottingham Forest kits on or anything like that, but five of the players had shirts without the sponsor Holsten on them after a cock-up in the dressing room – the problem was rectified in the second half as all 11 managed to wear the same kit.

19. BRIGHTON CHIPPER IN A CHOPPER

Instead of boarding the team bus in their suits to get to Wembley for the 1983 final against Manchester United, Brighton arrived at Wembley via helicopter, landing in a nearby school field ('The Seagulls have landed,' announced the pilot) and then jumping on a coach to the ground. That's the way to arrive at a cup final.

18. MALCOLM ALLISON'S HAT

In a bid to match Jack Tinn's lucky spats, Crystal Palace manager Allison wore a wild fedora hat throughout the club's 1975-76 cup run, which took them all the way to the semi-finals. After seeing off the might of Walton & Hersham, Millwall and Scarborough, the Third Division Eagles then took on Leeds, Chelsea and Sunderland – all away – and came home victorious every time. But the fedora's powers ran out when Palace were beaten by eventual winners Southampton in the last four.

17. RYAN GIGGS'S RUG REVEAL

It wasn't the breathtaking brilliance of the solo goal that won the semi-final replay for Manchester United and inspired the club's unprecedented Treble of 1999. Oh no, the Giggs effort was extraordinary, but the real genius lay underneath the shirt which was removed in the delirium of the moment as Giggs revealed an even more sensational shaggy carpet upon his chest and midriff. It's no coincidence that the trend for waxed chests among male footballers and celebrities started at precisely that moment.

16. FIRST PITCH INVASION

A couple of months before there were famously 'some people on the pitch' at Wembley, two other people were on the pitch during the 1966 final. When Mike Trebilcock (real name) equalised for Everton, who had been 2-0 down, it was too much for a couple of fans who ran on to the pitch to celebrate with their hero. One of them, Eddie Cavanagh, kept running and managed to avoid one policeman by removing his outer garment mid-run to leave the copper holding a jacket without him in it, and who then took a comedy tumble for good measure. Cavanagh kept going until he was felled by a perfect rugby tackle from another cop. Better still for the fan, Everton then grabbed a winner to lift the cup.

15. LOGAN'S FUN

The 1999 final between Manchester United and Newcastle saw a young Gabby Logan stationed in the old stadium's Olympic gallery meeting and greeting all the great and good of the game, armed with a BBC microphone. She obviously had her questions for everyone, as we do, except one of those slightly floored match referee Peter Jones: 'Who do you want to win?'

14. THE NAKED LUNCH *NEW ENTRY*

When non-League Histon beat Leeds in a live TV cup shock one Sunday lunchtime, the nation watched on with mouths wide open in surprise. But the jaws of the country then hit the floor when TV cameras were allowed to enter the Histon dressing room where celebrating players included one revelling non-Leaguer dancing around as naked as the day he was born.

13. PARDEW DANCES LIKE A DAD 

It's one thing for players to have an elaborate goal celebration, but managers really should stick to a clenched fist to retain their dignity. When Crystal Palace took the lead in the 2016 final through Jason Puncheon, manager Alan Pardew let the moment get to him and dad danced in the Wembley technical area.

12. THE DOC'S LIQUID BREAKFAST

Back in the 70s and 80s, TV cameras were given access all areas on cup final morning, so they were in the team hotels, on the team bus (or helicopter if you're Brighton) and sometimes in the players' bedrooms. Seriously. The 1976 final was no different and during a broadcast from the Manchester United hotel on the morning of the game, manager Tommy Docherty could clearly be seen thirstily supping a pint of lager. Cheers!

11. CHESTERFIELD IN THE SEMIS

The Spireites never really seem to get the plaudits they deserve for their astonishing cup run in 1996-97 which took the third tier side all the way to the last four where they were a bad refereeing decision away from the final. John Duncan's side beat Bury, Scarborough, Bristol City, Bolton, Nottingham Forest and Wrexham, and then held Premier League Middlesbrough to a 3-3 draw in the semi-final – a game in which they were denied a clear goal which would have put them 3-1 up against ten men. They lost the replay but won many fans.

10. BLAME IT ON TRAORE

Think of FA Cup own goals and you may remember Tommy Hutchison's belter in the 1981 final which earned Spurs a replay against Manchester City. But you'd be barking up the wrong tree, because the greatest cup own goal award goes to Liverpool defender Djimi Traore in a third-round defeat against Burnley in 2005, when he inadvertently danced round the ball, dragged it back and contrived to score the ultimate comedy OG. He had the last laugh though as he ended the season with a Champions League winner's medal.

9. STAY CLASSY, WEMBLEY

Back in the day (as the kids like to say), it may be hard to believe but both BBC and ITV screened the FA Cup final simultaneously.

You can imagine there was a healthy rivalry. Before the 1969 final, ITV arranged an exclusive matchday interview with all the Manchester City players in exchange for a nice donation to the players' kitty. Unfortunately for ITV, the BBC's Stuart Hall managed to grab Francis Lee and Mike Summerbee on their way to Wembley and broadcast a live interview, raining all over the commercial channel's parade. That was not the end of it. A couple of hours later, while Hall was broadcasting live from Wembley Way, he was ambushed by an ITV technician and a full-scale fist fight broke out between the two ITV and BBC crews in scenes reminiscent of the *Anchorman* movies. News team... ASSEMBLE!

8. LONG TO REIGN OVER US

She'll never live it down and it almost makes me feel guilty to include it here, but the 2016 final got off to the most hilarious start when singer Karen Harding forgot to sing the national anthem at Wembley. She missed her cue, and then remained silent for at least half of the anthem while the rest of us looked on bewildered. It was very noisy at Wembley that day, so it might just be possible that with everyone singing the national anthem so loud, Karen was distracted from singing the national anthem.

7. LEE CLARK'S T-SHIRT

Proud Geordie Lee Clark was one of around 40,000 Newcastle fans who attended the 1999 cup final against Manchester United, and there's nothing wrong with that. Like many of the Toon fans, Clark was kitted out in Newcastle regalia, except his particular t-shirt was emblazoned with the slogan 'Sad Mackem Bastards', poking fun at rivals Sunderland. Which is all well and good, apart from the fact that Clark was actually a Sunderland player at the time.

6. RONNIE RADFORD AND RICKY GEORGE'S HEROICS

Not just Ronnie Radford's tremendous equaliser for non-League Hereford against Newcastle in 1972, but Radford *and* George's goals, which created the greatest cup shock of the 20th century.

5. 1990 SEMI-FINAL DAY

Up until 1990, cup semi-finals were played on Saturdays at 3pm, and were never shown on the telly – that honour was reserved for the final only. Then some bright spark realised that was a ridiculous idea and decided that not only should they be screened live, but they should do so back-to-back on the same day. And with that moment of genius, the greatest-ever day of live football took place on 8 April 1990. It was all part of an amazing sporting weekend which also featured The Masters and the Grand National. The football started with underdogs Crystal Palace beating league champions elect Liverpool by the odd goal in seven after extra time – earlier that season The Eagles had been beaten 9-0 at Anfield. Before we'd even had time to recover from that, it was Manchester United v Oldham with trophy-less Alex Ferguson under pressure to deliver against Joe Royle's exciting Second Division side. They shared the spoils in a six-goal thriller which also went to extra time. Two matches, 240 minutes of football and 13 goals – somehow life would never be the same again. On the same weekend, Nick Faldo won The Masters.

4. LIVERPOOL'S WHITE SUITS IN 1996

Armani model David James took care of Liverpool's suits at the 1996 final, which must have seemed like a good idea at the time. And, other than the cream-coloured (white, to you and me) jacket and trouser combo, ridiculous red and cream striped ties and the white Gucci shoes, it *was* a good idea.

3. ROY ESSANDOH'S GOAL

Signed by third-tier Wycombe, after a plea made on Ceefax a week before the club's quarter-final against Leicester by manager Lawrie

Sanchez for a non-cup-tied striker to help his injury-hit side, Essandoh certainly fitted the bill. Recently released from Finnish side Vaasan Palloseura, he took his place on the bench for the Chairboys and entered the fray during the second half. With the match finely poised at 1-1, Wycombe appealed for a penalty which wasn't given – Sanchez appealed a bit too much and was sent off by referee Steve Bennett. As his manager watched the game tick into injury time on a TV monitor inside the Filbert Street tunnel, Essandoh, who had only signed a two-week contract, rose to guide a header into the net and send his side into the semi-finals. A truly unbelievable story that could only happen in the FA Cup.

2. GAZZA'S 1991 SEMI-FINAL POST-MATCH INTERVIEW

There are post-match interviews and then there is the Paul Gascoigne post-match interview after he inspired Spurs to beat arch-rivals Arsenal 3-1 in a Wembley semi-final to send him to his first final. After scoring a stunning, long-range free kick and playing out of his skin, Gazza was pumped up and could barely get his words out when Ray Stubbs suggested to him that it was all a bit of a fairytale.

'So happy! Couldn't sleep last night. Had a couple of injections because I was so nervous. I'm now away to get me suit measured, YES!' he screamed into the camera with clenched fist raised.

'What about your start to the game?' asked Stubbs.

'It wasn't bad, was it? EEEE!' gurned Gazza before muttering 'Must go!' and heading back to the dressing room.

'There we are, the shy and sensitive Paul Gascoigne,' dead-panned the great Des Lynam back in the studio, as only he could.

1. TREVOR SINCLAIR'S OVERHEAD KICK

Still with me? No surprises here, with Sir Trevor of Sinclair's moment of magic rightfully installed in its place as the greatest FA Cup moment ever.

We've had a good old look back over the course of this chapter, and I would like to continue that theme now with a little slice of the olden times. We are going way back. Prepare yourself for a #HistoryXI.

#HistoryXI

Team Name: JFK Athens
Reserves: Declaration of Independiente
Stadium: Ye Olde Trafford
Management Team: The Third Rijkaard, D-Day Deschamps, Gorman Conquest

First Team:
Poomsday Book

Sagna Carta
Breen Elizabeth the Hurst
Genghis Cannavaro

Dunnpowder Plot
The Great Dier of Rondon (c)
The Great Train Ribery
The 7 Windass Of The World

Edu Kanoute
Asprilla The Hun
Bojan Horse

Subs:
Beasant's Revolt
Bubonic Craig Bellamy
Tugay Fawkes
War Of The Moses
NapoLeon Osman
Anne Brolin
TutanKanu

A LOW

BLOW

I'm going to talk about Euro 2016 in this chapter, but let's just make a pact now to not mention England. Their exit was so embarrassing I think the best thing to do is pretend it never happened. It was my absolute pleasure to spend some time in the Wales camp over the course of that summer and I have to say they were getting everything right.

Not only were they playing good football, but there was a real togetherness in every aspect, from quiz nights to table tennis tournaments and the real business on the pitch. They had the shining star in Gareth Bale, who spoke so impressively to the media and seemed to embrace his role as team talisman but always emphasised the collective over the individual. They were based in the sleepy town of Dinard on the north-west coast, and I am sure they were short of things to do at times but there was clearly a strong bond not only between players and staff but also players and fans. They seemed to feed off each other, and everywhere you looked you saw the same message... #TogetherStronger. Let's be honest, the video of the squad celebrating England's demise didn't do that bond any harm either.

I arrived in the Welsh camp on the day the second celebration video hit the world of social media and amid the PR panic most of the players had no interest in speaking to the press, but Mr Bale was front and centre again. 'We've done nothing wrong. We are enjoying ourselves and we are still in the tournament.'

As we sat in the hotel restaurant for 20 minutes two days before that Belgian quarter-final, I asked him about how the Welsh seemed to enjoy the big occasion rather than be scared of it and freeze. England had been humbled by Iceland in Nice at the start of that week. He talked about the importance of knowing your job and embracing the challenge, rather than allowing it to control you. Those were words echoed by his manager Chris Coleman after that 3-1 win at the side of the pitch in Lille.

As the players were celebrating behind him, I asked Coleman if he had a message for the generation of young boys and girls who had stayed up far too late to watch Wales make the semi-finals of a major tournament for the first time in their history. 'Don't be afraid to dream,' was his answer. 'Four years ago we were a million miles away from where we are now. I've had far more failures than I have had success, but I am not afraid to fail.' Those words got a huge reaction in the press the next day and rightly so.

Bale demonstrating a near perfect example of the man-bun.

Wales weren't the only home nation who enjoyed themselves at the Euros. Did you see the Northern Ireland homecoming at Belfast airport? Will Grigg only left their bench during the European Championship in 2016 to warm up, but that didn't prevent him being one of the most famous players at the tournament and getting the loudest cheer on returning home.

I imagine it was quite a frustrating few weeks for the striker, but it's credit to the amazing Northern Irish fans that supporters from every nation knew the words, and dance, to 'Will Grigg's On

Fire' by the end of the first week. Other players and managers were being asked if they knew the words, and Robbie Savage spent at least a day trying to adapt it to fit Gareth Bale. In the end he gave up. You can't force these things, they have to develop naturally. I heard the receptionist in our Paris hotel humming it most mornings. She's either a massive fan of Gala's 'Freed From Desire' or she too succumbed to the magic of the Griggster.

His Euros heat map still makes me laugh every time I look at it. One French journalist asked me if Will Grigg was actually a real person. He was the same guy who watched in disbelief as fans of both countries stayed behind after Wales's round of 16 1-0 win over Northern Ireland to sing it together in the Parc des Princes.

Inspired by the Will Grigg chant, we had a BBC karaoke night one evening in our hotel and there were quite a few former footballers who've been hiding their lyrical lights under a bushel. Here is some of the set list:

Alan Shearer – totally nailed Lionel Ritchie's 'All Night Long' even the potentially tricky section of 'We're going to... party. Karamu, fiesta, forever. Come on and sing along!' The big man returned to the mic later for some Kings of Leon action and seemed to know all the words to Rick Astley's greatest hits. Alan also has the loudest voice of any human ever recorded. I have no factual analysis to prove this but ask anyone who has ever heard him sing. No amplification required.

Danny Murphy – very impressive when it came to judging the mood of the audience. He went for some classic James and 'Sit Down' and you might be surprised to hear he gave a very moving rendition of Whitney Houston's 'I Wanna Dance with Somebody', complete with a few closed-eye moments for added authenticity.

Dean Saunders – brother Saunders never took centre stage, which was a surprise considering that he has more stories to tell than everyone else put together – all of them hilarious. He was happy to provide backing vocals for the rest of us and when asked why he wasn't grabbing the limelight he said 'You lot can be Gladys Knight… I'm happy to be a Pip.'

Rio Ferdinand – took a while to make his mind up, but eventually settled on a bit of UB40. 'Red Red Wine' went down very well, and when he forgot the words he filled the gap expertly with some signature moves.

Jermaine Jenas – happy to sit on the sidelines and watch for the early stages, but was clearly inspired by Shearer's vocal range and volume and opted for a karaoke classic of 'Don't Look Back in Anger', which he confidently conquered.

Kevin Kilbane – it was the surprise of the night when Kilbane somewhat reluctantly came to the front of the room, but once he started wrecking 'Ice Ice Baby' things escalated quickly. Zinedine Kilbane received a standing ovation for a perfect performance and enjoyed it so much he backed it up with the 'The King of Wishful Thinking' an hour later.

To add to a somewhat random evening, Jim Magilton, Andy Keogh, Richard Dunne and Stephen Craigan wandered in and Craigan wasted no time in belting out 'The Gambler' by Kenny Rogers. Very tough for a debutant in front of a hostile crowd, but the big man delivered the goods.

Neil Lennon – the man loves the mic. When he realised Kenny Rogers wasn't off limits, he launched into a big triple, starting with 'Islands in the Stream', followed by Tom Jones's 'It's Not Unusual' (thankfully not 'Delilah' – I refer you to the chapter about China) and finished it off with 'Sunshine on Leith'. I joined him on this one to mirror The Proclaimers and, despite the fact neither of us is Scottish, we just about got away with it.

Jens Lehmann didn't turn up until after the karaoke session, but was easily one of the stars of the tournament for me. He remains one of the most magnificently stereotypical Germans you will ever meet, but he was really entertaining and had everyone laughing on a curry night. He is straight down the line, says exactly what he thinks and eats an awful lot of chicken. He had Alan Shearer in fits of giggles on at least ten occasions and completely changed most people's opinion of him in the space of a couple of hours and about 30 poppadoms.

I loved interviewing him, because he was just brutally honest and sometimes struggled to understand the British style. Maybe he did, but was just really funny. One of my interviews with him went like this:

Me: Jens, thanks for talking to us. When will the world champions turn up?
Jens: They are here. They are playing in Group C! [No smile]
Me: Yes, but they have been pretty ordinary so far, haven't they? Where is the team which won in Brazil?
Jens: They are here but they are a bit tired. They just need to relax a bit. Do not worry.
Me: Are you concerned that you don't seem to have a recognised striker?
Jens: I don't really care. We will be fine. We will just get it done.
Me: Are you worried about anything?
[Surprisingly long pause]
Jens: I have forgotten my shoes.
Me: Jens Lehmann... thank you.

Jens wasn't the only German making headlines in France during the Euros, as Joachim Löw was in the papers and on TV for an overly familiar touchline tickle.

I once had a bizarre gym session with the Germany boss in Brazil. It was at the draw for the 2014 tournament in Costa do Sauípe in December of the previous year. It was the day before the big event and there wasn't much to do in the complex. I'd already completed a lifetime ambition and had a friendly ruck with the World Cup mascot, Fuleco, and in the early afternoon I'd managed to find a small gym in the resort. The outside temperature was 32 degrees. The indoor temperature was also 32 degrees as the air con was having a fit.

I was in there alone, so just wandered around sweating profusely and occasionally putting in some effort on one of the machines. I was staring vacantly out of the window on the pec-fly machine when the door swung open and in walked Mr Löw. We nodded at each other, he stretched off for a few minutes and then asked if he could share the machine. For the next quarter of an hour he and I swapped on and off making our chests massive.

I practised some of my GCSE German and while I was still working out how to get *Schwarzwälderkirschtorte** into the conversation, he was ready to move on.

He said 'thanks', I said '*danke*' and he made his way to the hamstring curler.

At no point did he put his hands down his trousers. That is what he got in trouble for at the Euros. All men everywhere have played the occasional frame of pocket billiards, but Joachim not only 'rearranged'... he then went for the full finger sniff!

He was already trending on social media by the time he decided to do something that would cause millions of people watching around the world to say 'uuurgggh' at the same time. The German manager inexplicably went for a back-door excavation and then sniffed his hand again!

This was getting close to a diplomatic incident. Herr Löw was quizzed about it in his press conference and blamed it on 'adrenaline and concentration. I will try to behave differently in the future,' he said, adding 'I saw the pictures and obviously sometimes you do things subconsciously. It happened and I am sorry.'

That didn't prevent one newspaper revisiting the famous 'Wally with the Brolly' headline and offering the 'The Minger with the Finger'. You get the feeling he will never make the same mistake again.

*Black Forest Gateau

19 FOOTBALL STARS WHO MADE GERMANY BECOME THE GOOD GUYS

There was a time when it came naturally to every England fan to hate the German football team with a passion stronger than the love they had for their own side. But then something changed.

It turned out that the Germans weren't such bad eggs after all – as we can see from Joachim Löw's antics. How did this happen and who is responsible for such a reversal of our instinctive gut feelings? Allow me to present to you the 19 Germans who made their footballers the good guys.

BERT TRAUTMANN

In 1949, Manchester City signed former Hitler Youth member and German prisoner of war Bert Trautmann to play in goal for them – as controversy goes, this was up there with Mo Johnstone going from Celtic to Rangers. Facing abuse on a weekly basis from home and away fans, Trautmann remained defiant and seven years later played in the FA Cup final against Birmingham City. He was well on his way to a winner's medal as Manchester City led 3-1, but a collision with Birmingham's Peter Murphy broke the German's neck. Did he go off the pitch given the severity of his injury? No, he did not. Trautmann played on to help City win the cup and in the process helped to change some preconceived notions about Germans.

RUDI VÖLLER

He may not have played through the pain like Trautmann, but Völler was an amusing character, especially to look at, thanks to his quite superb mullet and moustache combination. Here was the German who taught us it's OK to laugh at ourselves. He was also on the end of a phlegm double from Frank Rijkaard in the 1990 World Cup. Somehow Völler was sent off for his part in the fracas too, but was probably pleased to have an early bath as the Dutchman's second spit landed right in Völler's curly barnet.

JÜRGEN KLINSMANN

Nobody could believe it when Spurs signed one of the great footballing villains in 1994 – Klinsmann was the epitome of all things about German football that the English despise. He was arrogant, confident and quite brilliant. Accusations of diving followed him everywhere, but Jürgen nipped them in the bud after scoring his first goal for Spurs, when he sprinted across the White Hart Lane pitch and launched himself into a full-scale diving goal celebration. In an instant, he was loved.

UWE RÖSLER

Around about the same time Klinsmann was changing perceptions in north London, another German was doing the same in the blue half of Manchester. Rösler's goals helped City fans forgive and forget, and they even produced a t-shirt celebrating their new star with the motif 'Rösler's granddad bombed Old Trafford'.

DIDI HAMANN

Not only did he play for Newcastle and then win loads of trophies with Liverpool, but the German midfielder integrated into British culture so well that he ended up becoming a cult figure who made regular appearances as a pundit, and several starring roles in BBC comedy panel show *Fighting Talk*. All that after he had the temerity to score the last-ever goal at the old Wembley which saw Germany defeat England. Now *that's* acceptance.

JOACHIM LÖW

So, other than his scratch 'n' sniff incident at the Euros, what has the man they call Jogi Love done to further the cause of Germans in this country? For a start there's that unfortunately very public display of his human side which is endearing. And then there's the cool, calm, suave persona and sideline style with which he led his side to World Cup glory, playing some fantastic football along the way. It was impossible not to love Löw and his team. Which brings us nicely on to...

THE XI WHO SMASHED BRAZIL

The complete dismantling of Brazil in the 2014 World Cup semi-final was one of those football moments where the world stops and looks on with mouths wide open. A victory for the ages won Germany many fans, not least their vanquished Brazilians who were so happy when their conquerors then went on to defeat their arch-rivals Argentina in the final. Five-nil up after just 29 minutes, Germany eventually prevailed 7-1 with one of the most complete displays in history against a hapless Brazil who had no answer to their free-flowing football. And for that, Manuel Neuer, Philipp Lahm, Jérôme Boateng, Mats Hummels, Benni Höwedes, Bastian Schweinsteiger, Sami Khedira, Thomas Müller, Mesut

Özil, Toni Kroos and Miroslav Klose are also all players who made Germany become the good guys.

A special mention here to one of my wonderful colleagues, Rob Facey, who managed to get a ticket for the game against Brazil. It involved a nine-hour bus journey there and the same back. The bus left in the middle of the night from Rio, and Rob was desperate for the toilet and a bite to eat when they eventually got there. In the time it took him to relieve himself and buy some grub, he'd missed four goals. Well worth the 18-hour round trip.

ROBERT HUTH

In 2001, Chelsea boss Claudio Ranieri signed a young German defender called Robert Huth. Opportunities were limited for the German to make any impression at Stamford Bridge as Ranieri left in 2004, and Huth followed a couple of years later. But he made a career for himself in England first at Middlesbrough, then at Stoke where he was a reliable centre-back, but not someone who would've made you think differently about Germans. In 2015, reunited with Ranieri at Leicester, everyone suddenly saw Huth in a different light as he was part of the Leicester team that rewrote the club's and Premier League history – now, here was a German who everyone was rooting for. After 14 years in England, Huth was a Premier League champion and also held the record for the most Premier League appearances by a German. *Jawohl*, Robert!

His name also lends itself to a series of wonderful headlines:

The Huth, the Huth, the Huth Is on Fire!
You Can't Handle the Huth
The Huth, the Whole Huth and Nothing but the Huth
Huth, There It Is!
Huth Had Thought It?
Pizza Huth
The Huth Can Set You Free
Huth Dunnit?
Huth Dares Wins
The Huth Hurts
The Huth Is Out There

I think I need to stop typing.

JÜRGEN KLOPP

Way before he arrived in England, the Dortmund manager was already a cult figure in this country, popular with the press and football fans for his honesty and humour. Klopp could publish a quotes book on his own, given the number of zingers he has come out with over the years (when Mario Götze left Dortmund for Pep Guardiola's Bayern Munich, Klopp said: 'He's leaving because he's Guardiola's favourite. If it's anyone's fault, it's mine. I can't make myself shorter and learn Spanish.'). Alongside the personality comes the extremely pleasing way that his sides play football – and there you have the perfect recipe for another German who made them the good guys.

Klopp is another one whose name is a headline writer's dream:

Run of bad games – Klopp Kop Flopp
Relegation – Klopp til You Drop
Leaves for a bigger club – Klopp Goes the Weasel
Klopp of the Pops
Top of the Klopps
Klopp Gear
Don't Klopp

You might also notice that he appears in almost every single themed XI at the end of the chapters of this book. His name is pun gold.

8 ENGLAND v GERMANY GAMES THAT YOU PROBABLY DIDN'T KNOW ABOUT

Joachim Löw is definitely the studious type – you don't turn your country into world champions without knowing a thing or two about the beautiful game. But I wonder if he knows about all of these England v Germany matches that are steeped in history but not talked about anywhere near as often as the likes of 66, 70, 90 and 96? Students of football, this one's for you.

DATE: 23 November 1899
SCORE: Germany 2 England 13
IMPORTANT STUFF: Not an official international, as the German FA wasn't formed until 1900, but let's not give Germany an excuse if they're not looking for one. The teams met again two days later and Germany fared better, losing only 10-2 this time. But England weren't done yet. Two further tour matches were played against a combined Austrian and German team, which England won by the far more respectable scores of 6-0 and 7-0.

DATE: 4 December 1935
SCORE: England 3 Germany 0
IMPORTANT STUFF: The first international between the sides played in England against the backdrop of Nazism, England ran out comfortable winners at White Hart Lane.

DATE: 14 May 1938
SCORE: Germany 3 England 6
IMPORTANT STUFF: The infamous match in Berlin where England players were badly advised by the FA to perform the Nazi salute before the match – the result was emphatic, with Cliff Bastin and Stanley Matthews among the scorers.

DATE: 1 December 1954
SCORE: England 3 West Germany 1
IMPORTANT STUFF: West Germany were reigning world champions, but sent an under-strength team to Wembley for this friendly, which turns out to have been a bit of a mistake as England won comfortably.

DATE: 23 February 1966
SCORE: England 1 West Germany 0
IMPORTANT STUFF: A World Cup final rehearsal, not that anyone knew about it at the time, saw England hand a debut to a West Ham striker called Geoff Hurst. He wasn't on the scoresheet on that particular day. Nobby Stiles scored the only goal.

DATE: 1 June 1968
SCORE: West Germany 1 England 0
IMPORTANT STUFF: Franz Beckenbauer scored the goal that gave the Germans their first-ever victory over England. That's right, it took them until 1968 to beat England. And even then it was against a massively weakened England team compared to the side that had taken on the world two years earlier. Problem was, it gave Germany the taste for victory...

DATE: 29 April 1972
SCORE: England 1 Germany 3
IMPORTANT STUFF: This was the first leg of the Euro 72 quarter-final (they did things differently back then) after which the *Observer* described England as having been 'comprehensively outclassed'. A 0-0 draw in the second leg a fortnight later was no consolation and England were out of the tournament, two years after the

Germans had defeated them in the World Cup in Mexico. It would become a familiar pattern.

DATE: 17 June 2000
SCORE: England 1 Germany 0
IMPORTANT STUFF: Let's end on a high. With all the other defeats, many people forget that England defeated Germany in a tournament this very century (21st, if you happen to be reading in a different one). It was Euro 2000 in Charleroi, Belgium, and Alan Shearer's goal gave England the win – it was ultimately in vain as both sides failed to progress to the quarter-finals, but let's gloss over that.

THE BARMIEST MEMBERS OF THE GOALKEEPERS' UNION

Every team has one and we all love to laugh at their wacky antics – except when it's Joe Hart in a major tournament, in which case it's not funny. Spending time with Jens Lehmann reminded me that it's high time the weird and wild species of the goalkeeper was celebrated.

Please note that René Higuita, Rogério Ceni and José Luis Chilavert are card-carrying Union members and would obviously be right at the top of this list were it not for the fact that we've already covered their heroics elsewhere in this book.

FABIEN BARTHEZ

A stereotypically eccentric French goalkeeper who probably would have been a surrealist artist had he not been half-decent between the sticks. Barthez was famous for having his head kissed by Laurent Blanc before every France World Cup match in 1998, and also for not bothering to stop Paolo Di Canio's FA Cup winner for West Ham at Old Trafford, instead appealing for an offside that never was. Best of all was a story told by Southampton manager Gordon Strachan in 2001, following a game between the Saints and Manchester United at St Mary's. Barthez had come off with a mysterious ailment at half time and Strachan was asked if he'd heard what was wrong with the Frenchman. Said the Scot: 'It didn't look like there was much wrong with him when I found him in my office with his feet on the desk, smoking a cigarette.'

BRUCE GROBBELAAR

As much as he'll be remembered for his sense of humour, punching his own defender during a match and walking on his hands during trophy-winning celebrations, Brucey will always be known for the wobbly legs routine which helped Liverpool win the 1984 European Cup. The match against Roma went to penalties and Grobbelaar's antics of appearing to make his legs go all loose and wobbly as each Roma player prepared to shoot seemingly made the difference as Liverpool won the shoot-out 4-2.

JENS LEHMANN

The former Arsenal and Germany keeper was a fiery character on the pitch, as a career haul of 65 yellow cards and seven reds (including one in the 2006 Champions League final) testifies. But the German's strangest habit was a propensity for urinating on the pitch, which he was caught doing at least twice during his career.

JORGE CAMPOS

The Mexican was short for a goalkeeper but incredibly athletic, making him a superb shot-stopper. But he'll forever be known for his wonderfully flamboyant and borderline hallucinogenic taste in goalie jerseys. Not many men could get away with them, but one called Campos certainly could.

ITUMELENG KHUNE

The South Africa and Kaizer Chiefs goalkeeper makes it on to this list purely because he made a René Higuita scorpion kick save during the Chiefs' 2015 league game against Mpumalanga Black Aces. At least Higuita had the good sense to wait for a friendly to do it.

HUGO GATTI

The former Boca Juniors goalkeeper was known as El Loco, which tells you almost everything you need to know. He always wore a headband on the pitch and was famous for leaving his penalty area, dribbling around opponents and generally being a total liability.

He also called Maradona 'a fatty who plays well', which was funny until the fatty scored four goals past Gatti in their next game.

RAMÓN QUIROGA

The Peruvian was another South American goalkeeper who preferred to play outside of his penalty area, much to the joy of fans of any team he played against. He is most famous for his antics in the 1978 World Cup when he embarked on regular dribbles outside the box, and against Poland managed to get all the way into the opposition half (seriously) before fouling Grzegorz Lato and picking up a yellow card. Manuel Neuer's sweeper-keeper routine is old hat compared to Quiroga's revolutionary midfielder-keeper shenanigans.

GERMAN BURGOS

He may have been called German, but Burgos was an Argentinian who was known as El Mono, the monkey. Burgos has lead a colourful life and career, including serving an 11-game ban for punching another player, and once saving a Luís Figo penalty with his face. Another stopper who was unafraid to charge out of his area, Burgos usually took to the field in a cap and garish goalie jersey (think Campos but without any of the flamboyance). He ended up working as assistant manager to his compatriot Diego Simeone at Atlético Madrid after beating cancer, playing in a rock band and appearing on a reality TV show. There's undoubtedly more to come.

After all this talk of goalkeepers who love their on-pitch Hollywood moments, it must be time for a #MovieXI.

#MovieXI

Team Name: Clear & Present Rangers
Stadium: Bernabeu After Reading
Management Team: RoboKlopp, Dead Poyets Society, 12 Years A Slade

First Team:
Dudek Where's My Carr

The Neville Wears Prada
Shittu Shittu Bang Bang
Dunne & Dummett
Teenage Mutu Ndah Skrtels

The Tchoyi In The Striped Wanyamas (c)
Tinkler, Taylor, Sodje, Cabaye
PS Mulumbu

Educating Lita
Amokachi If You Can
Slumdog Aliadiere

Subs:
An Inconvenient Huth
The Mexes Chainsaw Massacre
Bigfoot & The Henderson

EPILOGUE:

I love my job. I realise I am very privileged to do it and it has taken me to some amazing places. Of all the trips, I don't think I ever have been or ever will be involved in anything that will come close to the 5,000-mile road trip we were asked to undertake in 2010 for the World Cup in South Africa.

The plan was to start in Cape Town on the opening night and then drive a double-decker bus around the whole country, broadcasting the cultural sights and sounds back to the UK and visiting each of the host cities.

I'm sure you can all remember the football. Another miserable England campaign unravelled in Bloemfontein as Fabio Capello's side were swatted away by the Germans. I still like to think things would have been so different had Frank Lampard's clear goal been given but maybe I'm just kidding myself. Lots of people say the defeat to Iceland in 2016 was the worst ever England performance but the goalless draw with Algeria in Cape Town can't be far behind. It was the one where Wayne Rooney 'thanked' the fans down the camera as he sloped off the pitch at the end.

England were long gone by the time of the quarter-final between Uruguay and Ghana in Johannesburg. It was a truly amazing game to experience. The whole of Africa was behind the Black Stars but they were cruelly robbed by footballer/volleyball villain Luis Suárez. It was his handball that gave Asamoah Gyan the chance to score what would have been a decisive late penalty in that game. He missed and I will never forget the red-carded Suárez running back up the tunnel to celebrate his misfortune and receive the full force of the locals' fury.

Aside from the stuff on the pitch, as a student of history, it was breathtaking to visit the scene of Rorke's Drift and learn about the 96 inaccuracies from the film *Zulu*. I'm still disappointed that Michael Caine's character never said 'Zulus... fowsands of em' but the real life accounts were far more harrowing than anything that appeared on the big screen. Whatever the rights and wrongs of colonial imperialism, standing on the spot where thousands of men (both British and Zulu) lost their lives at Isandlwana churned the stomach and sent shivers down the spine at the same time.

When it came to the wildlife we managed to tick off two of the 'Big Five' on the trip, clapping eyes on a few rhino and elephants but no lions, leopards or buffalo, who kept will hidden in the bushes. Being stalked by a five-tonne miffed pachyderm in Pilanesberg National Park was a little unnerving but thankfully the big lad decided to have a swipe at some Argentina fans in a Volvo rather than our little people carrier.

Top animal gong went to the bird which we watched swallow an entire fish whole. It took a while and was a bit like observing a human trying to nail a watermelon in one go!

I can still remember what fellow presenter Rob Walker (no relation) said to me the day we left for South Africa at Heathrow airport. 'Give it a few weeks and Africa will get you.'

Rob was right. The football was brilliant, the scenery, wildlife and travel were unforgettable, but it is the people who never leave you.

In Cullinan, we stumbled upon Moira, a 24-year-old who was training a marching band to play at the closing ceremony. The band members freely admitted that without Moira's help they would be struggling with drink, drugs and teenage pregnancy, just like huge numbers of the young people that lived in their township.

I often think about a lady called Georghina who we met in Nelspruit. She lived just 500 yards from the brand new stadium and was surviving by making food for the workers but was terrified that she wouldn't be able to provide for her family once the World Cup circus shut down.

Setting up the television signal took a while but was well worth it.

On one of the middle Saturdays our bus visited the Zenzele orphanage in the township of Finetown, about 30 miles outside Johannesburg. We were going to show a group of 60 kids their first football match on a TV rigged up to our BBC bus.

I hold my hands up and admit that I went to South Africa with preconceived ideas about what I would see and the people I would meet. The trip to the orphanage was an absolute game-changer. It was the day that Africa got me. When we turned up at Zenzele, the children were all outside waiting for us. They sang us a song and some of them read a script they had specially written for our arrival.

A lady called Winnie Mabaso was the founding mother of the orphanage. She used to feed more than 1,000 children a week out of her own kitchen before fundraisers in England bought the building which was run by a remarkable lady called Miriam.

All of the children we saw were HIV positive and had lost their parents as a result of the virus. They were happy, vibrant and full of life. Much of that was down to Miriam and her incredible team, who cared for them, fed them three times a day and took them to the clinic when they started to show any symptoms of the virus.

The heartbreaker for me came when Miriam said she too was HIV positive and had lost her own mother to Aids. The emotion we all felt listening to her remains hard to describe – a mixture of anger, frustration and guilt at the life we have back in the UK.

It made us all think about the legacy of these huge money-spinning world cups. Surely they should be making a difference to places like Zenzele, to people like Miriam?

The overriding feeling was one of helplessness. I held a little lad called William, who was the same age as my eldest daughter, and it's hard not to feel angry at the world. But, we kept being told that the kids at Zenzele were actually the lucky ones. Statistics tell you that those with Aids who lived outside the gates were far more likely to die before they reached adulthood. That explained why – during the day – there were children jumping the walls to get in.

When we finally rigged the TV up, all the kids gathered on a crop of rocks in the driveway. With no running water and limited electricity, this was a totally new experience. This was Ghana v Australia.

Miriam showed them how to cheer if a goal went it – and they soon had the opportunity to practise when the Aussies took the lead. They were delighted when Ghana equalised but the highlight was the advert for *Doctor Who* at half-time. 'What was that?' said El Rico. 'I want to see that show,' added Thabiso. Once the game had finished and our piece on the orphanage had been broadcast, we showed it to them on the screens. Imagine seeing yourself on TV on the first day you had ever seen a TV. Dancing broke out and the occasional yelp was followed by pointing at the faces they

Miriam is in the South Africa kit behind me. The kids loved it.

William was great company and stayed up there for some time.

recognised. Miriam broke down when she was told how many people were watching them back in the United Kingdom.

We left just after dark with warm hugs all round and promises that we would never forget the people we had met and the friends we had made. The world cup left South Africa many years ago and it remains an incredibly complicated country with huge social problems. I know it sounds clichéd and glib but those kids in Zenzele really do put the sport we love into perspective. I wasn't sure whether to put this chapter in the book because I don't feel I have the words to do this subject justice. I suppose all I can do is explain what we saw and the profound effect it had on us.

Things have improved since our visit. Zenzele is now a full-time community centre and there is a brand new orphanage nearby called Ilamula House. The Winnie Mabaso Foundation has enough financial support to work in local squatter camps, plant vegetable gardens, establish a pre-school, set up a mobile library, run a feeding station and distribute school uniforms.

Maybe I should leave you with the words of a guy called Michael who I met in a church in Soweto the Sunday after our visit to Zenzele. As a South African, his opinion carries far more weight than mine and strikes at the heart of it...

'I have lived in South Africa my whole life. Over the last forty years, I can barely remember a day when I haven't felt frustrated by what I see around me. I love this country. At times, it makes me laugh and cry in equal measure but I am confident that, before I die, I will live to see a better South Africa because there are so many people desperate to make a difference and change it.'

I hope and pray that Michael is right.

And so to this bit, where I would like to take the opportunity to thank everyone who has helped in putting this little baby on the shelf.

I have no idea of the order you are meant to do these things in but I'll start with my wonderful family. My wife Sarah is an absolute superstar. Not only does she put up with my really annoying habits but she also allows me to go gallivanting around the globe to pick up stories for this book. She is patient, kind, gorgeous and a wonderful mother to our three kids. She always knows what to say, is a beautifully harsh but fair critic when required and even paid close attention to *Match of the Day* when we first started seeing each other, to show her dedication to the relationship. That love for football has long since dissipated to the extent that in the 86th minute of England's 0-0 draw with Slovakia at Euro 2016 she texted me to say she'd only just realised that England were playing in red!

I need to mention my mum and dad for giving me a footballing education which involved an appreciation of Glenn Hoddle and a love of Crawley Town. There were a few bad decisions – like the full-size poster of Garth Crooks that hung on my wall for three years in the 1980s – but it's important to come through hardship in your youth.

As well as my 'dad', I also wanted to thank my heavenly father. Many of you will know that I am a Christian and I believe that everything I have comes from God. I am always grateful for the gifts he has given me and the doors he has opened in my life.

The rest of my family are also excellent (ticks box) and we have a dog called Winnie who I should thank for urinating on an early draft of some notes on the chapter on Afghanistan. I had to rewrite it and I think it's a lot better post-wee than it was pre-wee.

A huge hug goes in the direction of the magical human who is Gershon Portnoi. I don't know about you but I've never met anyone else called 'Gershon' and I've never come across the surname 'Portnoi' anywhere else. To bring the two together in one bloke seems like a wonderful conjunction of the planets and he is very much the golden child of literature. His advice, research and wordsmithery have been far more significant than any dog urine. Portnoi... I salute you.

It would also be remiss of me not to thank the lovely humanoids at Simon & Schuster. Led by the sporting titan Ian Marshall, they have been great to deal with from the outset and their encouragement and guidance along the way has made this a memorable experience. I have always enjoyed writing and they have only added to my desire to keep going.

It was great to get the magnificent Susie Dent to write the foreword to *The Thronkersaurus* and I was delighted that Big Alan Shearer agreed to be involved with this one. I have seen first-hand how many demands there are for his time so I am hugely thankful for his foreword which was warm, insightful and didn't hammer me too much. Working closely with him, it's so easy to see why he was successful on the pitch. His preparation and dedication to doing things well really set him apart and, on top of that, he doesn't spend his life existing in the celebrity bubble. The fact that this book is in the Shearer family toilet means an awful lot to me. I am aware that sounds a bit weird.

All books like this require a sounding board and they don't come much better than my pal and agent Jonny McWilliams. He may have a slightly dodgy shoe collection but he knows the industry inside out and is a trusted colleague and friend. Without Jonny, I probably wouldn't have written this and you wouldn't be reading it. I guess what I am really saying is... if you think this is utter rubbish, then address your hatred towards him.

Just a few more 'thank yous', I think. The first of those is to all the people whose shoulders I have stood on during the course of my career. It is to my eternal frustration that in the TV industry those in front of the camera are referred to as 'talent'. I've been privileged to work with some amazing people over the years – cameramen, camerawomen, producers, soundies, planners, runners, fixers, bookers, floor managers, autocue operators, sparkies, subs and statisticians. Some of them are mentioned in this book but many go unnamed but never unnoticed. All of the stories in here would be much poorer, and many impossible, without the people I've had the pleasure of working alongside.

I can't put the pen down without thanking you lot. It never ceases to amaze me that people enjoy reading my guff. I have kept all the emails, letters, texts and tweets that people sent me about the first book and hopefully you have enjoyed this one too. I better keep working for a few more years because I have now almost completely run out of stories and pictures. The goblet is empty. I know a lot of kids will read this book and I have tried my best to keep it as friendly to that audience as possible. We can't sanitise the beautiful game entirely but I hope you feel this tome is suitable for ears of every age.

Thanks to you all,

Dan

BIBLIOGRAPHY

90mins.com
Back Home: England and the 1970 World Cup, Jeff Dawson (Orion, 2002)
bbc.co.uk
Bend It Like Bullard, Jimmy Bullard (Headline, 2014)
bleacherreport.com
dailymail.co.uk
express.co.uk
esquire.co.uk
eurosport.co.uk
fanatix.com
football365.com
fourfourtwo.com
givemesport.com
goal.com
guardian.com
gamespot.com
heraldscotland.com
independent.co.uk
liverpoolecho.co.uk
metro.co.uk
mirror.co.uk
nationalclubgolfer.com
pastemagazine.com
PA Sport
shortlist.com
skysports.com
soccerbase.com
sport.co.uk
sportkeeda.com
soccerlens.com
talksport.com
telegraph.co.uk
the42.ie
thesportster.com
thesun.co.uk
Who Are Ya? The talkSPORT Book of Football's Best Ever Chants, Gershon Portnoi (Simon & Schuster, 2011)
whoateallthepies.tv
youtube.com

CREDITS

Images on pages 1, 4, 8, 9, 10, 12, 13, 32, 33, 44 (bottom), 45, 46, 47, 62, 82 (bottom), 93 (bottom), 95, 110, 126, 128, 135, 160, 161, 162, 163, 174 (bottom), 175, 177 (top), 190, 191, 205 (middle), 206, 207, 217, 220, 221 (top), 234, 235, 266, 283, 284, 285 and end papers courtesy of Dan Walker.

Images on pages 6, 11, 26, 34, 36, 41, 48, 49, 51, 64 (top), 70, 71 (bottom), 76, 84, 85, 89, 96 (bottom), 99 (bottom), 104 (top), 112, 117, 119, 123, 130, 137 (right), 140 (middle), 142, 150, 152, 155, 166, 168, 171 (top), 196 (top), 199, 203, 211 (top), 213, 221 (bottom), 223, 237 (top), 240, 247, 255, 262, 273, 276 and 279 © Getty Images.

Page 90 (top left) by Richard Bartz, Munich aka Makro Freak – own work; 90 (bottom right) Gilad Rom; 148 (top) contributor: Andrew Hendo; 149 (top) contributor: SwanseaJack4Life; 149 (bottom) contributor: Auz. Files licensed under the Creative Commons Attribution-Share Alike 3.0 Unported license. Page 151 This file is licensed under the Creative Commons Attribution-Share Alike 4.0 International license. Owner: Bears1996.

All other images © Shutterstock.com. Page 79 (top) SamJonah / Shutterstock.com; 118 (bottom) Emilio100 / Shutterstock.com; 144 (bottom right) dean bertoncelj / Shutterstock.com; 159 (top right) kay roxby / Shutterstock.com; 188 Denys Prykhodov / Shutterstock.com; 192 burnel1 / Shutterstock.com; 194 gcpics / Shutterstock.com; 218 (top right) Nicescene / Shutterstock.com; 218 (bottom left) Ivan_Sabo / Shutterstock.com; 218 (bottom) Rasdi Abdul Rahman / Shutterstock.com; 275 (left) arda savasciogullari / Shutterstock.com; 275 (right) Andrey Lobachev / Shutterstock.com; 281 Rob Wilson / Shutterstock.com.

GALVI
WE NEVER
unicef